THE HISTORY OF THE COMMEDIA DELL'ARTE IN MODERN HISPANIC LITERATURE WITH SPECIAL ATTENTION TO THE WORK OF GARCÍA LORCA

David George

The Edwin Mellen Press
Lewiston/Queenston/Lampeter

Library of Congress Cataloging-in-Publication Data

George, David J. (David John)
   The history of the commedia dell'arte in modern Hispanic
literature with special attention to the work of García Lorca /
David George.
      p.   cm.
   Includes bibliographical references and index.
   ISBN 0-7734-9001-9
   1. García Lorca, Federico, 1898-1936--Sources. 2. Commedia
dell'arte--History and criticism. 3. Spanish literature--Italian
influences. 4. Catalan literature--Italian influences. I. Title.
PQ6613.A763Z6472 1995
892'.62--dc20   94-47050
                                                               CIP

A CIP catalog record for this book is available from the British Library.

Copyright © 1995 The Edwin Mellen Press

   The Edwin Mellen Press   The Edwin Mellen Press
           Box 450   Box 67
      Lewiston, New York   Queenston, Ontario
       USA 14092-0450   CANADA L0S 1L0

                        The Edwin Mellen Press, Ltd.
                          Lampeter, Dyfed, Wales
                        UNITED KINGDOM SA48 7DY

                  Printed in the United States of America

For my parents, Catherine and David

Contents

List of Illustrations

ABBREVIATIONS

MLR   *Modern Language Review.*

PMLA   *Publication of the Modern Language Association of America.*

ALEC   *Anales de la Literatura Española Contemporánea.*

BHS   *Bulletin of Hispanic Studies.*

ACKNOWLEDGEMENTS

Gratitude is expressed to the University of Wales Press, for permission to reproduce material from *Lorca: Poet and Playwright*, ed. by Robert Havard, and from *Studies in the commedia dell'arte*, ed. by David J.George and Christopher J.Gossip.

Gratitude is also expressed to *Antípodas*, *Theatre Research International* and *Forum for Modern Language Studies*, for permission to reproduce material from articles published in these journals.

The illustrations in this volume have appeared by kind permission of the following:

Figs. 1-4: Prensa Española: ABC/ Blanco y Negro.

Figs. 12-16: Design and Artists Copyright Society.

I am grateful to old friends Roger and Mercedes Mills of University College of Wales, Aberystwyth for helpful comments on Latin American poetry; to the following colleagues of the University College of Swansea for their helpful comments in the preparation of this manuscript: to Dr Paul Garner of the Department of Hispanic Studies and to Dr Susan Harrow of the Department of French; and especially to Professor Derek Gagen of the Department of Hispanic Studies and to Wynn Thomas of the Department of English, both of whom read drafts of the book and contributed many perceptive comments; to Roger Davies, the Faculty of Arts technician, for the preparation of the illustrations. Dr Jesús Rubio Jiménez of the University of Zaragoza drew my attention to the valuable material in *Por esos mundos*, and offered numerous insightful comments. Amparo Martínez, also of Zaragoza, was responsible for providing photographs for the illustrations from *Por esos mundos*. A special word of thanks is due to John Duigenan of the Department of Computer Science at Swansea for patient hours spent with me at my word processor. Finally, the preparation of the book would not have been possible without the patience and understanding of my wife, María Antònia Babí, and my three daughters, Elisenda, Carys and Mair, who were not able to play on 'their' computer when daddy was writing his interminable book.

David George
May 1994

All translations of quotations are my own. In quotations from plays and poems I have maintained the names of *commedia* characters in the original Spanish, Catalan or French, but have used the standard English equivalent on all other occasions. In those instances where characters from plays have generic names I have used the English equivalent (e.g. Young Man instead of Joven).

Introduction

In common with other European countries, late nineteenth and particularly early twentieth-century Spain was interested in the *commedia dell'arte*. Although there was a *commedia* tradition in Spain (to be discussed in chapter 2), this was nowhere near as strong as in some other countries, particularly France. The turn-of-the-century revival owed much to foreign, particularly French, influences. Contemporary Spanish, Catalan and Spanish-American authors were steeped in French culture.[1]

Critics have discussed the presence of the *commedia* in Spanish and Spanish-American works, but they have invariably considered such works in isolation, and have not attempted to set them in a wider international context. Díaz-Plaja, for instance, writing in 1965, recognises the existence and even the possible importance of the *commedia*, but leaves the way wide open for further research:

> El tema de la restauración de las máscaras de la *commedia dell'arte* en el simbolismo europeo, es más importante de lo que a primera vista parece. Probablemente fue Verlaine su máximo vulgarizador, y a través de él llegó a Rubén Darío que espolvoreó de Pierrots y Colombinas todo el modernismo hispánico: en el teatro, el "tinglado de la antigua farsa" fue restaurado, como es bien sabido, por el Benavente de *Los intereses creados*. Pero ¿cuáles fueron las etapas y cuál el hondo sentido de esta restauaración?[2]

> The topic of the restoration of the masks of the *commedia dell'arte* in European symbolism is more important than at first sight it appears to be. Verlaine probably did most to popularize it, and through him it reached Rubén Darío, who sprinkled the whole of Hispanic *modernismo* with Pierrots and Columbines. In the theatre, the "intrigue of ancient farce" was restored, as is well known, by Benavente in *Los intereses creados creados* (*The Bonds of Interest*). But what were were the stages and what was the deep meaning of this restoration?

Although there was certainly an increase in *commedia* activity after the
publication of the Benavente play in 1907 (see especially chapter 2), *Los intereses
creados* was by no means the first example of the *commedia* revival. Díaz-Plaja
correctly underlines the importance of the Nicaraguan *modernista* poet Rubén Darío
in the diffusion of the *commedia*. *Modernismo* was the dominant literary movement
in Spanish America and, to a lesser extent, in Spain around the turn of the century.
Modernismo corresponds to *art nouveau* in France, *Jugendstil* in Germany and
pre-Raphaelitism in England, while possessing, of course, its own specific
features. In Catalonia the movement is known as *modernisme*. Although there are
important differences between *modernismo* and *modernisme*, certain Catalan
modernistes shared an 'art for art's sake' philosophy with their Spanish and
Spanish-American counterparts, which to a large extent accounts for their mutual
interest in the *commedia*.[3]

Díaz-Plaja's problem is that he views the subject purely as a *modernista*
phenomenon, which accounts for a certain failure on his behalf to understand its
'stages' and its 'deep meaning'. Something similar happens with critics of García
Lorca, probably the best-known Spanish writer to use the *commedia*. For example,
both C.B.Morris and R.Utrera find it hard to accept that Harlequin can move in an
urban environment. Morris writes: 'the harlequin figure who moves through *Viaje a
la luna* - and who reappears in *El público* - is more at home in the canvases of
Picasso than in this city of violence',[4] while Utrera considers similarly that 'la
figura del arlequín es más habitual en los cuadros de Picasso que en la violenta
ciudad neoyorquina en la que el poeta vive; por ello, la ropa del clown, antes que
incitadora a la risa, está utilizada como objeto portador de agresividad'[5] ('the figure
of the harlequin is more at home in the canvases of Picasso than in the violent city
of New York in which the poet lives; as a consequence, the clown's costume does
not provoke laughter but is the bearer of aggresssion').

Even specific criticisms of the *commedia* in individual Spanish authors have
suffered from lack of completeness.[6] The present study aims to avoid the pitfalls of
the fragmented approach and to examine the *commedia* in its entirety as a multi-
faceted feature of Hispanic culture during the period in question. This, as far as I

am aware, is the first study to contextualize well-known Hispanic *commedia* works, both in terms of popular culture and of each other.[7] Some authors are dealt with in more than one chapter, as it is felt that a thematic approach is more fitting than an author-by-author analysis, and because the view of the *commedia* in certain writers, in particular Benavente, varies greatly from work to work.

There is historically a considerable overlap between the *commedia* and analogous paratheatrical forms such as the carnival, mime and the circus. This is recognised where appropriate, although it is intended to limit detailed discussion specifically to the *commedia*. It is hoped that this will have the advantage of clarity and will allow for a tighter structure than would otherwise be the case. For similar reasons, the period for discussion is limited to 1890-1935, and earlier periods are discussed only insofar as they have a bearing on this one. I am aware that the *commedia* appears in and influences contemporary authors, such as the Catalan Joan Brossa, but these should be the subject of a separate study.

The main analysis of the *commedia* in Hispanic culture is found in chapters 3 to 6. The first two chapters set the context for this analysis by considering first the development of the *commedia* in Europe from the seventeenth century to the early twentieth century (chapter 1), and secondly the Spanish manifestations of the theme prior to the twentieth century, together with a brief analysis of the theme in journalism, the carnival and the work of minor dramatists and composers in early-twentieth-century Spain (chapter 2). Readers of the Mellen series on the *commedia dell'arte* will not require a detailed history of the original *commedia dell'arte* in Renaissance Italy,[8] but it will be convenient to summarise its principal characteristics both to highlight more effectively later developments and also because of the interest in the Italian original on the part of early twentieth-century Spanish and Catalan authors, who saw it as the epitome of popular theatrical culture (as chapter 3 will illustrate).[9]

The *commedia dell'arte*, as is well known, was performed by itinerant troupes of players. Texts were not written down, but the performers were expected to improvise the whole play around a basic plot. Since each play was different, there grew up a great number of variations centred around certain themes. The subjects of the different plays were known as scenarios, the most famous of which is the collection of Flaminio Scala. The scenarios ususaly contained set patterns and intrigues, which imposed certain limitations on the actors. However, these rules were flexible and actors had plenty of scope to reveal their talents. This they did most of all in the short scenes known as *lazzi*, which were inserted into the main action of the play with the specific aim of entertaining the audience and allowing the actors to reveal their powers of imagination and technical skill. Actors often displayed considerable physical skills as well as verbal wit, and many of them wore either full or half masks.

The *commedia dell'arte* is famous for its stock characters, the best-known of whom are the comic servants, who ostensibly assisted and schemed on behalf of their masters and mistresses, the Innamorati, but who were really the controllers of the action themselves. Some of these became household names, in particular Harlequin, Pierrot and Columbine. The development in France of Harlequin and Pierrot is discussed in chapter 1, but it should be stressed that the original Italian models, Arlecchino and Pedrolino, were comic dolts. Colombina is one of the servants and is often the mistress of Harlequin or Pierrot. As time went on, she frequently played the part of the coquette. Harlequin, Pierrot and Columbine formed a love triangle, with Pierrot the sad victim of a cuckolding on the part of Harlequin.

Other stock characters are Pulcinella, the blustering, sometimes violent character with his characteristic humps, the boastful Spanish Capitano, the pedantic Dottore and the stingy merchant Pantalone. Specific characters are associated with specific Italian towns: Arlecchino with Bergamo, Pulcinella with Naples, Pantalone with Venice, and so on. Many of the original characters have not survived the transformation of the *commedia* through the ages, and names such as Brighella, Mezzettino and Isabella are now remembered only by *commedia dell'arte* specialists. Practically all of the Hispanic authors who will be discussed in this book deal with a limited number of *commedia* characters, normally Harlequin, Columbine, Pierrot and Pulcinella. There are some exceptions, notably Benavente, whose *Los intereses creados*, to be discussed in chapter 3, contains a much wider range of characters.

Although drama is naturally the focus of attention in this study, manifestations of the *commedia* in prose writing, poetry and the visual arts are also explored. Chapter 3 is concerned with the general revival of interest in the original *commedia dell'arte* in early twentieth-century Spain, and with plays written in the *commedia dell'arte* style. Harlequin is the most popular figure in these plays, while Pierrot is the main focus of attention in chapters 4 and 5. Examples of essentially sentimental approaches to the poor Pierrot figure are studied in chapter 4, while chapter 5 investigates how certain authors subvert the sentimentality through irony. Finally, chapter 6 concentrates once more on the harlequin figure who is now menacing and dehumanised. This chapter is dedicated entirely to the work of García Lorca, and allows us to highlight the originality of Spain's best-known twentieth-century writer.

---

1 The term *Hispanic* is used throughout to refer to literature written in Spanish (be it from Spain or Spanish America) and Catalan.
2 Guillermo Díaz-Plaja, *Las estéticas de Valle-Inclán* (Madrid: Gredos, 1965), p.217. James Fisher's recent book on modern manifestations of the *commedia dell'arte* has a chapter on Spain, but this is of necessity an overview; see James Fisher, *The Theatre of Yesterday and Tomorrow: Commedia dell'arte on the Modern Stage* (Lampeter/Lewiston/Queenston: The Edwin Mellen Press, 1992).
3 The adjective from *modernismo* is *modernista* (plural *modernistas*); the adjective from *modernisme* is likewise *modernista* in the singular, but *modernistes* in the plural. *Modernismo* and *modernisme* must be distinguished from Modernism, which is a fundamentally different movement.
4 *This Loving Darkness* (Oxford: OUP [for University of Hull Press], 1980), p.134. Both *Viaje a la luna* and *El público* will be be discussed in chapter 6.
5 *García Lorca y el cinema* (Sevilla: Edisur, 1982), p. 81.
6 An example is Robert Lima's 'The *Commedia dell'Arte* and *La marquesa Rosalinda*', in *Ramón del Valle-Inclán: A Critical Appraisal of His Life and Works*, ed. by Anthony Zahareas (New York: Las Americas, 1968), pp. 386-415.
7 Uribe's book on the *commedia dell'arte* is not concerned with the modern period. See María de la Luz Uribe, *La comedia del arte* (Madrid: Destino, 1983).
8 The bibliography on the *commedia dell'arte* is vast. The most complete bibliographical source is Thomas F. Heck, *Commedia dell'arte: a Guide to the Primary and Secondary Literature* (New York and London: Garland, 1988).
9 I use the term *commedia dell'arte* to refer specifically to the Italian original, and simply *commedia* or *the commedia* in all other instances

Chapter 1

The *Commedia* in Europe

The *commedia* in seventeenth- and eighteenth-century France

Although the home of the *commedia dell'arte* was Italy, several Italian companies, such as the famous Gelosi, performed in other European countries in the late years of the sixteenth century, particularly France. However, it was not until the mid seventeenth century that the Italian comedians really established themselves in Paris.[1] They remained there until almost the end of the century before being expelled in 1697.

When they returned to France in 1716, the *Nouvelle Troupe Italienne*, as the 1716 players who were led by Luigi Riccoboni were known, found that interest in the *commedia* had waned with the absence of the Italians, and also faced the danger that the troupe would be compared unfavourably with the théâtres de la foire. Riccoboni lacked an author of stature and found the language barrier disconcerting, although he began taking steps remarkably quickly to make a direct appeal to his French audiences. French subject matter was introduced into a play as early as two months after the troupe's arrival in France; the French-speaking actor Dominique, son of the famous Harlequin of the previous century, was engaged in 1717; and scenes in French appear to have begun to figure from about the beginning of 1718. A major breakthrough came when the painter Jacques Autreau produced for Riccoboni's company a *commedia* play, *Le Naufrage au Port-à-l'Anglais*, which, with its performance on 20 February 1718, began the process of refinement of the *commedia*, which was one of the important French contributions to the genre. A further significance of Autreau's play was that the text was written down and not improvised as it had been previously, thus increasing the role of the individual author and lessening that of the actor. Goldoni, one of the most important writers of *commedia* theatre, took a similar path in Italy. Although he recognised that improvisation had a certain value, Goldoni is an important figure in the movement away from improvised scenarios to the written text and the consequent growth in the significance of the individual author.

The Italian players continued to perform in Paris until 1762, when the Italian Comedy at the Hôtel de Bourgogne secured the amalgamation of the opéra-comique into their company. Those actors who could play only in Italian were pensioned off and in 1779 the State Council ordered that the company of Italian players, now 63 years old, should be abolished and a new company formed to perform purely in French. According to Goldoni, the only Italian player retained was the 70 year old Carlin, the Harlequin of the company, who died of apoplexy in 1783.

The development of Harlequin

The best-known and best-loved *commedia* figure in the seventeenth and eighteenth centuries was Harlequin, whose evolving character was shaped by a number of great actors during this period. The original Bergamasque was a doltish character, a foil to his cunning Bergamo counterpart Brighella. Harlequin was the stupidly naive buffoon who delighted audiences with his mistakes. With time he acquired cunning, and it is as a scheming rogue that he has passed down the centuries. Harlequin's character was changed radically in the seventeenth century by a number of celebrated performers: Dominique, Gherardi, Thomassin and Carlin, especially Dominique and Thomassin. All these actors could perform in the spirit of the crude Arlecchino prototype, but each added a characteristic of his own to the role, with an emphasis on refinement, sensibility, grace and elegance.

Giuseppe-Domenico Biancolelli, the father of the French-speaking actor who was appointed to Riccoboni's troupe in 1717, was born in 1640 in Bologna where his parents were actors. In 1659 he was a member of a troupe that was invited by Cardinal Mazarin to perform in France, where he achieved his greatest successes, and where he was known as Dominique. Renowned for his wit and physical agility, and a favourite with King Louis XIV, Dominique began the process of refining Harlequin. This trend was further accentuated by another actor, whose Italian name is given variously as Tommaso Visenti, Tommaso Vicentini,

Tommaso-Antonio Vicentini, Antonio Vicentini, but who is best known by the name he adopted in France, Thomassin. Born in Venice, he played in Italy for a long time before going to France with Riccoboni's *Nouvelle Troupe Italienne* in 1716. Like Dominique, Thomassin achieved his greatest successes not in Italy but in France, and was able to convey emotions of mirth and pathos to his audiences. Beaumont writes:

> He had a brilliant career. Agile, gay and always original, he would set the house in roars of laughter by some inimitable display of buffoonery, then, passing almost imperceptibly from comedy to tragedy, he would cause the same public to shed tears of sorrow - no light achievement when it is remembered that his face is covered by a mask. His physical dexterity was remarkable. In this respect he is said to have attained such a degree of perfection that he could turn a somersault with a full glass in his hand and alight on his feet without having spilt a single drop of the wine.[2]

Thomassin was one of Marivaux's favourite actors, and was the inspiration for all of the Arlequin roles he wrote, from his earliest important theatrical success, *Arlequin poli par l'amour* (1720), to the last play in which he included the character, *Les Fausses confidences* (1737). Some of the other actors never acquired a good command of French, and the ability of the company to survive under these conditions is a testimony to their great miming technique, their ability to express by body movement, synchronisation and ultimately by pregnant silences: some critics have stated that the *école du silence* had its roots in such a style of acting.

By the early part of the twentieth century, Harlequin had reverted to *commedia dell'arte* type, having been largely supplanted as the favourite *commedia* figure in the nineteenth century by Pierrot. Before looking briefly at Pierrot's development in nineteenth-century France, we shall cite briefly one essay on Harlequin, by Banville, who was a significant influence on Hispanic *modernista* poets. In his 1869 Banville: 'Arlequin', Banville evokes

> Ce rêve d'agilité, de tendresse et de folie que Watteau penchait au bord de ses fontaines aux urnes murmurantes, dans ses grands parcs silencieux dont les vastes et clairs ombrages ensoleillés frissonnent comme des chevelures! Mais, ô maître, qui dans ta divine féerie mêlas les masques du théâtre aux enchantements des paysages, comprenant bien que tu avais ainsi créé le seul paradis qui soit à la

portée de l'homme, le riant démon aux mille couleurs que ton génie a transfiguré.[3]

> That dream of agility, tenderness and madness whom Watteau painted leaning over fountains with their gently murmuring water, in his great, silent parks where the vast, bright, sunlit shadows glisten like a golden head of hair! But you, oh Master, in your divine fantasies are able to blend the masks of the theatre with charming landscapes, and you know that by so doing you have created the only paradise that is within man's reach, the smiling devil of a thousand colours transformed by your genius.

This Arlequin encapsulates the element of idealism which is central to Banville's vision of the *commedia*. Harlequin both inhabits and personifies a world of fantasy which provides relief from life's tedium. Although the expression 'le riant démon' brings to mind the roguish, even the sinister side of Harlequin's character, Banville's evocation of Harlequin is essentially escapist and sentimentalised.

The nineteenth-century French Pierrot

Many of the important developments in the *commedia* tradition during the nineteenth century occurred in France, and involved the figure of Pierrot. This character has received extensive critical attention, and would not concern us were it not for the fact that Pierrot is a central *commedia* character in Hispanic literature. This is especially so in the early part of the twentieth century, before he is later replaced by the menacing Harlequin figure. What follows is a summary of the main characteristics of the Pierrot that had emerged by the end of the nineteenth century, and which will be of relevance to chapters 4 and 5.

In the work of many a Romantic and post-Romantic Pierrot is a frustrated, but also an elegant dandy, whereas he was little more than a comic simpleton when he was first introduced into France. A key figure in the transformation of the *commedia* in general and Pierrot in particular is the eighteenth-century French painter Antoine Watteau, in whose *Gilles* the *commedia* dolt acquires an air of melancholy loneliness. Watteau, like Marivaux, refined the *commedia dell'arte*, and hinted at the presence of frustration beneath the apparently gay and frivolous masks worn by *commedia* characters and other participants in his *Fêtes galantes* paintings.

Watteau's transformation of the *commedia dell'arte* greatly influenced nineteenth-century French poetry. The Goncourt brothers are generally credited with stimulating interest in Watteau among poets such as Hugo, Gautier and Verlaine. Verlaine's *Fêtes galantes* captures the playful yet melancholy elegance of the Watteau world, and highlights the sadness and ocasionally the bitterness behind the fantastic disguises. Other Verlaine *commedia* poems, specifically the sonnet entitled 'Pierrot' from *Jadis et naguère*, evoke a world of silence, negation and vacancy which seems, in some ways, to anticipate a kind of postmodernist void.[4]

The importance of Watteau, then, or at least the vision of Watteau conveyed by the Goncourt brothers and Verlaine, is central to the development of the *commedia dell'arte* in eighteenth- and nineteenth-century France away from the farce and earthy humour associated with its Italian source. However, as far as Pierrot is concerned, perhaps the key figure in his development in nineteenth-century France was the famous mime, Jean-Gaspard Deburau. Robert Storey in *Pierrot: The Critical History of a Mask* emphasises less the popular inspiration of Deburau than his role in the transformation of the figure:

> A mime whom Gautier later praised as "the most perfect actor who ever lived" and whose talents became legendary for several generations of performers, Deburau created a stage Pierrot that eclipsed all previous interpreters of the *zanni* and hung, like a white shade, over most of his pantomimic successors. This actor has often and justly been acknowledged as the godparent of the multifarious, moonstruck Pierrots who gradually found their way into Romantic, Decadent and Symbolist literature; but Deburau's real role in the transmission of the type from the popular to the literary world -- and its transformation from *naïf* to neurasthenic pariah -- has been only imperfectly understood, when it has been understood at all.[5]

To such an extent had the moonstruck Pierrot penetrated not only French poetry but also Parisian popular culture by the middle of the nineteenth century that Lehmann was able to note: 'Leaving aside posterity, we remark simply that around 1850 Paris appeared to an onlooker like Gavarni to be alive with Pierrots.'[6] By the late nineteenth century, Pierrot, despite (perhaps even because of) the fact that he maintains something of his innocence, clearly symbolises tragedy rather than comedy. Yet in Laforgue's poetry, in particular, Pierrot is able to maintain a certain ironic detachment from his own tragic, or potentially tragic, situation. As Lehmann puts it: '[Laforgue's] Pierrot, the fascinated but entirely lucid victim, attempts both to participate and to stand outside; to remain alive, "a dupe", and to stand outside, "a dilettante" '.[7] Indeed, Laforgue's Pierrot contains the essential duality of the nineteenth-century Pierrot figure. As King has it, he is 'both the frivolous dilettante and the Christ-like prophet-victim, but a prophet who proves to offer no positive message, he is the elegant, superior black-costumed Hamlet-like dandy, Lord Pierrot, yet he chooses to play the role of the white-faced, white-costumed simpleton'.[8]

Another characteristic of the Decadent Pierrot is his sexual impotence, which converts him into almost a cult figure for some artists and writers. To quote Hueurre:

> C'est justement à cause de son inhibition sexuelle que Pierrot s'est imposé d'office comme héros de la période décadente, comme héros de l'impuissance. En effet, à cette époque, les esprits sont marqués par le pessimisme qu'a engendré la défaite de 1870 et par l'inquiétude métaphysique qui accompagne les débuts du scientisme ...... L'amour devient chez Huysmans et Oscar Wilde un culte raffiné de cette impuissance.[9]

> It's precisely because of his sexual inhibitions that Pierrot has become a hero of the Decadent period, like a hero of impotence. In reality, the spirit of the era was marked by the pessimism engendered by the defeat of 1870 and by the metaphysical anxiety which accompanied the beginnings of the scientific revolution... Love became in Huysmans and Oscar Wilde a refined cult of this impotence.

Both the whiteness of Pierrot's costume and his liaison with the moon were symbols of sterility. Starobinski's view is that the nineteenth-century clown/dandy figure consciously struggles to transcend his physical reality and inhabit a purely spiritual world: 'le *dandy* est précisément l'homme qui s'efforce de transcender le donné contingent de l'existence corporelle. Par la magie des artifices de la toilette, le dandy cherche à s'absenter de son corps'[10] ('the dandy is precisely the man who struggles to transcend the confines of physical existence. Through the magic of the artifices of dress, the dandy looks to separate himself from his body').

Perversity is a part of this cult, and Lehmann even goes a step further and highlights a philosophical side to the Pierrot/dandy figure of late nineteenth-century

France: 'Pierrot - dandy, dilettante, artist - proceeds to develop his Schopenhauer pessimism, unobtrusively, into a veritable aesthetic [...] as Schopenhauer has taught - the worship of Art is a liberation from the Will, a voluntary sterility.'[11] Sterility and frustration have thus taken on a consciously aesthetic, even philosophical, dimension in the *fin-de siècle* portrayal of Pierrot.

Pierrot was often a reflection or projection of the persona of the poet or the painter in the Romantic and post-Romantic periods, and to some extent the vision of the frustrated, even tragic Pierrot was a way for creative artists to wear their hearts on their sleeves. Nevertheless, Laforgue, at least, is able to set some ironic distance between himself and his Pierrot persona.[12] This is one characteristic of his Pierrot poems which has led critics to point to Laforgue's modernity.

The albeit faltering and incomplete transformation of Pierrot from doltish *commedia* servant to cynical dandy exemplifies the growing gulf between the popular strand of *commedia* revival and the version of the *commedia*, notably of Pierrot, which emerges in *fin-de siècle* French poetry. King puts in a nutshell the general trend in nineteenth-century French poetry away from realism:

> The gulf separating the realm of art from the realm of lived experience and objective reality was an ever increasing one, and the clown, as a blatantly proclaimed actor and champion of artifice, set himself in total contrast, physically and spiritually, with his audience and society in general. A rebel against realism, or rather his audience's conception of realism, he perceived more profoundly than his audience the comedy of life, that "all the world's a stage"; and, symbolically, by rejecting surface realism, by means of his make-up, costume and comic mask, he was demonstrating a deeper consciousness of the illusory nature of life and death.[13]

The persistence of the popular *commedia* tradition

All the while that Marivaux and later the Symbolists were refining the *commedia* almost out of recognition, the comic spirit of the *commedia dell'arte* was surviving in the popular theatre of the fairs and the boulevards, and, in the nineteenth century, the théâtre des Funambules. The théâtres de la foire originally replaced those of the Italian comedians when the latter were expelled from France at the end of the seventeenth century, but they became rivals when the Italians returned. The théâtres de la foire were constantly at loggerheads with the authorities and were forced, because of the numerous prohibitions placed upon them, to draw upon their inventive skills. For instance, at one stage dialogue was prohibited, so they turned to the use of dumb characters and mime. The musical side of the theatre developed, and, as time went on, the entertainment became more diversified. Acrobats and rope dancers became part of the scene and marionette shows were included alongside harlequinade spectaculars. The théâtres de la foire, however, became associated with low humour and were often the subject of scorn; but their contribution to the development of the *commedia* was extremely important, and they changed some of the masks, such as Pierrot and Pulcinella.

Although in general the théâtres de la foire lacked authors of high quality, certain dramatists succeeded in raising the plays performed there to a level of literary if not moral respectability. The best-known writer for the Fair theatres was Lesage, whose plays use *commedia* characters to explore the relationship between high and low culture, and to make statements about questions of power structures within eighteenth-century society.[14]

In a sense, the successor to the théâtres de la foire was the théâtre des Funambules. Earlier in this chapter the role played by Deburau in the transformation of Pierrot from comic dolt to a key symbol of nineteenth-century poetry was emphasised. All the same, one should remember that writers such as Banville were attracted to the Funambules mainly because of their popular spirit, which they idealised.The distinction between popular and high culture is never, of course, a clearcut one. Banville polemically used his *commedia* sources as a stick to *épater le bourgeois*. Hueurre makes the point that, after Deburau, Pierrot as portrayed in the nineteenth century was for some writers and painters a figure of the people, and his attraction for them reflected their interest in the people and democracy. She refers specifically to Banville, a staunch Republican, who juxtaposes Pierrot with the Bourgeois, for whom he had a deep-rooted hatred:

> Le Pierrot [of *Les Folies-Nouvelles*] représente l'artiste idéaliste et pauvre que le bourgeois est incapable de comprendre, d'apprécier et de soutenir. Banville croit profondément que la classe bourgeoise, centrée sur ces propres intérêts, a trahi les espoirs de la République et du peuple.[15]

> The Pierrot [of *Les Folies-Nouvelles*] represents the idealistic, impoverished artist whom the bourgeois is incapable of understanding, of appreciating or enduring. Banville believes deeply that the bourgeois class, centred as it is on its own self-interests, has betrayed the hopes of the Republic and the people.

The general tendency in eighteenth- and nineteenth-century France towards the appropriation of a model, deeply rooted in Mediterranean culture, and its refinement by the Symbolists in particular, is countered by the persistence of the popular, often subversive, spirit in the théâtres de la foire, the carnival and mime theatre. The contradicton, if contradiction it is, is epitomised by Banville, whose populist vision is essentially idealistic and, in reality, more closely linked to subsequent refinement than at first it may appear to be. To quote King: 'Ridicule of bourgeois realism informs Banville's aesthetics, with the poet's often proclaimed preference for non-realist fantasy and the cult of form. Banville, the skilled craftsman and author of *Petit Traité de poésie Française* (1872), parallels the supremely skilled acrobatic clown'; and 'so Banville's acrobatic clown remains predominantly a hopeful spiritualist.'[16] The following stanzas from 'Les Folies-Nouvelles' illustrate King's point:

> Voyez! C'est Arlequin avec sa Colombine,
> Ce joli couple en qui le poète combine
> L'âme avec le bonheur se cherchant tour à tour,
> Et l'idéal avide, en quête de l'amour!
> ....
> Et le plus grand de tous, calme comme un Romain,
> Le plus spirituel, le plus vraiment humain,
> Formidable, et toujours plus grand que sa fortune,
> Mon cher ami Pierrot, le cousin de la lune! [17]

> Look! It's Arlequin with his Colombine, that handsome couple in whom the poet combines soul with happiness, searching for each other in turn, and the covetous ideal, in search of love! And the greatest of them all, calm as a Roman, the most spiritual, the most truly human, formidable, and always greater than his fate, my dear friend Pierrot, the cousin of the moon.

As has been observed, Banville's evocation of Arlequin in 'Arlequin' similarly emphasises spiritual qualities. Although very different as regards sensibility and aesthetic distance between persona and author, the Banville Arlequin and Pierrot and the Laforgue Pierrot have in common their distaste for vulgarity.

A harsher vision of the social reality surrounding the Pierrot figure occurs in the paintings of Rouault. Here is a striking example of Pierrot as *homme du peuple* where the use of the 'poor' Pierrot stereotype owes more to social than to aesthetic concerns. For Rouault Pierrot symbolised not the misunderstood clown or dandified aesthete but the travails and the exploitation of the lower classes. Picasso too in his Rose Period paintings of circus acrobats and *saltimbanques* has a similar social mesage to convey.[18]

The *commedia* in Modernism and the avant-garde

A more general identification of the *commedia* with popular tradition appears in Modernist and avant-garde culture, which believed the real and vital forms of art to be the *commedia*, carnival, circus and mime. The Modernists in general, and the Expressionists, Dadaists and Surrealists in particular, saw in the *commedia* an example of primitive art which could act as a revitalising force. As Starobinski puts it: 'la culture la plus avancée, qui se croit extenuée, cherche une source d'énergie dans la primitive'[19] ('the most advanced culture, which believes itself to be worn-out, looks for a source of energy in primitivism'). The Surrealists explored to the full the possibilities of mask inherent in the *commedia*, being especially interested in multiple personality or *döppelganger* and the interchangeability of human and non-human characters.

Susan Harrow links the revival of the *commedia* to the pessimism and sense of life's absurdity felt by the Modernists:

> The sense of pessimism which overtakes the modern sensibility is the comfortless refuge of the artist whose confidence in the new century is broken by the events of 1914-18 [...] In an age dominated by the consciousness of life's absurdity, of its non-sense, the artist turns to the consciously absurd - to comic shows and pantomime arts - in his search for a structured space in which to play out his obsessions and desires.[20]

Harrow emphasises that the Modernists had first to recognise the existence of the tradition before they could displace and then transform it:

> Such instances of the multi-facetted *commedia* and circus-inspired production of the modern era confirm our suggestion of a double conclusion for the relationship between the traditional popular arts and Modernist high culture, one which links figurative continuity to the Modernist imperative to 'make it new'. Here we touch on the paradox at the centre of modern art: to be radically new is to declare a major stylistic difference in respect of the prevailing or preceding tradition as a first step towards displacing that tradition. However, the active negation of tradition is predicated on a recognition (valorization) of tradition without which there is no impetus for change, no urge to 'make it new'.[21]

It was precisely this recognition of the *commedia* tradition, coupled with a desire to 'make it new' that led certain early twentieth-century European writers and theatre directors to see in the *commedia* a possibly fertile source of regeneration of the theatre. Craig in England and Meyerhold and Blok in Russia were influenced by the *commedia*.[22] Especially interesting for the study of Spanish authors in chapter 3 is the work of Jacques Copeau in France. It is not suggested that there was any direct contact between Copeau and the Spaniards, merely that there are some striking parallels between them. What follows is a brief analysis of those aspects of Copeau's experiments with the *commedia* that will have a bearing on the discussions in chapter 3.

The links between *commedia dell'arte* and festive street drama are highlighted in an article Copeau wrote for the programme of the *Cahiers de la Maison de la Culture de Grenoble* as late as 1945. On the use of mask exercises, he writes:

> Begun as a school exercise, a research, the mask allows us to see a world which could give an actor a whole new life. One thinks of the magic masks from Africa and Polynesia, of what the *commedia dell'arte* must have been on the planks of the public squares. We left behind us altogether the naturalistic way of acting, and yet the characters possessed a greater reality and a greater vitality.[23]

According to Copeau, the revival of the *commedia* goes hand in hand with anti-Naturalism. He explains how the younger writers of the early 1940s were freer than those who

> grafted their popular movements onto the Boulevard Theatre of 1899 and the *Théâtre-Libre* of 1897... They are more or less disencumbered from Naturalism. That is the chief service that the art theatre movement of 1920-40 has done them. They benefit from a technical liberation which was no easy task. Lyricism is not taboo. The development of mime does not frighten them. They know what play is, what it means to establish a sense of play among themselves and even between themselves and the public. They have established a contact with the classics. Molière is alive for them. They are not unaware of the theatre of the Far East. They have had some contact with the *commedia dell'arte*. They have great confidence in the actor and make no attempt to produce illusion by a change of scenery.[24]

Critics have stressed that Copeau's achievement as far as the *commedia* was concerned was not so much to reproduce the original version on a modern stage as, in effect, to write 'new' *commedia*. Rudlin, for instance, writes:

> But even Arlequin, Colombine and Pierrot [...] had lost their universality, having become sentimentalised by the eighteenth century and turned into a spectacle by the nineteenth. Little by little, said Copeau, their comedy had been sterilised, so that the present task was not to revive them, so much as to re-populate their stage.[25]

Finally, in a 1928-29 article on Charlie Chaplin as inheritor of the *commedia*, Copeau's claim that there exist connections between the *commedia* and the cinema parallel views expressed by Rivas Cherif in Spain (as chapter 3 will illustrate): 'Charlie Chaplin belongs to the lineage and family of those great characters of the *commedia dell'arte* who, for more than two centuries, have supplied modern theatre with their offspring.' Chaplin's problem, says Copeau, is that he is the only one of his kind:

> Now, let us suppose that in addition to Charlie's character, others as well developed as his appeared; suppose that one day when the masses, even the least cultured of his crowd of admirers, would be able to *identify* at a glance *all the characters* of the comedy as they can Charlot. Suppose that they recognised them all, loved or hated

them, remembered them as Renaissance audiences remembered; loved or hated the flesh and blood creations of Arlecchino, Pantalone, Pulchinella and Brighella. Does it not seem that, in one fell swoop, modern theatre would be transformed, would regain its grandeur and its meaning, and finally, in Shakespeare's words, would become the mirror of the world and the chronicle of the times?... I may add that it is perhaps the great virtue of cinema that it returns dramatic art to its sources and forces it to revive its roots...[26]

With the rejection of Symbolist aesthetics in the early part of the twentieth century, something else happened as the *commedia* evolved. During the nineteenth century, as we have seen, Harlequin, who had hitherto been the most popular of the *commedia* servants, was largely supplanted by Pierrot, since the latter accorded better than Harlequin with the sensibilities of the age. As the values of Symbolism and Decadentism were rejected and satirised by the Modernists, Harlequin came back into favour. His roguishness, amorality and emotional detachment were better suited to the twentieth-century sensibility, and he was perceived as an important link with the original spirit of the *commedia dell'arte* by writers who saw in popular art forms a rejuvenating force.

Max Jacob encapsulates the difference between Pierrot and Harlequin in a letter to Jacques Maritain in 1936. Commenting on the shift from the Symbolist mode which had prevailed at the end of the nineteenth century to a more radical Modernist consciousness in the early twentieth century, Jacob refers to an 'art arlequin' ('la connaissance des effets à produire et leurs moyens' -'the knowledge of the effects to be produced and their means') replacing the 'art pierrot' ('l'humble confession des états d'âme' - 'the humble confession of emotional states') of the previous generation.[27]

In many ways, the Harlequin/Pierrot dichotomy summarises the shifts in the perception and presentation of the *commedia* in Europe. Parnassianism, Symbolism and Decadentism represented in part a reaction against the populism and vulgar excesses of Romanticism, while the exponents of Modernism in their turn reacted simultaneously against what they felt were the stifling limitations of Naturalism, the smug commercialism of middle-class theatre and Western culture in general, and the élitism and refinement of Symbolism and Decadentism.

During the eighteenth and nineteenth centuries the *commedia* underwent far-reaching and sometimes contradictory changes. Almost all of the important developments took place in France, which adopted the original *commedia dell'arte* and converted it into a French rather than an Italian phenomenon. An excellent example is the figure of Pierrot, who, although based on Pedrolino, is perceived as a thoroughly French character. In eighteenth-century France the *commedia* lost a lot of the directness and even the humour of the Italian comedy. Watteau and Marivaux refined the genre, with even Harlequin relinquishing some of his coarseness. In nineteenth-century French poetry the refinement became even more accentuated, and the *commedia*, and specifically the lonely figure of Pierrot, acquired symbolic overtones. The popular side of the *commedia* survived, however, and the distinction between high and low culture became ever more difficult to draw in the nineteenth century. In the early twentieth century the original *commedia dell'arte* once more captured the attention of writers and artists as the Modernists looked to revitalise Western art through the revaluation of such paratheatrical forms as the circus, the carnival and the *commedia*, not only in France but across Europe. Hispanic literature of the period 1890 to 1936 is marked by both the popular and refined sides of the *commedia*. The summary in the present chapter has set a context for an analysis of this literature.

---

1 For a detailed account of the absorption of the *commedia dell'arte* into France, see Bruce Griffiths, 'Sunset: from *commedia dell'arte* to *comédie italienne*', in *Studies in the Commedia dell'Arte*, ed. by David J.George and Christopher J.Gossip (Cardiff: University of Wales Press, 1993), pp. 91-105.
2 Cyril W.Beaumont, *The History of Harlequin* (New York: Benjamin Blom, 1967 [reprint]), p.57.
3 Théodore de Banville, 'Arlequin', in *Critiques*, ed. by Victor Barrucand (Paris: Charpentier, 1917), pp.204-5 (p.204).
4 The poem may be read in Paul Verlaine, *Œvres poétiques complètes*, ed. by Jacques Borel (Paris: Gallimard, 1962), pp.320-21.
5 Robert Storey, *Pierrot: A Critical History of a Mask* (Princeton: Princeton UP, 1978), p.94.
6 A.G.Lehmann, 'Pierrot and fin de siècle', in *Romantic Mythologies*, ed. by I.Fletcher (London: Routledge & Kegan Paul, 1967), pp.209-23 (p.215).
7 *Ibid.*, p.217.
8 Russell P.King, 'The Poet as Clown: Variations on a Theme in Nineteenth-Century French Poetry', *Orbis Litterarum*, 33 (1978), 238-52 (p.250).

9 Pauline Baggio Hueurre, 'Étude du personnage de Pierrot' (unpublished doctoral thesis, Stanford University, 1976), p.100.

10 Jean Starobinski, *Portrait de l'artiste en saltimbanque* (Geneva: Albert Skira, 1970), p.66.

11 Lehmann, pp.218-19.

12 A similar position will be detected in the work of Lugones and Valle-Inclán (towards Pierrot and Harlequin respectively), to be analysed in chapter 5.

13 King, p.244.

14 See George Evans, 'Lesage and D'Orneval's *Théâtre de la foire*, the commedia dell'arte and power', in *Studies in the Commedia dell'Arte*, ed. by David J.George and Christopher J.Gossip, pp.107-20.

15 Hueurre, p.44.

16 King, p.241, p.242.

17 In *Odes funambulesques* (Paris: Librairie Alphonse Lemerre, n.d.), 108-37 (p. 129). King's comment on Banville's use of the clown figure is particularly relevant here: 'for Banville the common denominator of artist and acrobatic clown resides less in their comic mask or their function as entertainers than in their "vertical" aspirations, from reality to ideality, from the physical to the spiritual' (King, p.240).

18 For a selected bibliography of the *commedia* in Picasso, see chapter 6.

19 Starobinski, p.120. Richard Sheppard's view on the Dadaists' use of mythical and magical figures is also apposite here: 'behind the nonsensical surface of the Dada poems lies a therapeutic purpose. In Jung's thinking, the exteriorisation of psychic energies in the archetypes has the same function as the expression of those energies in the rites of Carnival in Bakhtin's: the maintenance of individual and/or collective psychic health in a universe which is, at one and the same time, naturally protean and yet over-burdened by superimposed, man-made forms. For all their attacks on its bourgeois forms, art should, in the Dadaists' view, have an analogous function. By conjuring up those unconscious energies repressed by Western civilisation and hence depriving them of their harmful potential, art should reaccustom people to them and thereby assist them to attain a state of dynamic balance within a universe of fluctuating opposites. The fantastical, magical figures of Dada poetry are not only dancing demigods amid such a universe, they are also embodiments of that theoretical belief and existential possibility, and if the poems in which they are celebrated seem like so much unintelligible and outrageous nonsense to the average reader, then that may well be because there is considerable truth in Jung's and Bakhtin's contention that the educated bourgeois has lost touch with the complexities of his own, most primitive nature and those of external Nature, and, simultaneously, much of his instinctive feeling for the myths, images and rituals which pictorialise the relationships between those two realms' ('Tricksters, carnival and the magical figures of Dada poetry', *Forum for Modern Language Studies*, 19 [2] [1983], 116-25 [p.123]).

For a detailed and challenging study of Surrealism and Spanish Drama, see Andrew A.Anderson, 'Bewitched, Bothered and Bewildered: Spanish Dramatists and Surrealism, 1924-1936', in *The Surrealist Adventure in Spain*, ed. by C.Brian Morris, Ottawa Hispanic Studies, 6 (Ottawa: Dovehouse, 1991), pp.240-81.

20 Susan Harrow, 'From Symbolism to Modernism - Apollinaire's Harlequin-Acrobat', in *Studies in the Commedia dell'Arte*, ed. by David J.George and Christopher J.Gossip, pp.199-236 (p.200).

21 *Ibid.*, p.200

22 There is a large bibliography on these three figures. On Craig, see James Fisher, 'Commedia Iconography in the Theatrical Art of Edward Gordon Craig', in *The Commedia dell'arte from the Renaissance to Dario Fo*, ed. by Christopher Cairns (Lampeter/Lewiston/Queenston: The Edwin Mellen Press, 1989), pp. 245-75. Fisher's recent book in the Edwin Mellen *Studies in the Commedia dell'arte* series has a full and detailed study of, and bibliography on, all three writers: see James Fisher, *The Theatre of Yesterday and Tomorrow*. See also W.Gareth Jones, '*Commedia*

dell'arte: Blok and Meyerhold, 1905-1917', in *Studies in the Commedia dell'Arte*, ed. by David J.George and Christopher J.Gossip, pp.185-97.

23 In *Copeau: Texts on Theatre*, ed. and trans. by John Rudlin and Norman H. Paul (London and New York: Routledge, 1990), p. 237. In their book on the *commedia dell'arte*, Kenneth and Laura Richards write: 'as the mingling in performance of masked and unmasked figures suggests, the improvised drama of the *commedia dell'arte* was stylized and non-naturalistic' (*The Commedia dell'Arte* [Oxford: Basil Blackwell, 1990], p.2). Richards and Richards also point out that the vision of *commedia dell'arte* presented by many practitioners since the mid-eighteenth century did not conform with the reality of the *commedia* itself: 'a stress on the simplistic is no less evident at times in the work of some practitioners, particularly those who, attracted by the myth of pristine innocence, play up "low" farce and facile buffoonery, and lean heavily on the stage interpretation of the "masks" as infantile grotesque' (p.304).

24 *Copeau: Texts on Theatre*, pp.192-93.

25 John Rudlin, *Jacques Copeau* (Cambridge: CUP, 1986), p.97.

26 *Copeau: Texts on Theatre*, pp.164-5.

27 This unpublished letter is quoted by J.de Palacio in 'La Posterité du Gaspard de la Nuit', in *Max Jacob I - Autour du poème en prose, Revue des Lettres Modernes* (Paris: Minard, 1973), p.187. Susan Harrow comments:
'The meaning of Jacob's statement has to be sought in the new stylistic temper and the emergence of a Modernist temper that develops in opposition to the dominant canon of the past century - Romantico-Symbolism, a sensibility predicated on the pursuit of sentimentality, lyrical effusiveness, and a preoccupation with subjectivity which posits the text as the vehicle for the expression of the more profound self of the artist. With scientific progress and material innovation leading to heightened human expectations towards the end of the nineteenth century, there occurs a significant displacement within the artistic sensibility. Lingering Romantic *ennui* gives way to a new spirit in the arts and to approaches which stress creativity over expressivity, objectivity over subjectivity. Consistent with this is a new emphasis on the work of art as self-referential object. And so the artist turns from an art of lyrical expression to one of objective construction. For Jacob, the ousting of the pitiful Pierrot by the agile Harlequin metaphorises the shift from the subjective art of the late nineteenth century to a more formalist-inclined art of creation whereby a more detached, critical imagination now prevails over the more purely lyrical sensibility of Romantico-Symbolism' (*Studies in the Commedia dell'Arte*, ed. by David J.George and Christopher J.Gossip, pp.211-12).

Chapter 2

The *Commedia* in Spain

The history of the *commedia* in Europe is, as has already been shown, full of contradictory trends and counter-trends. In Spain, there is no analogous refinement and polishing of the *commedia* until the late nineteenth century. When the *commedia* is taken up by turn-of-the-century Hispanic writers, the French influence is decisive, and native Spanish traditions are largely ignored. Yet Spanish writers before the late nineteenth century whose work contains allusions to the *commedia* normally have in mind precisely the native version of the genre which is almost always manifested in the Shrovetide carnival.[1] Furthermore, they tend not to idealise its pre-bourgeois popular essence, but rather adopt a detached *costumbista* approach or, in the case of Bécquer, are hostile to it. What follows is a brief historical survey of the development of the *commedia* in Spain prior to the late nineteenth century, and its links with the indigenous carnival tradition. Finally the continuation of these links in the early twentieth century is examined.

The *commedia* in sixteenth- and seventeenth-century Spain

In addition to their long and successful visits to France, the Italian players of the *commedia dell'arte* travelled to Spain. The person chiefly responsible for the production of Italian improvised comedy in Spain was the famous Harlequin actor Alberto Ganassa. He first came to Madrid in 1574 and put on plays in the *corral* theatres of the capital.[2] The Ganassa company also went to other Spanish cities, and by 1579 he had acquired such a reputation that he was summoned by Philip II to Toledo to play in the Corpus Christi celebrations before the King and the Queen.[3] He stayed in Spain until 1584 and is said to have returned in 1603.[4]

Ganassa and other *commedia dell'arte* players so caught the imagination of the organisers of the Spanish carnival, that in 1592 *ganassas* and *botargas* - an allusion to the actor Estafanelo Bottarga - are found in a carnival procession in Valencia. These figures also appear in other contemporary festivities.[5] This is important, in that not only was Ganassa's influence felt, and felt decisively, on the legitimate theatre, but also, at a very early date, a link is established between the *commedia* and the carnival in Spain. Two other Italian companies came to Spain: *los Corteses* (in 1583) and *los Confidentes* (in 1587). There is, however, no evidence that any others visited Spain after Ganassa until the eighteenth century.

Memories of Ganassa and others nonetheless survive, as is illustrated by scattered references in literature and the continued appearance of the masks in festivities. In 1667 *alriquines* appear on the back of the *tarasca* that it was proposed to construct for the Corpus Christi procession in Madrid.[6] Later in the seventeenth century, Bances Candamo writes of 'Comedias Mímicas, y Pantomímicas... que llaman de purichinela'.[7] This is the first reference to Punch in Spanish, but Bances is referring to the theatre in Italy rather than in Spain.

The eighteenth century

In 1703 a group of Italian comedians known as *los Trufaldines* came to Madrid and eventually established there their own theatre, the Caños del Peral.[8] They took their name from Trufaldin, or Truffaldino, one of the masks of the *commedia dell'arte*. Another Italian troupe came to Spain in 1713 and a letter addressed to the King on 21 March 1714 begins as follows: 'Señor *Florindo* y *Columbina*, puestos a los pies de V.S....'[9] The part of Colombina was played by Vicenta María Gardelini, wife of Francisco Neri, head of the company, and another character in the troupe was 'Covielo'.[10]

In the late eighteenth century there is evidence that *commedia* characters appeared as part of the repertoires of Italian troupes who were in Spain at the time. These troupes also performed mime theatre, acrobatics and puppet shows, and so a phenomenon similar to that of the French théâtres de la foire seems to have existed in Spain. Valuable information on the work of these Italian players is provided by J.E.Varey:

> También salieron en el tablado los descendientes de la *commedia dell'arte* italiana: Arlequín no falta nunca, y Hergueta es el primero que hace el papel de la época que nos interesa, saliendo en 1760. Escaramuza aparece en 1776, y en casi todos los años sucesivos; en 1786 dice Santiago Hergueta que ha servido a Madrid en este papel "desde mi nacimiento, sufriendo la impertinencia de tantos porrazos". En 1769 las dos compañías que actuaban en Madrid ostentaban sendos Escaramuzas y Arlequines. Trufaldín sale en 1768 y Colombina en 1783. En 1788 el papel de Colombina es remediado por un hombre, Juan López, que recibe una gratificación por "el esmero y propiedad con que ha vestido, tanto en los bailes como en las pantomimas, en que se le han ocasionado muchos gastos por imitar la propiedad del carácter de mujer en las Columbinas de dichas pantomimas". Por fin, vemos también a Pierrot, mencionado en el cartel de Angeli.[11]

> The descendants of the Italian *commedia dell'arte* also appeared on stage: Harlequin is ever-present, and Hergueta is the first to play the role in the period that interests us, appearing in 1760. Scaramouche appears in 1766 and in almost all of the following years; in 1786 Santiago Hergueta says that he has served Madrid in that role "since my birth, suffering the indignity of all those blows". In 1769 the two companies that were performing in Madrid each had a Scaramouche and a Harlequin. Truffaldino appears in 1768 and Columbine in 1783. In 1788 the part of Columbine is played by a man, Juan López, who receives a reward for the "care and faithfulness of his dress, in the dances as well as in the mimes,[12] in which his expenses have been great because he has represented with accuracy the character of a woman in the Columbine parts in these mimes". Finally we see Pierrot, who is referred to in Angeli's theatre bill.

Harlequin appears again in 1774, as part of the repertoire of these acrobats. Varey explains:

> La acción de una de las pantomimas de 1774 se localizó en un molino... El cartel de este año la llama "una mui lucida diversión nueva, que será una Comedia Inglesa, que han hecho en París la Quaresma pasada: el título es, las Desgracias de Arlinquin, y las Picardías del Molinero, volando al aire Casas, Ventanas, Molinero y Arlinquin todo junto, adornado de Tramoyas, todas de buen gusto".[13]

> The plot of one of the mimes of 1744 was set in a mill... The bill of that year called it "a splendid new entertainment, which will be an English Play, which was performed in Paris during the last Shrovetide carnival: its title is the Misfortunes of Harliquin, and the naughty tricks of the Miller, with Houses, Windows, Miller, Harliquin and all flying through the air, adorned with Stage Machinery, all in good taste".

The link between the *Arlinquin* and the carnival (the reference to 'Quaresma') provides further evidence of the early connection between the *commedia* and the carnival in Spain.

In an article on the activities of a Spanish troupe in the Canaries in the 1790s, Varey points out that the *commedia* masks formed part of the repertoire of this company: 'la segunda parte de la diversión es la pantomima española de magia; y los *dramatis personae* son Pantaleón, Arlequín, Colombina, Pierrot y un Médico anatomista'[14] ('the second part of the entertainment is the Spanish magic mime; and the cast list is Pantaloon, Harlequin, Columbine, Pierrot and an Anatomist'). As with the Italian troupes in Spain in the late eighteenth century, this company included puppet shows, shadow puppets, mime, juggling, conjuring and dance in their repertoire. Among the wealth of data provided by Varey is a curious advertisement of 1817 by an Italian company which offered acrobatics and an entertainment of performing dogs including 'una Columbina baylando el valsé' ('a

Columbine dancing a waltz'), and 'dos Columbinas dando algunas vueltas de paseo'[15] ('two Columbines going for a stroll').

Commedia dell'arte, puppets, mime and carnival were all part of the same popular culture and are often indistinguishable from one another. Both the *commedia* and the carnival appear in the work of a number of eighteenth- and nineteenth-century Spanish painters and writers. Goya, for instance, has an engraving showing *commedia* players. This is entitled *Los cómicos ambulantes*, which depicts an open-air performance, taking place in the country, attended by a large number of people including Columbine, Harlequin, Pantaloon and the Doctor. The date is not known, but it seems that it belongs to the mid or late 1790s.[16]

The Shrovetide carnival also forms the subject of a number of Goya's paintings and drawings. Nigel Glendinning, in an article on the carnival in the works of Goya and Alas, makes some interesting and important observations on Goya's use of carnival. In the earlier paintings, such as *El pelele*, he suggests, Goya is more restrained than, for example, in the drawings of the *Disparates*. Glendinning writes of *El pelele* that 'carnival, in fact, is a subject for observation rather than comment'.[17] The tossing of the *pelele* in a blanket was part of the traditional Shrovetide carnival celebrations, as was the burial of the sardine, which forms the subject of another Goya painting in which the artist is more concerned with the disorderly aspects of carnival than he was in *El pelele*. Disorder, and the concern with the grotesque, increased in Goya's later drawings of carnival, for example in *Disparate de carnaval*. During the carnival people were able to hide their normal identity behind a mask. It was a time of licentiousness, when barriers were broken down, and when links were reestablished with a primitive society. The carnival, of course, was an unusual or abnormal period, in which respectable people could let their hair down, their identities hidden behind their mask. Bakhtin and his followers have explored the subversive, anti-establishment aspects of such manifestations of popular culture as the carnival,[18] and indeed Julio Caro Baroja has a full-length study of the carnival phenomenon in Spain.[19]

Commedia and carnival in nineteenth-century Spanish literature

The carnival theme appears in the work of a number of nineteenth-century Spanish writers, such as Larra and Alas, while Bécquer deals in his essays with both the carnival and the *commedia*. In an essay from *Ensayos y esbozos* entitled 'La ridiculez' (1862), Bécquer chooses Harlequin to represent the absurd anti-hero: 'la ridiculez... es Arlequín que cambia su espada de madera por otra de acero, asesina con ella en broma y dice después a su víctima una bufonada por toda oración fúnebre'[20] ('ridiculousness ..is Harlequin who swaps his wooden sword for one of steel, kills with it in jest and then recites a joke to his victim instead of a funeral oration'). There is an interesting contrast between the Harlequins of Bécquer and Banville. In the latter's 'Arlequin' (published six years after 'La ridiculez') Harlequin is idealised, while Bécquer's character is anti-hero rather than hero, a grotesque and absurd figure.[21]

Bécquer's view that the adulation of heroes is absurdly out of date emerges clearly from another essay, 'El carnaval' (from *Escenas de Madrid*), in which the *commedia* and the carnival are once more inextricably linked, as Harlequin is again the butt of Bécquer's biting satire: 'la política y el amor pedían prestado su traje a Arlequín, y el alegre ruido de los cascabeles del cetro del bufón urdían la trama de su novela sangrienta o sentimental'.[22] ('politics and love borrowed its Harlequin costume, and the joyful sound of the bells of the clown's sceptre contrived the plot of its bloody or sentimental novel').

Commedia and carnival in the early twentieth century

The tradition of harlequins, columbines and pierrots taking part in the Shrovetide carnival continues in Spain well into the twentieth century. However, its appearance not only in the carnival but also in *zarzuelas*, operettas, film[23] and in journalism in the early years of the century, probably owes less to Spanish carnival tradition than to the fact that the *commedia* was 'in the air' in both popular and high culture at the time. Interestingly, whereas it was Harlequin who appeared in the Spanish carnival of earlier centuries, it is Pierrot who predominates in the early years of the twentieth, which tends to confirm that French influence was at work.

This was as much true of Catalonia as it was of Castilian-speaking Spain. To quote Xavier Fàbregas:

> Dins la iconografia modernista hi trobarem un lloc destacat els mims, que amb robes folgades i emblanquinats de Pierrot sospiraren sota una lluna plena penjada dels telers dels escenaris, tot protagonitzant quadres entendridors.[24]

> In *modernista* iconography we find a special place for mimics, who with their wide costumes and whitened Pierrot faces sighed beneath a full moon hanging from the backcloths of the stages, as they acted out sentimental scenes.

The most famous of these Catalan Pierrots was Enric Adams, who began his stage career in Barcelona in 1892. He acted mainly in music halls, and also performed outside Catalonia in places as far apart as Paris, Moscow, London and Alexandria.[25]

A special place in the development and spread of the *commedia* in Catalonia is occupied by the Quatre Gats café in Barcelona. This was the meeting-place for such *commedia* practicitioners as Picasso and Rusiñol, and marionette and shadow puppet shows were performed there. The Quatre Gats epitomised Catalan *modernisme*, and did much to cement the close link between popular and high art that is characteristic of the movement.[26]

There is no analogous institution in Madrid, but this does not prevent the *commedia* from playing an important part in the popular culture of the Spanish capital. In 1908, for example, a *zarzuela* entitled *La tragedia de Pierrot* (*The Tragedy of Pierrot*) was put on in Madrid, and was reviewed several times in *ABC* during the following years. Its setting is a stereotyped *modernista* moonlit garden, and the reviewer of 1911 praises particularly the effectiveness of the lighting.[27] The title of the *zarzuela* suggests the sentimental 'poor' Pierrot already analysed in chapter 1, and which will be discussed in the Hispanic context in chapters 4 and 5. Pierrot is also the subject of an operetta enitled *Sueño de Pierrot* (*Pierrot's Dream*), which was performed in Barcelona and Valencia and reviewed in *ABC* on 16 February 1914. The reviewer stresses the play's Romantic characteristics, highlighting its lyrical tenderness and passionate love. Pierrot also dominated the Madrid carnival during these years. Many floats were decorated by his elegant presence, the trend reaching its peak in 1915, when a float of *pierrots* entitled *Juego de Bolos* won second prize in the procession (see fig.1).

If Pierrot 'wins first prize' for the number of appearances he makes in the carnival, and in musical drama, then he is followed by Harlequin and Columbine. The latter is Pierrot's companion in many of the carnival processions, and Arlequín appears several times in plays such as *El arlequín*, reviewed in *ABC* on 9 March 1909:

> Nuestro querido compañero Manolo Soriano y su consorte literario Luis Falcato estrenaron ayer, con éxito completo, *El arlequín*, juguete cómico que une a la gracia de sus escenas una correctísima y fluyente versificación.
>   Para *El arlequín* han compuesto los señores Cristóbal y Barte unos cuantos números de música retozona, de los que se repitieron un dúo muy bonito, una vibrante jota y un 'cake-val' intencionado.
>   *El arlequín* se lo tomó muy a gusto el público, y a los insistentes aplausos de la paroquia se presentaron cuatro veces en escena los autores...

> Yesterday our dear colleague Manolo Soriano and his literary consort Luis Falcato staged a highly successful first performance of *El arlequín*, a comic sketch which adds a most correct and fluent versification to the humour of its scenes.
>   For *El arlequín* Messrs Cristóbal and Barte have composed a few cheerful little numbers, and they did an encore of a very nice duo, a lively *jota*[28] and a meaningful cake-walk.
>   The audience really enjoyed *El arlequín*, and the authors responded to the persistent applause by taking four curtain calls.

It will be observed from the review that the work is a comic sketch, which could possibly indicate a Bakhtinian celebration of the ludic content of popular culture. Much more likely, however, is that *El arlequín* contains the sort of commercial trivia against which the likes of Valle-Inclán, Rivas Cherif and García Lorca constantly railed. For them, their version of *commedia* and popular culture in general possessed the cleansing spirit which could help rid the Spanish theatre of the scourge of plays like *El arlequín*.

The same would appear to be true of an opera entitled *El triunfo de Arlequín* (*The Triumph of Harlequin*), which, according to the *ABC* reviewer (17 November 1918), is a sentimental work whose most impressive moment was the dream of Pierrot (not Harlequin, despite the title) in the third act:

> El cartel inaugural no podía ser más tentador; el estreno de una ópera de un joven maestro español y la presentación de un excelente cuadro de artistas de reconocida valía. Hay que reconocer que a la natural expectación ha correspondido el éxito. *El triunfo de Arlequín*, principalmente en lo que a la partitura se refiere, y con especialidad al valor de su técnica, duestra [sic] en el joven compositor que con tanta fortuna reveló su talento al estrenar su primera partitura, *El príncipe bohemio,* un avance considerable.
> El libro es una nueva versión del viejo poema de la comedia italiana: la veleidosa Colombina y sus eternos admiradores de sus gracias, Pierrot, Arlequín y Polichinela.
> Sobre el poema, escrito por González Rendón, el maestro Millán ha escrito una partitura muy estimable, avalorada por los procedimientos orquestales y por la elegante línea melódica, en la que se destacan con vigoroso relieve los diversos caracteres de los personajes-símbolos de la farsa...
> El número que mayor efecto produjo fue el sueño de Pierrot, del segundo acto, que fue repetido entre grandes aplausos.

The opening bill could not be more tempting; the first performance of an opera of a young Spanish maestro and the presentation of an excellent team of artists of recognised quality. It must be said that with its success the play lived up to expectations. With *El triunfo de Arlequín*, especially in the score and technical aspects, the young composer who revealed his talents in his first opera, *El príncipe bohemio (The Bohemian Prince)*, has shown considerable progress.

> The book is a new version of the old poem of the Italian comedy; the flighty Columbine and the eternal admirers of her charms, Pierrot, Harlequin and Pulcinella.
> The composer Millán has written a superb score on the poem by González Rendón, enhanced by excellent orchestral touches, and by the elegant melody in which the personalities of the various characters-symbols of the farce really stand out...
> The biggest hit was Pierrot's dream, in the second act, which was repeated to great applause.

The real-life 'popular' theatre, it seems, was a long way removed from the idealised version of it portrayed by García Lorca and others.

Por esos mundos

One of the main sources of articles, playlets and short stories on the *commedia* theme in early twentieth-century Spain was *Por esos mundos*. Published mainly on a monthly basis between 1900 and 1916, it was a general arts and travel journal, which produced a number of splendidly illustrated items on the *commedia*, mime, the circus and the carnival. A number of leading Spanish writers, including Benavente and Valle-Inclán, published there. It was an important forum both for well-known authors such as these and for minor writers who were interested in the *commedia* and analogous themes (see figs. 5-11).

Some of the works which appeared in *Por esos mundos* are discussed elsewhere in this book, but one regular writer deserves special mention here. Manuel Abril wrote some extremely perceptive articles on the tradition of the macabre in art (August 1913) and two on the carnival (February 1914 and March 1915), as well as an excellent piece on the *commedia* in modern art entitled 'Pierrot y Colombina', which was published in the April 1913 number of the journal.

The last-mentioned article reveals Abril's knowledge of the history of the *commedia dell'arte*, as well as his sensitive appreciation of the development of

Pierrot in the nineteenth century, particularly of how he became a refined decadent. According to Abril, suffering became an important ingredient of the *fin-de-siècle* Pierrot: 'pero cuando Pierrot deja de representar el sufrimiento del hombre y pasa a ser hombre que sufre, lo amargo se acentúa' ('but when Pierrot stops representing man's suffering and becomes instead the man who suffers, bitterness is accentuated') (p.459). Abril, however, believes that Pierrot always retains some of his clown's characteristics, which are set against the refinement and the sensitivity: 'es el Pierrot que se arma de una escoba para hacer rabiar a las porteras, el Pierrot del barullo, la trapacería y la desfachatez - *il s'en fiche, lui* - el bohemio, en una palabra' ('it is Pierrot who arms himself with a broom to frighten the [women] caretakers, the noisy, gossiping, impudent Pierrot - *il s'en fiche, lui* - in short, Pierrot the bohemian') (p.459).

Abril sums up Pierrot as follows, and links him with the figure of Hamlet:

> Si a esta condición de sarcástico histérico y de macabro histérico se añade la manía filosofadora, se tiene en sus tres características principales al Pierrot definitivamente representativo, a ese Pierrot que viene a ser un Hamlet vestido de Payaso. (pp.453-54)

> If to this condition of hysterical sarcasm and macabre hysteria one adds that of a philosophising mania, then one has the three chief characteristics of the final version of the representative Pierrot, of that Pierrot who is a Hamlet dressed as a clown.

Abril is acutely aware of the setimentality/irony dichotomy of the early twentieth-century Pierrot, as *art pierrot* collides head on with *art arlequin*. This dichotomy finds expression in Abril's essay in the image of a juxtaposition between prose and poetry:

> Pero su destino quiso envolverle hasta el final en una suprema ironía: por ser irónico y poner un escarmiento amargo-burlesco a todo, incluso su vida misma es burla, es la ironía de entrometer

prosa prosaica en una historia que se había inventado para poetizar las aventuras del querer. (p.460)

But his destiny decided to involve him right to the end in a supreme piece of irony: as an ironist himself who always moralises in a half-bitter half-burlesque way about everything, even his own life is a joke; it is the irony of inserting prosaic prose into a story which was invented to poeticise adventures of love.[29]

From enthusiasm to disillusionment

Por esos mundos illustrates how the *commedia* had permeated Spanish cultural life by the early years of the twentieth century. Another illustration is the appearance in 1912 (the same year in which Valle-Inclán's *La marquesa Rosalinda* received its first performance) of two journals entitled *Arlequín* and *Polichinela*. *Polichinela* never appeared again after 1912, but *Arlequín* did re-emerge later in the decade, with several numbers being printed in 1919 and 1920.

The tone of these contrasts sharply with that of the 1912 number. Gone are the joy and the gaiety of the former, and in their place one finds a sense of disillusionment with the *commedia* and the carnival. Clearly, by the late 1910s the *commedia* was such a well-worn topic in Spanish musical comedy, and particularly carnival, that weariness with it was exhibited in press articles. For instance, a review of the *zarzuela, El pan nuestro (A Daily Event) (ABC,* 1 January 1917) makes the point that the Pierrot theme is beginning to grow stale:

La acción es en Madrid, y el panecillo, por lo tanto, está falto de peso; y, como es más ligero que el aire, sube y sube hasta alizar (véase aterrizar) en el astro de la noche. Allí le recibe Pierrot, cantando a la luna, como de costumbre.

The setting is Madrid, and the little bread, as a consequence, lacks weight; and since it is lighter than the air, it rises and rises until it lands on the star of the night. There it is met by Pierrot, who as usual is singing to the moon.

The key phrase is 'as usual', which emphasises the familiarity of the theme. Press review articles of the carnival stress weariness with what was viewed as repetitive fare. The enthusiasm for the elegance and gaiety of the floats of *pierrots* and *colombinas* of the early years of the century is tempered, until the following review of the 1920 carnival appears (*ABC*, 17 February):

> No es de extrañar, por tanto, que en el desfile de carrozas y de coches - salvo contadas excepciones - brillara por su ausencia el arte y el buen gusto, ofreciéndose en cambio el desfile de los tan conocidos 'clowns', 'pierrots' y 'colombinas'.

> It is not surprising, then, that with a very few exceptions, artistic merit and good taste are notable for their absence in the processions of floats and carriages. What one gets instead is a procession of the all-too-familiar clowns, pierrots and columbines.

The phrase 'all-too-familiar' parallels the 'as usual' of the 1917 review of *El pan nuestro* and suggests that around this time disillusionment with the *commedia* and with the carnival increased. It is perhaps no coincidence that these pieces were published either during the latter stages of the Great War or in the years immediately following it, when escapist spectacles which were perceived as lacking *gravitas* would seem to be inappropriate.[30]

Equally important, the enthusiasm for 'popular' *commedia*, carnival, and circus, which was felt by some of the avant-garde writers and artists not only of Spain but also of Europe in general, was clearly not shared by hack reviewers of the Spanish daily press. The *commedia* in early twentieth-century Spain was obviously little more than a fashion or a fad as far as musical comedy and the popular theatre were concerned, and its practitioners were not innovative either thematically or technically. A very different picture emerges from painters and writers like Picasso, Dalí and García Lorca (the first of whom was painting Cubist Harlequins *before* some of the press reviews which have been studied), who explore the liberating potential of the ludic traditions of the *commedia*, in particular of Harlequin, as well as the interplay between civilisation and primitiveness, and the multiple persona associated with the masks of Harlequin, Pierrot or the clown. It would be left to the forward-looking theatre critics like Pérez de Ayala and Rivas Cherif, and the painters and the writers of the avant-garde, to explore the exciting possibilities of the *commedia*.

---

1 This link, of course, is not limited to Spain. It is also a feature, for instance, of the Nice and Venice carnivals.

2 For an account of Ganassa's work in Spain and his contribution to the Spanish commedia of the Golden Age, see N.D.Shergold, 'Ganassa and the *commedia dell'arte* in the Sixteenth-Century Spain', *MLR*, 51 (1956), 359-68. For details of Ganassa's second visit to Spain in 1603, see J.E.Varey, 'Ganassa en la península ibérica en 1603', in *De los romances-villancico a la poesía de Claudio Rodríguez. 22 ensayos sobre las literaturas española e hispanoamericana en homenaje a Gustav Siebenmann*, ed. by José Manuel López de Abadia and Augusta López Bernasocchi (Madrid: José Esteban, 1984), pp.455-62. I am grateful to Professor Varey for drawing my attention to this article. For a guide to primary and secondary sources to the *commedia* in Spain, see Thomas F.Heck, *Commedia dell'arte: a Guide to the Primary and Secondary Literature*, especially pp.161-65.

3 Shergold, p. 360.

4 Casiano Pellicer, *Tratado histórico sobre el origen y progresos de la comedia y del histrionismo en España*, 2 vols (Madrid: Imp. del Real Arbitrio de Beneficencia, 1804), I, 72.

5 Shergold, pp.364-65.

6 The drawing is reproduced in J.E.Varey and N.D.Shergold, 'La tarasca de Madrid: un aspecto de la procesión del Corpus durante los siglos XVII y XVIII', *Clavileño*, 4 (1953), no.20, 21.

7 *Theatro de los theatros*, ed. by Duncan Moir (London: Támesis, 1970), p.14.

8 E.Cotarelo y Mori, *Orígenes y establecimiento de la ópera en España hasta 1800* (Madrid: n.pub.,1917), pp.27 ff; J.E.Varey, 'The First Theatre on the Site of the Caños del Peral', *Dieciocho*, 9 (1986), 290-96. I am grateful to Professor Varey for drawing my attention to this article.

9 Cotarelo y Mori, p.45. For detailed information on the Italian companies in Spain in this period see N.D. Shergold, J.E. Varey and Charles Davis, *Fuentes para la historia del teatro en España, XI. Teatros y comedias en Madrid: 1699-1719. Estudio y documentos* (London: Támesis, 1986).

10 Cotarelo y Mori, pp.46-7. On Covielo, or Coviello, see K.M.Lea, *Italian Popular Comedy*, 2 vols (Oxford: Clarendon, 1934,), II, 485 *passim*.

11 *Los títeres y otras diversiones populares de Madrid: 1758-1840* (London: Támesis, 1972), p.23.

12 I have translated the Spanish *pantomima* as *mime*, *mime theatre* or *mime show* throughout, in order to distinguish it from the traditional English pantomime.

13 J.E.Varey, *Los títeres y otras diversiones*, p.25.

14 J.E.Varey, ' "Mucho ruido y pocas nueces": un episodio teatral canario de 1784', *Segismundo*, no.3 (1955), 115-34 (p.127).

15 *Los títeres y otras diversiones populares*, plate 8.

16 The picture is reproduced in Pierre Gassier and Juliet Wilson, *The Life and Complete Works of Francisco Goya* (London: Thames and Hudson, 1971), p.110.

17 'Some Versions of Carnival: Goya and Alas', in *Studies in Modern Spanish Literature and Art Presented to Helen F.Grant*, ed. by Nigel Glendinning (London: Támesis, 1972), pp.65-78.

18 See for example Mikhail Bakhtin, *Rabelais and his World*, trans. by Helene Iswolksy (Cambridge, Mass: MIT, 1968). For interesting background material on the themes of disorder and

topsiturviness in literature, see Helen F.Grant, 'El mundo al revés', in *Hispanic Studies in Honour of Joseph Manson*, ed. by Dorothy M. Atkinson and Anthony H. Clarke (Oxford: Dolphin, 1972), pp.119-37. The 'planned disorder' of carnival, in the seventeenth century, is also the subject of an article by J.E.Varey, 'La creación deliberada de la confusión: estudio de una diversión de carnestolendas de 1623', in *Homenaje al Prof. William L.Fichter* (Madrid: Castalia, 1971), pp.745-54.

19 Julio Caro Baroja, *El carnaval* (Madrid: Taurus, 1979).

20 G.A.Bécquer, *Obras completas* (Barcelona: Ferma, 1966), p.580.

21 On the grotesque in Bécquer, see Paul Ilie, 'Bécquer and the Romantic Grotesque', *PMLA*, 83 (1968), 312-31.

22 *Obras completas*, p.1197.

23 I have a record of two films whose titles include the names of commedia characters: *La señorita Arlequín*, and *¿Polichinelas?* The last showing of *La señorita Arlequín* was advertisd in *ABC* on 31 March 1919; *¿Polichinelas?* was reviewed in *ABC* on 2 May 1920.

24 Xavier Fàbregas, *Història del teatre català* (Barcelona: Millà, 1978), pp.193-94.

25 *Ibid.*, p.194.

26 The use of the Pierrot figure as a polemical Catalan *modernista* symbol will be discussed in chapter 4. Since the completion of the text of this book, my attention has been drawn to an unpublished Ph.D. thesis on the subject of Pierrot in Catalan *modernisme*, which, unfortunately, I have not been able to consult. The thesis in question is Jordi Lladó Vilaseca, 'Pierrot i la literatura catalana modernista', Universitat Autònoma de Barcelona, 1992. I am grateful to Dr Enric Gallén, of the Pompeu Fabra University of Barcelona, for drawing my attention to the existence of this thesis.

27 See *ABC* for the following dates: 1 April 1908; 5 June 1909; 17 June 1910; 9 and 10 March 1911. I have not been able to see a text of this work or of the others referred to in this chapter. I have to presume that they are lost.

28 The *jota* is a dance from Aragon.

29 A clear parallel will be noted with Valle-Inclán, whose *La marquesa Rosalinda* will be discussed in chapter 5.

30 Here the parallel is with Benavente's *La ciudad alegre y confiada* (1916), which will also be analysed in chapter 5.

Chapter 3

The Comic Spirit of the *Commedia*

As Chapter 1 showed, one of the most important reasons for the revival of interest in the *commedia dell'arte* in the early twentieth century was that it was believed to typify the essence of popular theatre and street spectacle. The rediscovery and recreation of the *commedia* was linked to a rediscovery of man's primitive roots, which had been stifled by centuries of Western civilisation. Also, directors like Craig and Copeau saw the *commedia* as anti-Naturalist and a source for the regeneration of the theatre.

The present chapter will do two things. First, it will examine this rediscovery and recreation in early twentieth-century Spain, and its specific relevance to the regeneration of Spanish and Catalan theatre, by taking into account the theoretical views of writers and directors such as Gual, Benavente, Pérez de Ayala, Rivas Cherif, Valle-Inclán and Lorca.[1] It will consider how the attraction of the *commedia* to these authors is that it encapsulates an eternal comic spirit, which should be recreated as an essential part of the contemporary theatre's recapturing of its popular roots. At the same time, it will argue that for certain writers the *commedia* seems to possess the freshness and vitality which are associated with youth, and even with childish playfulness. The roguish innocence is exemplified above all by the figure of Harlequin.

Secondly, Chapter 3 will examine the extent to which the theories which have been outlined are put into practice in specific plays in which modern authors attempt to recreate the comic spirit of the *commedia*, with its roguish innocence.

Three plays will be analysed: Baroja's *Arlequín, mancebo de botica* (1927-28), Gual's *La serenata* (1916), and Benavente's *Los intereses creados* (1907).

The *commedia* and regeneration: Pérez de Ayala

Pérez de Ayala discusses the history of the *commedia* in an undated essay from *Las mascaras*, 'El gran teatro del mundo' ('The Great Theatre of the World'). He sees the the *commedia* as a purified, stylised version of Latin comedy. It is, he says, typical of the type of theatre in which characters are not profound creations but serve as pretexts for social comment of the most trivial and fleeting kind. Ayala does not mean this in any derogatory sense, but emphasises that this type of theatre precludes profound characterisation, in contrast to Greek, Spanish and English drama:

> Este es el procedimiento de la *commedia dell'arte*, en la cual el asunto y los personajes no son sino pretexto y ocasión para comentar la vida contemporánea, en su aspecto urbano más trivial y pasajero; las preocupaciones, prejuicios, necedades, gustos y modas burguesas de una época. La *commedia dell'arte* es así e inadvertiblemente el arquetipo de un género teatral, el más difundido y más artificioso, por más hacedero.
> El otro procedimiento - el del teatro griego y el de los teatros español e inglés clásicos - es inverso: comienza por tomar una personalidad excepcionalmente poderosa, como núcleo genético de la obra.[2]

> This is the way of the *commedia dell'arte*, in which the plot and the characters are merely a pretext and an opportunity to comment on the contemporary scene, in the most trivial and transient setting of polite society; the concerns, prejudices, foolish deeds, tastes and bourgeois fashions of a period. The *commedia dell'arte* is therefore inevitably the archetype of a theatrical genre, the most widespread and ingenious because it is the most practical.
> The other method - that of Greek drama and of Spanish and English Classical drama - is the exact opposite: it begins by taking an exceptionally powerful personality as the generative nucleus of the work.

Pérez de Ayala sets the *commedia* in the context of popular European puppet tradition, as he evokes the kind of street entertainment associated with popular culture by Bakhtin and his followers. He also sees the *commedia* as belonging essentially to the craftsman stratum of medieval Italian society:

> Aparentemente, por lo que se ve, la *commedia dell'arte* era un tinglado dominical de plazuela, al modo del Guignol, en Francia, y el Punch and Judy, en Inglaterra. El nombre completo que se le daba era: «comedia improvisada por menestrales». La palabra «arte», que figura en el nombre de esta forma de divertimiento callejero, no está empleada en el sentido estético de hoy en día. Las «artes», en las ciudades italianas de la Edad Media, eran los gremios o corporaciones de menestrales, por oficios. (p.571)

> The *commedia dell'arte* seems to have been a Sunday street entertainment, like the French Guignol and the English Punch and Judy. Its full title was *improvised artisan comedy*. The word *arte*, which appears in the name of this kind of street entertainment, is not used in the modern sense of he word. The *arts*, in medieval Italian cities, were artisan associations or corporations, organised by profession.

The *commedia* and regeneration: Pío Baroja

Another Spanish writer, Pío Baroja, sees the *commedia* as anti-Naturalist: 'pensar que se pueden llevar figuras de hombre reales al Teatro, creo que es una ilusión con que se engaña un poco a la gente joven'[3] ('it seems to me that young people are labouring under an illusion if they believe that one can bring to the Theatre the characters of real people'). In another comment which recalls Copeau, Baroja believes that *commedia* characters represent comic tradition, brought up to date for the modern audience: 'el que quiera hacer algo en el Teatro tiene que emplear figuras ya viejas, aunque con etiquetas modernas' ('if one wishes to work in the Theatre one must use ancient characters, albeit with modern labels') (p.8). Baroja here expresses a sentiment that one finds time and again in relation to progressive theatre in the early twentieth century, namely that popular comic tradition, modernised and adapted to new movements, represents the best hope for the regeneration of what the progressive thinkers saw as an ossified commercial theatre.

The *commedia* and regeneration: Rivas Cherif

Rivas Cherif, who played the part of Arlequín in a production of Baroja's *Arlequín, mancebo de botica* during the 1925-26 season at the Baroja household,[4] points to the dynamic possibilities of the *commedia* in the creation of improvised drama and, in words that echo Copeau on Charlie Chaplin, even an improvised film-script:

> Buen ejercicio de *commedia dell'arte* es el de improvisar un diálogo de clowns sobre un truco conocido. Y luego, espiritualizándolo paulatinamente, pasar a algunos temas o guiones de *comedia italiana* de las mascaras e inventar, sobre los caracteres del Arlequín, la Colombina, el Polichinela, el Pantaleón, una comedia de estilo; para pasar por último a un argumento moderno de película, improvisando los actores las palabras del guión, a base de unas cuantas frases, o chistes obligados, que rellenar con el diálogo corriente.[5]

> A good *commedia dell'arte* exercise is to improvise a dialogue between clowns on a well-known routine. And then, while making it gradually more spiritual, to move to themes or scripts of the Italian comedy of masks and to invent a stylised play based on the characters of Harlequin, Columbine, Pulcinella, Pantaloon; and then finally move to a modern film plot, with the actors improvising the script, based on a few phrases or standard jokes with which to fill out the everyday dialogue.

Like Valle-Inclán, Rivas considered that the cinema, far from representing a threat to the theatre, was an exciting art form which could open up new horizons for the theatre.[6] In a 1920 article on new European theatre, in which he reveals his penchant for *teatros de arte* and in which he expresses his admiration for ventures such as Copeau's Le Vieux Colombier, Rivas Cherif sees the creation of a universal comic type as a way of maintaining the purity of drama. Harlequin and Charlie Chaplin are both cited as archetypal comic figures, as, curiously, is Don Juan:

Mientras subsista la organización actual de la sociedad, corresponde al artista mantener el fuego sagrado del arte puro, es decir, trascendente. Ha de suscitar la creación del tipo cómico universal, en el espectáculo de cuya pasión purgue la Humanidad su afán, el Arlequín, el don Juan, el Charlot. Para ello es preciso luchar sin tregua contra el rebajamiento industrial del teatro.[7]

As long as society continues to be organised as at present, it is the artist's role to maintain the sacred flame of pure, that is to say vital, art. He should promote the creation of a universal comic type, in the spectacle of whose passion Humanity may purge its anxiety: Harlequin, don Juan, Charlot. In order to achieve this, we must fight against the commercial abasement of the theatre.

In the article, Rivas Cherif links the search for a pure, uncontaminated theatre with popular dramatic culture, and refers to a Spanish production of Ibsen's play, *An Enemy of the People:*

La reciente representación de *Un enemigo del pueblo* de Ibsen, interpretado por actores bisoños, ante un público popular, en el Teatro Español, con motivo del último Congreso de la Unión General de Trabajadores, ha revelado hasta qué punto es fácil la regeneración de nuestra escena a base de actores y espectadores no contaminados por el ambiente.[8]

The recent performance of Ibsen's *An Enemy of the People*, played by inexperienced actors, before a lower-class audience in the Teatro Español on the occasion of the recent Conference of the UGT,[9] has shown how easy is a regeneration of our stage based on actors and spectators who have not been corrupted by the environment.

The *commedia* and regeneration: García Lorca

These sentiments are very similar to those of Lorca, particularly in puppet plays like *El retablillo de don Cristóbal* (*The 'retablillo' of Don Critstóbal*) (1931). This play contains, strictly speaking, only two brief references to a recognisable *commedia dell'arte* character: Arlequín, who is mentioned in the Director's epilogue, and a certain 'don Pantaleón' whom don Cristóbal says he served as a young man in France and Italy. However, this widely-travelled don Cristóbal is himself a Spanish version of Pulcinella or Punch, his full name being don Cristóbal de Polichinela. The Director presents him in the epilogue as a cousin to the Galician Bululú, brother-in-law of la tía Norica of Cádiz, brother of Monsieur Guiñol from Paris, and uncle to don Arlequín from Bergamo. They are all part of one big happy European puppet family, an idealised popular tradition, which embodies that purification of the Spanish theatre which Lorca judged was so urgently needed.[10]

The Director refers to 'esta viejísima farsa rural' ('this most ancient rural farce'), and to the Andalusian *cristobita* theatre as one where 'sigue pura la vieja esencia del teatro' ('the ancient essence of the theatre is preserved in a pure form') (p.697). His words, which reflect those of Crispín in the prologue to the much earlier play *Los intereses creados*, also belong to the *beatus ille* convention, and are very much in the Romantic tradition of folk literature.[11]

The main focus of Lorca's attention is, however, the regeneration of the Spanish theatre, as the Director makes clear in the epilogue: 'llenemos el teatro de espigas frescas, debajo de las cuales vayan palabrotas que luchen en la escena con el tedio y la vulgaridad a que la tenemos condenada' ('let's fill the theatre with fresh ears of corn, beneath which will be found swearwords which will fight on the stage against the boredom and the vulgarity to which we have condemned it') (p.697). Similar sentiments are expressed in the following :

> El teatro debe abandonar la atmósfera abstracta de las salas reducidas, su clima estrecho de experimentación, de *élite*, e ir a las masas [...] Eso es lo que trato de hacer yo en *Bodas de sangre* y en *La zapatera prodigiosa*. Las cosas están puestas aquí, las palabras, los matices, las ocurrencias, lo delicioso, lo dramático, lo simple y lo complicado, de una manera 'popular'.[12]

> The theatre must abandon the abstract atmosphere of minority theatre, with its narrow experimental and élite climate, and turn to the masses [...] That is what I have tried to do in *Blood Wedding* and in *The Shoemaker's Prodigious Wife*. Everything that is

contained there - words, nuances, events, delicious, dramatic, simple and complicated things - is treated in a 'popular' fashion.

The main body of the text of *El retablillo*, too, contains the idea that popular puppet types could be an agent of the regeneration of the middle-class commercial theatre. In a piece of humorous banter between the Poet and the Director, the former surreptitiously complains to the audience:

> Si el director de escena quisiera, don Cristóbal vería las ninfas del agua y doña Rosita podría llenar de escarcha sus cabellos en el acto tercero, donde cae la nieve sobre los inocentes. Pero el dueño del teatro tiene a los personajes metidos en una cajita de hierro para que los vean solamente las señoras con pecho de seda y nariz tonta y los caballeros con barba que van al club y dicen: Ca-ram-ba. Porque don Cristóbal no es así, ni doña Rosita (p.691).

> If the director wished, don Cristóbal would see the water nymphs and doña Rosita could fill her hair with frost in the third act, when snow falls on the innocent people. But the theatre owner has the characters locked up in an iron box so that they may be seen only by silk-breasted and foolish-nosed ladies and by bearded gentlemen who go to the club and exclaim: Good gracious! For don Cristóbal is not like that, and neither is doña Rosita.

Here the Poet's criticism is directed at the theatre owner, who is more powerful than the Director, and whose vision of popular types epitomised by puppets is so limited that he is afraid to allow them to come to life and be real. The complaint seems to be that they have been consigned to little more than museum pieces. One may compare the situation of the puppets referred to in the above reference with Zapatera's longing to be allowed onto the stage in the prologue to *La zapatera prodigiosa*, and with the situation of the puppets in *Los títeres de Cachiporra*, who were locked up, but who have escaped and have come to entertain their audience, whoever the latter may be.[13]

Lorca's own opinions on the importance of the Director are summed up in the sentence: 'un teatro es, ante todo, un buen director'[14] ('a theatre is, above all else, a good director'), while his well-known views on the incompatibility of commercial interests and artistic integrity reflect a wider debate on the subject in the Spain of the 1920s.[15] In short, *El retablillo de don Cristóbal*, like Lorca's other farces, enabled him to explore a part of Andalusian folklore, linking it with a wider European tradition. It also allowed him to experiment with themes and techniques which are more ambitiously and fully developed in the Surrealist plays and the folk tragedies, and which acted too as a vehicle for his views on the regeneration of the Spanish theatre. Although Harlequin has only a minor part in the play, he is clearly seen by Lorca as belonging to the same extended happy family of puppets as his European relatives.[16]

The *commedia* and regeneration: Gual

In the first part of the twentieth century the most innovative theatre director in Catalan drama, and possibly in Spanish drama in general, was Adrià Gual. In the introduction to his 1912 'fair farce', *Arlequí vividor* (*Harlequin the Wide Boy*), Gual sees comedy as the essence of popular culture which endured in a time of absurdly imitative Classicism. The grotesque and the carnivalesque blended with allegory as popular art survived in clandestine fashion for some fifteen centuries.

The *commedia dell'arte* raised the triumphal flag of this comic tradition in the Renaissance, epitomising the whole Latin tradition of 'ingeni i astúcia'[17] ('skill and cunning'). It did not deal with contemporary themes, but concerned itself instead with more general, universal ones, 'afectant a una moralitat colectiva' ('affecting a collective morality') (p.9).

The eternal nature of the *commedia* is highlighted in the figure of Harlequin:

> Es que la raça dels Arlequins es l'eterna raça còmica, es la condensació de tots els temps, l'esprit de totes les èpoques, decorat

amb trajos particulars, emancipant-se de tot moment exclusiu que pogués empetitir-la. (p.10)

The race of Harlequins is the eternal comic race, the résumé of all times, the spirit of all epochs, wearing their own particular costumes, freeing themselves from any particular or exclusive moment which could diminish them.

Gual views Harlequin as a direct descendant from Latin comedy, and, emphasising his universality, believes that he belongs to a larger family of comic figures, very much in the manner of Lorca's Arlequín and Cristóbal in the epilogue to *El retablillo de don Cristóbal*: 'tots els creadors, poetes, músics i pensadors s'han fet seus els individus de la gran família arlequiniana, perquè aquesta els ha sabut acaparar amablement mercès a l'universalitat del seu màgic comés' ('all creators, poets, musicians and thinkers have made the great family of Harlequins their own, because this family has been able to appropriate them thanks to the universality of their magic mission') (p.12).

The reference to 'creators' and 'poets' gives a clue to the spiritual dimension of Harlequin to which Gual, in Banvillian fashion, draws attention. If a guardian angel watches over our spiritual salvation, then the Harlequin, which 'portem en nosaltres, ... amb ses coloraines ramplones i estridentes' ('which we carry within us, with his coarse, jarring colours') (p.11), is the 'salvació dels accidents irrisoris de la vida' ('salvation of life's absurd accidents') (p.11). There is something 'magical and prophetic' about the *commedia* troupe of improvising actors.

The Gual Harlequin retains some connections with the roguish servant of the *commedia dell'arte*, but without, for example, any of the menacing irony of Arlequín in Lorca's *Así que pasen cinco años,* or the earthy coarseness of the Dario Fo Arlecchino. His essentially innocent roguishness is summed up in the phrase 'mal bon home' ('a bad good man') (p.11).

Like Pérez de Ayala, Baroja, Lorca, Valle-Inclán and Rivas Cherif, Gual saw the *commedia* as a genre whose comic spirit remained as vital and as dynamic as ever, and could serve as a regenerative force in the contemporary theatre: 'ells han sigut i segueixen essent el veritable geni de la comèdia moderna, [...] l'etern carnaval de ses follíes [...] han sapigut rencarnar la comedia del món en el mateix món de la comedia' ('they have been and still are the real essence of modern comic theatre, [...] the eternal carnival of their mad escapades [...] they have been able to reincarnate the theatre of the world in the world of the theatre') (p.12).

The innocence and spontaneity of the *commedia*: Benavente

For a number of Hispanic authors in the early twentieth century, the attraction of the *commedia* was that it possessed an innocence and a spontaneity which were associated with youth, and which represented a refreshing change from the ossified, stale commercial theatre. As Crispín said in the prologue to Benavente's *Los intereses creados* (*The Bonds of Interest*), 'el mundo está ya viejo y chochea; el Arte no se resigna a envejecer'[18] ('the world is old and doddery; Art is not prepared to grow old'). He asks the audience to enter into the light-hearted spirit of the play: 'el autor sólo pide que añinéis cuanto sea posible vuestro espíritu' ('the playwright asks only that you do your best to appreciate the play as children would'), and ends by promising pure entertainment: 'y he aquí cómo estos viejos polichinelas pretenden hoy divertiros con sus niñerías' ('I will show you how these old puppets will entertain you today with their childish activities'). Like Lorca in his farces, Benavente asks his audience to suspend belief, and to accept that they will not be witnessing the type of realism to which they were accustomed in the theatre. The *commedia* belongs to the new form of art encapsulated and propagated by Ortega y Gasset in *La deshumanización del arte* (*The Dehumanisation of Art*) (1925) and brings to mind once more Copeau's emphasis on the anti-Naturalist essence of the 'new' *commedia*. However, as we shall see later in the chapter, Crispín has a subtle awareness and even appreciation of the sophistication of modern audiences.

Benavente, of course, had a particular interest in children's theatre.[19] The January 1912 edition of *Por esos mundos* published Benavente's translation of an English Punch and Judy farce, under the Spanish title *Las diabluras de Polichinela* (*Punch's Pranks*). The prologue to this short play, which contains the characteristically innocent violence of a Punch and Judy show, refers to a private performance of the play organised by Benavente. Having lamented that modern-day children, unlike their counterparts of former times, are no longer capable of appreciating puppet theatre because they have become accustomed to other types of theatre and to the cinema, he declares his satisfaction at the result of his own enterprise:

> En una agradable fiesta, celebrada en casa de los Príncipes Pío de Saboya, pude, por unas horas, ilusionarme con un Renacimiento del Guignol.
> Más orgulloso que pudo estarlo Talma ante su público de reyes, tuve yo un público de niños, de verdaderos niños, que sabiamente educados, aún saben reir como niños con los muñecos del Guignol.

> In a pleasant gathering held in the house of the Prince and Princess Pío de Saboya, I was able to enjoy for a few hours a Guignol Renaissance.
> Prouder than Talma could be before his audience of kings, I had an audience of children, of real children. Whilst they were intelligently educated, they knew how to laugh like children with the puppets of the Guignol.

Innocence and spontaneity: Ramírez Angel, Gual, Pérez de Ayala and García Lorca

Similar sentiments are evoked in the prologue to E.Ramírez Angel's *Drama en un bazar* (*Drama in a Bazaar*), which was published in the December 1911 number of *Por esos mundos* (for illustrations of the play see figs. 8 and 9). This play may be considered as a predecessor of Jacinto Grau's *El señor de Pigmalión* (*Mr Pygmalion*) (1921), in that puppets, led in this case by Arlequín, revolt against their human owners. Although the play itself contains a political element, in the presentation of Arlequín as a demagogue unable to control the revolt of the puppets when it comes, the prologue possesses the same eulogy of the eternal youthfulness of popular art as in Benavente and other authors. It evokes 'uno de esos bazares donde florece, eternamente renovada, la juventud, en toda ocasión jovial, de los juguetes' ('one of those bazaars where the youthfulness of toys flourishes, eternally rejuvenated, always jovial'). For Gual, too, the *commedia* was linked with youthful, even childish playfulness. He makes the point clearly in a lecture given at the Catalan School of Dramatic Art in Barcelona: 'la farsa italiana representa ésser els jòcs d'infantesa de l'artista teatral' [20] ('Italian farce represents the childish games of the theatrical artist').

Pérez de Ayala prefaces his *commedia dell'arte* section of *Las máscaras* with a spirited defence of the mime, which he appreciates for precisely the quality of childish innocence which leads other people to condemn it:

> Hay un género teatral, la pantomima, en que nada se puede escuchar porque nada se dice. La pantomima atrae y congrega multitudes populares en las salas de espectáculos. Se dice de una persona poco culta y enemiga de leer que «le estorba lo negro». Pudiera parafrasearse que a este mismo linaje de personas «le estorba el ruido de la voz». O lo que es lo mismo, que únicamente el vulgo gusta de la pantomima. A lo cual respondo que a mí también me gusta, y que he seguido muchas de ellas con mayor interés y deleite que algunas piezas habladas. No se olvide, además, que este género de la pantomima viene milenariamente desde Roma. Más aún: la pantomima es una fase infantil del teatro; y, como tal, incorpora una forma de teatro ingenuo e incompatible con las sofistaciones verbosas en que degenera el teatro al trasponer su postrera fase de senilidad. He aquí, pues, un teatro, la pantomima donde no puede haber sino espectadores (p.557).

> There is a theatrical genre, mime, in which nothing can be heard because nothing is said. Mime attracts and brings together the popular masses in theatres. It is said of an uncultured person who does not like reading that 'black bothers him'. Paraphrasing, one could say of the same type of person that 'the sound of the voice bothers him'. Or put in another way, that it is only the common people who like mime. To which I would reply that I too like it, and that I have followed many mimes with more interest and pleasure than some spoken pieces.[21] Moreover, it should not be forgotten

that this type of mime is age-old and derives from Roman times. And there is even more: mime is a childish phase of the theatre; and as such it includes a type of theatre which is innocent and incompatible with the sophisticated verbosity into which the theatre degenerates in its final stage of senility. So we have a type of theatre, the mime where there can be only spectators.

Two points emerge from this quotation. Firstly, the innocence and freshness of mime are contrasted with the senility of the contemporary theatre, a view which echoes Crispín's in the prologue to *Los intereses creados*, although Crispín does not appear to despise this sophisticated audience in the way that Pérez de Ayala does. Secondly, in his emphasis on mime, in opposition to the verbose and sophisticated language found in the commercial theatre, Pérez de Ayala clearly identifies himself with the anti-Naturalist tradition in the European theatre. Interestingly, he follows his section on mime with one on the silent cinema, before concentrating on the history of the *commedia dell'arte*, and seems to imply a link between *commedia* and cinema similar to that which both Copeau and Rivas Cherif specifically make in the Chaplin essay and *Cómo hacer teatro* respectively. A similar blending of genres occurs in Lorca's reference to the 'carácter de pantomima' of *La zapatera prodigiosa*. He refers to it as a 'pantocomedia [...] la obra es casi un "ballet", es una pantomima y una comedia al mismo tiempo'[22] ('a pantoplay[...] the work is almost a "ballet", simultaneously a mime and a play'), while the opening of Act II is described as 'casi una escena de cine'[23] ('almost a cinema scene').

Freshness and innocence are also, of course, features of Lorca's conception of popular puppet theatre in the farces. In the epilogue to *El retablillo de don Cristóbal*, the *commedia* belongs to this tradition. The Director declares that the context of countryside innocence converts crude language, which would be unbearable in a city environment, into something charming and attractive (p.697). In the prologue, too, which is delivered by the Poet, reference is made to the 'delicioso y duro lenguaje de los muñecos' ('delicious, harsh language of the puppets') , and there is idealisation of the popular puppet tradition in the sentence

52

'el guiñol es la expresión de la fantasía del pueblo y da el clima de su gracia y de su inocencia' ('the Guignol is the expression of the fantasy of the people and provides the climate of its charm and innocence') (p.675).[24]

An analysis of the three plays on which I shall now concentrate, *La serenata*, *Arlequín, mancebo de botica* and *Los intereses creados*, will highlight the way in which the three authors in question - Gual, Baroja and Benavente - put into practice some of the ideas on the comic spirit of the *commedia* that concern us in this chapter. The first two plays are what one might describe as farces of pure fun, while *Los intereses creados* is a more thoughtful presentation of the way the *commedia* spirit may be adapted to the modern age. The Gual and Baroja plays will be discussed before *Los intereses creados*, although they were written later, as this will enable us better to highlight the subtleties of the Benavente presentation of the *commedia*.

Gual: *La serenata*

Gual's *La serenata* (*estudi de farsa italiana*) (*The Serenade: [a Study in Italian farce]*), which was first performed at the Catalan School of Dramatic Art in 1916, captures the spirit of Gual's lecture which preceded the performance, in particular the sentiment that 'la farsa italiana representa ésser els jocs d'infantesa de l'artista teatral' ('the Italian farce symbolises the games the theatre artist played as a child'). The action of the play revolves around Matamoros's absurdly comic passion for Isabela, who is to be wed to Leandre. Arlequí, fulfilling his traditional servant's role, attempts to assist his master Matamoros to win his love. His concrete suggestion, around which much of the action of the play revolves, is that Scaramouche put to music a romantic poem Matamoros has written to Isabela, and which can be used by the lover to serenade his beloved.

The *commedia* characters in the play fulfil more or less their traditional roles. Arlequí, of course, has a number of traditional roles, which are varied and even contradictory. As chapter 1 observed, he was originally the dolt to Brighella's cunning, and later became the cunning servant himself. In Marivaux's work he was *poli par l'amour*, while his links with the devil are well known. In the nineteenth and early twentieth centuries amorality is a common trait of his. In the work of some authors he is an antidote to the Romanticism and Symbolism which are associated with Pierrot, while in others he possesses a liberating spiritual dimension representing the 'sublime, the unattainable, towards which mankind forever aspires'.[25] Gual's figure is a version of the cunning servant, a down-to earth character and a foil to his absurdly impractical and idealist master:

> MATAMOROS No hi ha justícia, amic Arlequí... No hi ha justícia! Si n'hi hagués, hom com jo no es trobaria com jo em trobo.
> ARLEQUI Anem a lo que interessa, i deixem tota filosofia pels temps d'estiu, que és quan els homes solen estar en vaga (p.159).

> MATAMOROS There's no justice, Arlequí, my friend... there's no justice! If there were, a man of my standing would not find himself in this situation.
> ARLEQUI Let's get down to business, and leave philosphy for the summer, which is when men can rest.

At times Arlequí is unable to contain his laughter at his master's absurd pretensions, such as when he first recites the poem he has composed for Isabela. He is fond of a joke at his master's expense, and displays the roguishness one associates with Arlecchino as he persuades Matamoros to part with money to pay Escaramouche for his services. On one occasion he parodies the romantic gestures of the serenade, in a scene in which he and Escaramouche are 'teaching' Matamoros this gentle art : 'Deixeu fer, i avanceu. L'heu vista, saludeula. *Ell ho fa grotescament* ('Relax and move forward. You've seen her, now greet her. *He does this in a grotesque fashion*') (p.166).

Another comic servant, Colombina, shows the same down-to-earth scepticism as Arlequí. She too finds it difficult to contain her laughter as Matamoros rehearses his serenade: *'canten, però que es vegi que [Matamoros] està insegur de la tonada, i que és Escaramouche qui li dicta, tot acompanyant amb la guitarra. Colombina és morta de riure'* ('they sing, but it must be obvious that [Matamoros] is unsure of the tune, and that it is Scaramouche who explains it to him while playing the guitar accompaniment') (p.166). A little later in the play, Colombina reveals her common sense, in the middle of a rumpus involving neighbours, one of whom complains that the din of the rehearsal has awakened his sleeping baby. He brings his baby with him to Matamoros's flat; it is then passed between various other neighbours, and a judge, who has been called to deal with complaints about the din. It ends up in Colombina's arms, and she rocks it gently to pacify it.

Other *commedia* characters also follow to an extent the models on which they are based. Matamoros is, of course, one of the names by which the *commedia dell'arte* Captain was known, and in some of the stage directions the Gual character is referred to as Capità. The *commedia* figure is known for his often blustering bravura, and Matamoros laments to Arlequí early in the play that he has lost his own 'bravura' because he is lovesick for Isabela. Escaramouche has one thing in common with his *commedia dell'arte* counterpart: his guitar playing. He is a much less sharp character than Arlequí, and is easily deceived by the latter when it comes to the question of Matamoros's payment for his services. The other *commedia* characters in the play, Tartaglia, Pantaló and Briguela, are neighbours of Matamoros, and have very small parts.

La serenata has elements of pure farce. For example, after an argument between Matamoros and his neighbours following their complaints at the din created by the night-time rehearsals for his serenade song, the would-be serenader receives a bucket of water over his head from a neighbour living in the flat above him. Further farcical humour is provided in the baby incident. Yet more humour occurs in the scene in which Arlequí, fearing that the judge will cart Matamoros (and perhaps himself) off to prison, slips some money into the latter's hat. The judge is then convinced by Arlequí's explanation of events, and orders the neighbours to return to their flats. One could perhaps see this episode as mild social satire, but it is hardly even that, and certainly no element of social criticism seems to be intended. *La serenata* is nothing more (and nothing less) than a well-constructed farce, lively and humorous, and a further example of an early twentieth-century attempt to recreate what was understood to be the true spirit of the *commedia dell'arte*.

Baroja: *Arlequín, mancebo de botica*

The plot of *Arlequín, mancebo de botica o los pretendientes de Colombina* (*Arlequín the Chemist's Assistant, or Colombina's Suitors*) is as uncomplicated as that of *La serenata*. It is expected that Colombina will marry one of her rich suitors, such as the pompous don Perfecto, who in the course of the play appear in the chemist's shop to woo her. Her father, Pantalón, has left his assistant, the *mancebo* Arlequín, who is in love with his daughter, minding the shop while he goes out. This gives Arlequín the opportunity to make fun of the succession of suitors and other customers who come into the shop One of these customers is The Duchess, who turns out to be Arlequín's mother. Now that Arlequín is a 'man of parts', he will be able to marry Colombina!

Even from this brief outline of the plot, it will be obvious that *Arlequín, mancebo de botica* is essentially an innocent farce. Baroja attempts to capture the spirit of the original *commedia dell'arte* in presentation of character and plot.

Arlequín is a mixture of innocent dolt and shrewd manipulator, but without any of the sinister connotations of his counterpart in, for example, Lorca's *Así que pasen cinco años*. His humorously innocent expression of love for Colombina is more typical of a puppet than a Lugones Pierrot: 'me muero por ti, Colombina. Mi corazón hace tipitín, tipitán, al verte a ti' ('I am dying for you, Colombina. My heart goes boom whenever I see you') (p.23). He undermines Colombina's would-be suitors, although, given their pretentiousness and stupidity, this is not a difficult

56

task. For instance, he manages to get rid of don Perfecto with a very simple trick by playing on Perfecto's vanity:

> ARLEQUíN Nada, que parece que le buscan en la plaza. Según dicen, están discutiendo un asunto muy grave, y han dicho: eso, el único que lo puede resolver es don Perfecto; únicamente si viene don Perfecto se arregla eso.
> DON PERFECTO (A Colombina.) Nada; veo que me necesitan. Antes es la obligación que la devoción. Me voy, encantadora Colombina. Ya sabe usted que si usted quiere iremos al mismo diapasón.
> ARLEQUíN ¡Adiós, don Perfecto! ¡Que le vaya a usted bien, don Perfecto! Váyase a la ... plaza, don Perfecto. Vamos, ya se ha marchado ese pelmazo. (p.55)

> ARLEQUíN I think they're looking for you in the square. It seems they're discussing a very important matter, and they said: that's it, the only one who can resolve it is don Perfecto; only if don Perfecto comes can this be sorted out.
> DON PERFECTO To Colombina) Well, it looks as if they need me. Duty before pleasure. I'm going, my delightful Colombina. You know that if it is your wish we can sing to the same tune.
> ARLEQUíN Good-bye, don Perfecto! Good luck, don Perfecto! Go to the... square, don Perfecto. Right, the boring old fool has gone!.

At one point Pantalón calls Arlequín 'a sceptic' (p.26), but this scepticism is characterised more by a refreshingly common-sense deflation of pretentiousness than by the sophisticated and elegant cynicism of the Arlequín of Valle-Inclán's *La marquesa Rosalinda* (see chapter 5).

Colombina, too, possesses Arlequín's innocent, yet slightly roguish freshness. Despite her protestations when Arlequín manages to get rid of don Perfecto, she is fond of Arlequín. She is happy to marry him (once, it has to be admitted, she knows of his noble origins!), but she keeps her feet firmly on the ground ('no creas que basta ser duque para tener mi corazón' ('don't think that being a duke is enough to win my heart') (p.74).

As far as the other characters are concerned, there are some clear parallels with the original *commedia dell'arte*, although on occasions these are none too precise. For instance, Pantalón seems to have more in common with the Dottore than with Pantalone. For example, he is fond of quoting in Latin to humorous effect: '¡jovialidad para nosotros! Tú recuerda siempre, en los casos apurados, aquella relación admirable, creo que de Celso: «Quis, quid, quibus auxilis, cur, quommodo et quando»' ('cheerfulness for us! Always remember when you're in trouble those splendid words of don Celso, I think it was: "Quis, quid, quibus auxilis, cur, quommodo et quando" ') (p.33). At the end of the play, however, even Pantalón has his feet firmly on the Spanish ground: 'boticario he sido y boticario quiero ser. No cierro la botica. Mi divisa será siempre la misma, «cito, tutto et jucunde» ('I have always been a chemist and always will. I'm not going to close the shop. My motto will always be the same: "cito, tutto et jucunde" ') (p.80).

Baroja owes more to Spanish popular types that to the Italian *commedia dell'arte* for some of the characters of the play. The Sargento, for instance, speaks very much like the stock Andalusian figure from the *zarzuela* tradition: 'el cazo es que el perro de uzted me ha dado un bocado y me ha quitado un peaso del pantalón, y grasias que no me ha arrancado un peaso de carne' ('what's happened, guv, is that this bleedin' dog's gone an' nipped a great chunk out of me trousers, and I can thank me lucky stars he ain't got a mouthful of flesh') (p.40).

The chief characteristic of *Arlequín mancebo de botica* is its humour. This, as we have seen, derives in part from Arlequín's deflation of other characters. Some of it is also verbal, including a liberal use of puns, as in the following exchange between Arlequín and El Veterinario: 'ARLEQUÍN: Aquí un señor asegura que un banco más de la ciudad se ha hundido. EL VETERINARIO: El mío es seguro. Es el Banco de la Isla de Madera, y una cosa de madera no se hunde tan fácilmente' (p.46). (The pun depends on the meaning of *madera*: it refers to the Island of Madeira and also means *wood*. The Vet is saying, in reply to Arlequín's point about a number of banks in the town going out of business ['sinking'], that his bank, the Bank of Madeira [Wood] will not 'sink' so easily.)

Some of the play's humour has a certain coarseness about it, although this, too, is fairly innocent and inoffensive, like that of Lorca's puppet farces. The difficulty in which the Old Woman finds herself at one point is a typical example: 'es para mi hija, para mi Fiammetta. A la pobre le ha engañado ese canalla de sargento tuerto de la gendarmería y le ha dejado en estado interesante....Y ahora va a dar a luz' ('it's for my daughter, my Fiammetta. That rogue the one-eyed sergeant from the *gendarmerie* has deceived her and left her in an interesting state. And now she's going to give birth') (p.30).

Another example of the slightly risqué yet innocent coarseness comes in Arlequín's words to Colombina in a conversation in which the latter expresses concern over the state in which Fiammetta finds herself:

> COLOMBINA ¡Pobre Fiammetta! Me voy a arreglar el canario.
> ARLEQUíN Pero si yo te quiero, Colombina.
> COLOMBINA No me importa nada tu cariño.
> ARLEQUíN No digas eso, mi amor. Yo no te haré nunca un chico... es decir, te lo haré si tú me das el permiso; si no, no, rica mía.
> COLOMBINA ¡Calla, desvergonzado!

> COLOMBINA Poor Fiametta! I'm going to see to the canary.
> ARLEQUÍN But I love you Colombina.
> COLOMBINA Your love means nothing to me.
> ARLEQUÍN Don't say that, my love. I'll never make you a baby..., well I will if you let me, but if not, I won't, my sweet.
> COLOMBINA Shut up, you shameless man!

Arlequín mancebo de botica is a play which attempts to recapture the comic spirit of the *commedia dell'arte*. It is anti-Romantic in its deflation of bombast and its light-hearted, humorous treatment of love. It does not experiment with language (as Lugones and Valle-Inclán do), nor shape new dramatic forms (as Lorca does in some of his plays). It is a *bufonada* (*a comic farce*), to use Brígida's expression near the end of the play, which fits very well into the mood of 1920s frivolity. Indeed, both this play and *La serenata*, while devoid of the declamatory melodrama of an Echegaray, the social seriousness of a Galdós or a Dicenta, or the folksy *costumbrismo* of the Quinteros, are hardly mould-breaking or innovative.

Benavente: *Los intereses creados*

Benavente's *Los intereses creados* is a more refined and much subtler version of the comic spirit of *commedia* than those found in the Baroja and the Gual plays. Probably the best-known and most influential Hispanic *commedia* work, it contains a larger number of *commedia* characters than most Hispanic plays of the period, including well-known figures like Harlequin, the Captain, the Doctor, Pantaloon and Pulcinella. Arlequín is a poet who lives in the past and impotently laments that his talents as a poet are no longer appreciated by society. He has lost his role as scheming servant, this having been taken over by Crispín. The other *commedia* characters fulfil more or less their traditional roles. The Captain is a blustering *matamoros*, the Doctor is pretentious and shows off his learning at every opportunity, Pantalón is extremely mercenary, while Polichinela is a powerful figure in society who is not averse to using violence to achieve his goals.

There are also two characters who are given much larger parts by Benavente than their place in *commedia* history warrants: the servant Crispín and his master Leandro. In fact, Crispín was basically a French creation, and Duchartre says that he is 'the French son of Scaramouche'.[26] He also has a lot in common with the stock servant character of Spanish Golden-Age literature. Crispín controls the action of the play, by scheming to win the hand of Polichinela's daughter Silvia for his master Leandro. He does this by making it in everybody's interest that the match should happen. His success, against the opposition of Polichinela, is based on his understanding and skilful exploitation of each individual's weaknesses and vanities, as he weaves a complicated web of interests that leads inevitably to his desired end.

In *Los intereses creados* there is a constant interplay, even tension, between the past and the present. Benavente uses *commedia* characters in a Renaissance setting to make a point about the disappearance of traditional values, and many of the characters seem to be out of place in the modern world, which is the case with the Captain and the poet Arlequín, who represent the two sides of the traditional debate between arms and letters (*armas y letras*). They realise that their particular talents are out of fashion, but they can only lament the fact that they are not appreciated by contemporary society, whose values are purely mercenary: The Captain, for instance, makes the following point to Arlequín: '¿Mi espada? Mi espada de soldado, como vuestro plectro de poeta, nada valen en esta ciudad de mercaderes y de negociantes... ¡Triste condición es la nuestra!' ('My sword? My soldier's sword, like your poet's plectrum, is worth nothing in this city of merchants and businessmen. Ours is indeed a sad lot') (p.76).

In the following scene a tension is created between Arlequín, who extols the traditional values of the poet and the soldier and laments once again the mercenary nature of contemporary society, and the Inkeeper, who scorns these traditional values, and represents, like his counterpart in *Don Quixote*, everyday reality:

ARLEQUIN ¿Creéis que todo es dinero en este bajo mundo? ¿Contáis para nada las ponderaciones que de vuestra casa hicimos en todas partes? ¡Hasta un soneto os tengo dedicado y en él celebro vuestras perdices estofadas y vuestros pasteles de liebre... ¡Y en cuanto al Señor Capitán, tened por seguro que él solo sostendrá contra un ejército el buen nombre de vuestra casa. ¿Nada vale esto? ¡Todo ha de ser moneda contante en el mundo!
HOSTELERO ¡No estoy para burlas! No he menestrer de vuestros sonetos ni de la espada del señor Capitán, que mejor pudiera emplearla. (p.78)

ARLEQUIN Do you think that everything in this miserable world comes down to money? Do you attach no value to the fact that we have been singing the praises of your establishment wherever we go? I have even dedicated a sonnet to you in which I celebrate your stewed partridges and your hare pies...! And as for the Captain, rest assured that he would uphold the good name of your establishment even if he were facing a whole army on his own. Is this worth nothing? Must it all come down to ready cash?
INNKEEPER I'm not in the mood for jokes! I have no use for your sonnets nor for the Captain's sword, which would be better employed elsewhere.

Crispín uses the old-fashioned values of characters such as the Captain and Arlequín just as he uses human emotions. He is subtle in his treatment of these two: instead of getting annoyed with them as the Innkeeper does, he flatters them, simply because he knows that this is the way to have them on his side. He retains the comic roguishness of the traditional servant, yet is perfectly at home in the modern world. He acts, in fact, as a bridge between the old and the new, having originated in an era when things were simpler and more black and white than in the present, yet having the resourcefulness to survive in the more complex modern world, and understanding how audiences have changed in keeping with society's values. Therefore, although he exhorts the audience to enjoy the spectacle they are about to witness as their humble counterparts of previous centuries would have done, he is aware that they are more sophisticated than their predecessors:

> Bien conoce el autor que tan primitivo espectáculo no es el más digno de un culto auditorio de estos tiempos; así, de vuestra cultura tanto como de vuestra bondad se ampara. El autor sólo pide que aniñéis cuanto sea posible vuestro espíritu. (p.70)

> The author knows full well that such a primitive play is not really worthy of today's cultured audience; he therefore must rely on your culture as well as on your good will. The author's only request is that, as far as possible, you try to appreciate the play as children would.

The Bakhtinian 'primitive play' is, it seems to me, seen to be only half possible by the wily and wordly-wise Crispín. The 'as far as possible' is a more cautious exhortation than, say, that of Lorca's Author in *El retablillo de don Cristóbal*.

Crispín, in fact, highlights an ambiguity on Benavente's part towards the comic spirit of the *commedia*. Like the roguish *commedia* comic servant, Crispín is never caught out, and is cynical about life in general and about human weaknesses in particular. The characters of the play, he informs the audience in the prologue, 'no son ni semejan hombres y mujeres, sino muñecos o fantoches de cartón y trapo, con groseros hilos' ('are not men and women, and do not even look like them, but are puppets of cardboard and rags with coarse strings') (p.70).[27] He realises that human beings are moved by self-interest, a realisation which enables him to manipulate them. In a conversation with the crude and violent Polichinela, he says:

> Soy ... lo que fuiste. Y quien llegará a ser lo que eres ... como tú llegaste. No con tanta violencia como tú, porque los tiempos son otros, y ya sólo asesinan los locos y los enamorados y cuatro pobretes, que aún asaltan a mano armada al transeúnte por calles oscuras o caminos solitarios. (p.97)

> I am... what you were. And I will get where you are... just as you did. With less violence than you, for times have changed, and now the only people who murder are madmen, lovers and a few poor fools who hold up passers-by in dark streets or on lonely roads.

This quotation highlights the essence of Benavente's adaptation of *commedia dell'arte* in *Los intereses creados*. The primitive crudeness of an earlier age has been replaced by a gentler but more devious 'modern' approach, as Polichinela's violence has been supplanted by Crispín's subterfuge.

In many ways, Crispín plays the role of the detached puppet-master in *Los intereses creados*. He pulls the strings that move the 'muñecos' and 'fantoches' in the 'farsa guiñolesca' that is the play. He is also subtly aware that disguise and even falseness are an important part of life. This is well illustrated in an important speech by Crispín, at the end of his exchange with doña Sirena in Act 2, Scene 3. She retains a nostalgic longing for past elegance and splendour, with which Crispín the manipulator typically plays:

> Vos sois siempre la noble dama, mi amo el noble señor, que al encontraros esta noche en la fiesta, hablaréis de mil cosas galantes y delicadas, mientras vuestros convidados pasean y conversan a vuestro alrededor, con admiraciones a la hermosura de las damas, al arte de sus galas, a la esplendidez del agasajo, a la dulzura de la música y a la gracia de los bailarines... ¿Y quién se atreverá a decir

que no es esto todo? ¿No es así la vida, una fiesta en que la música sirve para disimular palabras y las palabras para disimular pensamientos? Que la música suene incesante, que la conversación se anime con alegres risas, que la cena esté bien servida ..., es todo lo que importa a los convidados. (p.92)

You are always the noble lady, and my master is the noble gentleman. When you meet tonight at the party you will speak of a thousand gallant and exquisite subjects, while your guests mingle and engage in conversation, admiring the beauty and splendid attire of the ladies, the magnificence of your lavish hospitality, the sweetness of the music and the elegant grace of the dancers... And who will dare to say that there is more to it than this? Is this not life itself, a party in which the music cloaks language and language cloaks thoughts? Let the music play endlessly, let the conversation be lit up with happy laughter, let the meal be served in fine fashion... this is all that worries the guests.

The suggestion in Crispín's words is that life itself is one great *fête galante*, where elegance, disguise and a sense of ritual, although artificial, are somehow more real than so-called reality. Life itself, one feels, is cast in a theatrical mould. Crispín, of course, does not make the above comment with nostalgic or sentimental intentions: he is, after all, the cynical puppet-master who loves playing with his puppets, and does not want them to feel deep emotions. Indeed, it could well be that Benavente is questioning and even satirising *modernista* nostalgia.[28] Yet there is an element of nostalgia, even sentimentality, in the play that *Arlequín, mancebo de botica* and *La serenata* do not possess. This is particularly strong in the final words of the play, which are spoken by Silvia. Addressing the audience, she first reiterates the view that life is a farce in which people, like puppets, are controlled by 'cordelillos groseros, que son los intereses, las pasioncillas, los engaños y todas las miserias de su condición') ('rough strings, which are men's interests, passions and deceits, and all the miseries of their human condition') (p.131). However, says Silvia, there is one string that is light and delicate, the string of love, and it is this which saves life from being a complete farce, and ensures that at least a part of us is eternal and will not die when we do. Leandro and Silvia do not accept Crispín's cynical evaluation of love, believing instead that love cannot be involved with deceit and must depend on true, honest emotions.

Nevertheless, one must beware of taking the words of Silvia too seriously, since Benavente believed that, once having expressed his true feelings and beliefs in the rest of the play, an author should aim to please the public in the conclusion. If we are to believe this, then Benavente's real purpose in *Los intereses creados* is not to be found in the final words of the play. The overall picture of life to emerge from the play is cynical. Human beings are moved by self-interest, mere pawns in the hand of Crispín. He is aware of people's feelings, just as he is conscious of a nostalgia for the past, but for him they are just more *intereses* to be played with and used. *Los intereses creados* contains a harsh view of reality, and its comic spirit is an indication more of its author's cynical view of life than of an eulogy of a lost comic age.

1 On the question of the crisis in the theatre and debates on its possible remedies in Spain in the 1920s, see Dru Dougherty, 'Talía convulsa: la crisis teatral de los años 20', in Robert Lima and Dru Dougherty, *2 ensayos sobre teatro español de los 20* (Murcia: Universidad de Murcia, 1984), pp.87-155. On the issue of the regeneration of the Spanish theatre, see María Francisca Vilches de Frutos and Dru Dougherty, 'La renovación del teatro español a través de la prensa periódica: la página teatral del «Heraldo de Madrid» (1923-1927)', *Siglo XX/20th Century*, vol. 6, nos.1-2 (1988-89), 47-56.
2 R.Pérez de Ayala, *Las máscaras*, in *Obras completas*, 4 vols (Madrid: Aguilar, 1966), III, 570. Further quotations from the work are taken from this edition, and the corresponding page references are given in the body of the text.
3 Pío Baroja, *Entretenimientos* (Madrid: Caro Raggio, n.d.), pp.8-9. *Arlequín mancebo de botica* is part of this work. Further quotations from this prologue, and also from the text of *Arlequín mancebo de botica*, are taken from this edition, and the corresponding page references are given in the body of the text.
4 See Dru Dougherty and María Francisca Vilches de Frutos, *La escena madrileña* (Madrid: Fundamentos, 1990), p.83, p.186. An account of the production of the play appears in Julio Caro Baroja, *Los Baroja*, 2nd edn reprint (Madrid: Taurus, 1986), pp.171-72. Caro Baroja seems unsure of the precise dates on which this and other plays were performed by the group.
5 Cipriano de Rivas Cherif, *Cómo hacer teatro* (Valencia: Pretextos, 1991), p.152.
6 On the links between the cinema and Spanish literature of the 1920s and 1930s see C.B.Morris, *This Loving Darkness*.
7 'Divagación a la luz de las candilejas', *La Pluma*, I (June-December 1920), pp.113-19 (p.119).
8 *Ibid.*, pp.118-19.
9 The Unión General de Trabajadores, or UGT, is one of the two main trade unions in Spain, and is associated with the Socialist Party.
10 Federico García Lorca, *Obras completas*, 3 vols (Madrid: Aguilar, 1986), II, 697. The 'don Pantaleón' reference is on p.689. Further quotations from *El retablillo* are taken from this edition of *Obras completas*, and the corresponding page references are given in the body of the text. Sentiments similar to those expressed by the Director in the epilogue are found in the prologues to

two other farces, *Tragicomedia de don Cristóbal y la señá Rosita* (*Tragicomedy of Don Cristóbal and Miss Rosita*) (1922?) and *La zapatera prodigiosa* (*The Shoemaker's Prodigious Wife*) (1930). Lorca's interest in the puppet show is well documented: see, for example, William L. Oliver, 'Lorca: The Puppets and the Artist', *Tulane Drama Review*, VII (1962), 76-95; Virginia Higginbotham, *The Comic Spirit of Federico García Lorca* (Austin: University of Texas Press, 1976), pp.71-88; Ian Gibson, *Federico García Lorca*, 2 vols (Barcelona: Grijalbo, 1985), vol.1, *De Fuentevaqueros a Nueva York*, 300, *passim*; and Piero Menari, 'Un texto inédito de Lorca para guiñol: Cristobical', *ALEC*, 11 (1986), 13-37.

Interestingly, the *ABC* reviewer of the first performance of *La zapatera prodigiosa* used the image of a harlequinade in the context of praise of what he saw as the play's refreshing innocence: 'gustó mucho la farsa de García Lorca, sencilla, pueril, deliciosamente ingenua, con su aire de pantomima arlequinesca ...' ('García Lorca's farce was well received. It is simple, childlike, deliciously innocent, with its air of harlequinesque pantomime...') (quoted in María Francisca Vilches de Frutos and Dru Dougherty, *Los estrenos teatrales de Federico García Lorca* [Madrid: Tabapress, 1992], p.48).

11 The uncorrupted peasants of rural villages make up one of three 1920s Spanish audiences identified by Dru Dougherty in 'Talía convulsa'. For an analysis of the question of audiences see Chapter 5, and for discussion of the idealised rural audiences, see pp.116-17. See also Alison Sinclair, 'Elitism and the Cult of the Popular in Spain', in *Visions and Blueprints*, ed. by Edward Timms and Peter Collier (Manchester: MUP, 1988), pp.221-34.

12 Quoted in *La zapatera prodigiosa*, ed. by Mario Hernández (Madrid: Alianza, 1982), p.153.

13 See *Obras completas*, II, 308 and 106 respectively. An analysis of Lorca's prologues is found in Reed Anderson, 'Prólogos and advertencias: Lorca's beginnings', in C. Brian Morris (ed.), «*Cuando yo me muera*»: *Essays in Memory of Federico García Lorca* (Lanham: University Press of America, 1988), pp.209-32. Translations of *El retablillo de don Cristóbal*, *La zapatera prodigiosa* and *Así que pasen cinco años* by Gwynne Edwards are found in *Lorca: Plays Two* (London: Methuen, 1990).

14 Reproduced in Margarita Ucelay, 'La problemática teatral: testimonios directos de Federico García Lorca', *Boletín de la Fundación Federico García Lorca*, 6 (1989), 27-58 (p.45). This article contains useful information on Lorca's views on a number of subjects, including that of the commercial theatre.

15 See Dougherty, 'Talía convulsa', chapter 3.

16 Valle-Inclán, too, whose *commedia* play *La marquesa Rosalinda* will be examined in Chapter 5, saw the popular puppet theatre as an important source of regeneration of the theatre. In the words of Compadre Fidel, in *Los cuernos de don Friolera* (*The Horns of Don Friolera*): 'sólo pueden regenerarnos los muñecos del compadre Fidel' ('only the puppets of our friend Fidel can regenerate us'). *Los cuernos de don Friolera* is one of three plays in *Martes de carnaval*; the quotation is taken from *Martes de carnaval*, ed. by Jesús Rubio Jiménez (Madrid: Espasa Calpe, 1992), p.201.

17 *Arlequí vividor* (Barcelona: no publisher, 1912). Further quotations from the work are taken from this edition, and the corresponding page references are given in the body of the text.

18 *Los intereses creados*, ed. by José Díaz de Castro (Madrid: Espasa Calpe, 1990), p.70. Further quotations from the work are taken from this edition, and the corresponding page references are given in the body of the text. The play will be analysed more fully later in the chapter.

19 See, for example, Linda S.Glaze, 'The Tradition of the *Comedia de magia* in Jacinto Benavente's Theater for Children', *Hispania*, vol.76 no.2 (1993), 213-31.

20 The lecture is reproduced as a prologue to the Gual play which will be examined later in the chapter, *La serenata*. The prologue and the play itself may be read in vol. XVIII of *Lectura popular. Biblioteca d'autors catalans* (Barcelona: Ilustració Catalana, n.d.). The quotation cited is on p.155; all quotations from *La serenata* are taken from this edition, and the corresponding page references are given in the body of the text.

21 Unfortunately Pérez de Ayala does not say where!

66

22 Quoted in Federico García Lorca, *La zapatera prodigiosa*, ed. by Mario Hernández, p.148

23 *Ibid.*, p.88.

24 In his article on Grau's *El señor de Pigmalión*, Dru Dougherty cites a 1925 article by Grau on 'personajes mecánicos' ('mechanical figures') that he witnessed at a *verbena*: 'como los antiguos muñidores de ferias, son infantilmente sencillos, y en la propia acción encuentran la propia alegría, restituyendo el arte a su primitivo prestigio de la ilusión pura y del juego por el juego' ('like the ancient messengers at fairs, they are childishly simple, and they find their own pleasure in the plot itself, restoring art to its primitive status of pure illusion and of play for play's sake') ('The Semiosis of Stage Decor in Jacinto Grau's *El señor de Pigmalión*', *Hispania*, 67 [1984], 351-57 [p. 355]).

25 Thelma Niklaus, *Harlequin Phoenix* (London: The Bodley Head, 1956), p.186.

26 Pierre-Louis Duchartre, *The Italian Comedy*, trans. by Randolph T. Weaver (New York: John Day, 1966 [reprint]), p.249. There is a useful account of his development in seventeenth- and eighteenth-century French literature in the introduction to Alain René Lesage, *Crispin rival de son maître*, ed. by T.E.Lawrenson (London: University of London Press, 1961), pp.33-40.

27 Phyllis Zattlin considers that Crispín's words show him up to be an unreliable narrator, in 'Metatheatre and the Twentieth-Century Spanish Stage', *ALEC*, 17, 1-2 (1992), 55-74 (p.61). Her study, both of *Los intereses creados*, and of the twentieth-century Spanish stage in general, is a most interesting one.

28 His earlier *Teatro fantástico* (1892) contains a much more straightforwardly *modernista* view of the *commedia*, while a more thoroughgoing, but more bitter and less elegant, questioning occurs in his 1916 play, *La ciudad alegre y confiada*. These will be discussed in chapters 4 and 5 respectively: although *Teatro fantástico* predates *Los intereses creados* by some 15 years, with its emphasis on dream, it belongs thematically to chapter 4, while *La ciudad alegre y confiada* fits well into the context of a general questioning of the *modernista commedia* in chapter 5.

Chapter 4

Escapism and Sentimentality

Chapter 3 was concerned with dramatists and writers on the theatre who rejected Romanticism and melodrama and for whom the *commedia*, with its simplicity as well as its rich popular heritage, represented a possibility of injecting new life into a moribund national theatre. Other writers of the period viewed the *commedia* from a completely different, even a contrary perspective, with little hint of either humour or cynicism. Either they saw the *commedia* as a means of escape from the prosaic reality of ordinary life,[1] or they employed the Pierrot figure as the prototype of unrequited love, often with a tragic outcome. A sentimental approach is typical of these writers, and the tone of their works is often melancholy and even melodramatic.

An example of the sentimental approach is Benavente's *Cuento de primavera (Spring Tale)*, which is part of *Teatro fantástico* of 1892, and probably the first modern Spanish work to deal with the *commedia*. *Cuento de primavera* is very different in style and content to the later *Los intereses creados*: the Harlequin figure of the earlier play, despite containing the traits of his roguish antecedent, is basically an advocate of magical escapism. An analysis of this play, and a comparison with Benavente's essays on the circus and the carnival, will not only shed important light on the escapist *commedia*, but will also set the influential *Los intereses creados* in the context of Benavente's earlier work on the *commedia* and will suggest that the standard critical view of the early Benavente as basically a Naturalist should be questioned.

68

The colourful, but sometimes melancholy, flights from reality in the work of the Nicaraguan *modernista* poet, Rubén Darío, are also typical examples of escapism and sentimentality. Pierrot is the *commedia* figure who appears most frequently here: he is the stereotyped 'poor' character, typical of late nineteenth-century poetry. Another *modernista* writer, Enrique Gómez Carrillo, is also fascinated by Pierrot. Two examples are considered: the essay *El teatro de Pierrot* and the novel *Bohemia sentimental*. It is here, as well as in the plays of Fernando Mota and Eduardo Zamacois, that the sentimentality associated with the Pierrot figure most obviously acquires tragic dimensions, and where the melodramatic tone is most marked.

Although Arlequín is the main *commedia* character in Benavente's *Cuento de primavera*, it is Pierrot who dominates the study of escapism and sentimentality in this chapter. Emilio Carrere specifically expresses his preference for Pierrot over Harlequin in *Bohemia sentimental*. Pierrot is also a central character in two plays from Catalan *modernisme*, Santiago Rusiñol's *La cançó de sempre* and Apel.les Mestres's *Els sense cor*. Here Pierrot represents *modernisme* under threat from the *noucentista* movement, which began to dominate Catalan cultural life towards the end of the first decade of the twentieth century.

Benavente on the circus and the carnival

Benavente had a personal connection with the circus. One critic even claimed that he was a circus impressario in Russia for a time,[2] although others believe there is insufficient evidence to support the claim.[3] What is sure is that Benavente was acquainted with, possibly romantically attached to, the English trapeze artist known as La Belle Géraldine. His love for the circus was second only to that of the theatre, and he even went so far as to equate the circus with life.[4] In addition to his circus essays, Benavente also wrote two complete plays and the first act of an uncompleted one which have circus settings. The essays to which I shall refer are 'El circo' ('The Circus'), 'Los payasos del circo' ('Circus Clowns'), 'Los "clowns" ', 'El poema del circo' ('The Circus Poem') and 'Carnaval'.[5] As the titles suggest, the clowns were the chief circus attraction for Benavente, and in 'El circo' he lists a number of them he himself had seen act. His respect for the clown emerges from 'Los "clowns" ': 'es una gente digna de estudio, una raza especial, como los gitanos, sin patria, sin carácter de nacionalidad, políglota, cosmopolita, y con todo ello, conservadora de tradiciones inmemoriales' ('they are a people worthy of being studied, a special race, like the gypsies, with no homeland or distinctive nationality, polyglot, cosmopolitan, and yet preserving their own immemorial traditions') (p.526). He also recognises the circus as a vital influence on works of literature: 'si la Loie-Fuller dio sus colores al arte modernista, los Hanlon-Lees le dieron las líneas y fueron precursores. Sin ellos no hubieran sido posibles las odas funambulescas de Banville, y sin ellas, las fiestas galantes de Verlaine' ('if Loie-Fuller gave *modernista* art its colours, the Hanlon Lees gave it its form and were its precursors. Without them neither Banville's *Odes funambulesques* nor Verlaine's *Fêtes galantes* would have been possible') (p.688).

Two other points of interest emerge from Benavente's essays on the circus and the carnival which are of direct relevance to his portayal of the *commedia* in *Cuento de primavera*. First, the clown, despite the laughter he provides ('y bien debemos gratitud a los buenos payasos del circo, que sólo nuestra risa pretenden con todas sus dislocaciones')[6] ('we are, indeed, indebted to the good circus clown, whose antics are aimed only at making us laugh'), is no frivolous creature, and in 'Los "clowns" ' Benavente says that he can express profound sentiments, as is the case in Shakespeare: 'y por boca de clowns expresó Shakespeare quizá lo más profundo de su filosofía, con irónica suavidad, con burlona tristeza, con bufonesca fantasía, con ese humor que pudiera simbolizarse en una lágrima, sorbida por una sonrisa' ('through his clowns Shakespeare expressed perhaps the most profound part of his philosophy, with its ironic gentleness, mocking melancholy, clownish fantasy, and that humour which one could say was symbolised by a tear, through a smile') (p.525). This example also contains Benavente's appraisal of the clown's blend of sadness and ironic humour, and his ability to evoke a world of fantasy.

Secondly, Benavente's circus and carnival essays shed light on nostalgia and sentimentality. In 'Carnaval' he moves from his reflections on the Nice carnival to a nostalgic longing for a past world which modern man can evoke only as a dream. This past world is compared unfavourably with the twentieth century which Benavente despises: 'no somos todavía tan desgraciados los que podemos soñar, al recordarlos, con aquellos tiempos de mundo ilusionado que había de tener tan triste despertar apenas empezado el siglo XX' ('those of us who can recall and dream of a past world of illusion, so sadly destroyed with the coming of the twentieth century, are not so unfortunate after all') (p.102). In 'El poema del circo' Benavente evokes the colourful atmosphere of the circus and the physical skill of the clown and his fellow circus performers, who, like Banville's Arlequin, seem able to transcend their surroundings and inspire poetry with their physical skills and colourful costumes. Once more Benavente suggests a link between popular and high culture, as he evokes the spirit of those inspired if crazy nineteenth-century writers who assumed the identity of clowns and acrobats in their writings:

> Espíritu de Barbey D'Aurevilly, de Villiers de l'Isle-Adam, de Poe, de Banville, de cuantos decadentes satánicos y parnasianos, clowns, acróbatas y dislocados de entendimiento, admirasteis el genio corporal de clowns, acróbatas y écuyères: inspirad el poema del circo. Pirueteen, caigan en saltos mortales las estrofas, jueguen y brillen como esferillas metálicas, cuchillos y antorchas de malabaristas, dislóquense en neologismos incongruentes, hagan trampolín del Diccionario, sean colorines, lentejuelas, campanilleen el iris todo. (p.551)

> Spirit of Barbey D'Aurevilly, Villiers de l'Isle-Adam, Poe, Banville, all the Decadents, be they Satanists or Parnassians, clowns, acrobats and scatterbrains who admired the physical skill of the clowns, acrobats and écuyères: inspire the circus poem. Let the stanzas pirouette and turn somersaults, let them play and shine like little metal balls, knives and juggler's lamps, let them be twisted into incongruous neologisms, let them bounce the Dictionary around as if it were on a trampoline, let them be bright colours and sequins, and let them tinkle the whole of the rainbow.

Another Banville comparison comes to mind, that of poet and clown, in an 1879 essay entitled 'Le Clown et le poète'; the following quotation from that essay bears a striking resemblance to the views on the circus and poetry expressed by Benavente in 'El poema del circo':

> Ah! les mêmes caractères, les mêmes mots, les mêmes définitions s'appliquent à l'un et à l'autre, car il y a un rhythmeur dans tout acrobate, et il y a dans tout habile arrangeur de mots un acrobate, sachant accomplir des merveilles de pondération et d'équilibre. S'élancer avec agilité et avec certitude à travers l'espace, au-dessus du vide, d'un point à un autre, telle est la suprême science du clown, et j'imagine que c'est aussi la seule science du poète.[7]

> Ah! the same characters, the same words, the same definitions can be applied to both, because every acrobat is in part a creator of rhythms, just as in every skilful arranger of words there is an acrobat who knows how to accomplish wonders of balance. The supreme skill of the clown is to be able to hurl himself through space, beneath the void, from one point to the next, and I imagine that this is also the poet's only skill.

In another sentimental passage from 'El poema del circo' Benavente considers that by going to the circus we revive our childhood days: 'el circo es la infancia del arte, y en el circo reviven nuestros días infantiles' ('the circus is the childhood of art, and at the circus we revive our childhood days') (p.551). In both 'El circo' and Los "clowns" Benavente urges people to attend the circus as children, and as ordinary, simple people: 'no como artista rebuscador de sensaciones o símbolos, sino como pueblo, como niños, para confortar la otoñada de nuestro corazón aventajado, con las risotadas infantiles, frescas, primaverales, las risas que en nosotros murieron para siempre ('not as an artist searching for sensations or symbols, but as ordinary, simple people, as children looking for a source of comfort for the autumn years of our excellent hearts in the childlike, fresh, springlike peals of laughter that have for ever died in us') ('El circo', p.66; 'Los 'clowns", p.527). These sentiments recall Crispín's prologue to *Los intereses creados* and his *Las diabluras de Polichinela.* as well as Ramírez Angel, Gual, Pérez de Ayala and Lorca (cf chapter 3), seeming to reject Symbolism in favour of popular culture. Yet the passage is characterised by the same sentimentality that has been observed elsewhere.

Cuento de primavera

The dominant tone of *Cuento de primavera* is one of sentimentality. It tells in fairy-story fashion the loves and intrigues of court life and is set in an imaginary country, the mood being established in the prologue. In one example the page Ganimedes, who delivers the prologue, emphasises the youthful freshness and dream-like nature of the story which is about to be enacted:

> Pues en esa estación hermosa del año y en esa edad dichosa de la vida, por influjo de una en otra sin duda, nació este cuento, ensueño juvenil, sin fijeza, sin orden, tumulto de imaginaciones sin más realidad que la de un sueño. [8]

> The tale was born in that beautiful season of the year [spring] and in that happy period of life [childhood], and no doubt the one influenced the other. It is a youthful fantasy, with no solid base or order, but is a riot of the imagination, possessing only the reality of a dream.

In another part of the prologue the audience is advised not to expect intellectual or moral qualities in the play: 'los hombres sesudos y graves, preocupados de más arduos estudios' ('wise, serious men, occupied with more arduous studies '), says Ganimedes, should leave the theatre, 'que no es digno de su entendimiento espectáculo tan baladí' ('for such a trivial play is not worthy of your intelligence') (p.348).[9] This idea is repeated later in the prologue, when Ganimedes also urges the audience to enter into a world of fantasy which the author is trying to create: 'nada de reflexiones; vamos a soñar, y el autor, soñando, os invita a ello' ('no thinking here; let us dream, and the author, dreaming too, invites you to join him in his reveries') (p.349).

The remainder of the play is similarly sentimental (for example, the love aspect, and the presentation of the *pueblo* as a simple, innocent contrast to the court), and contains a strong element of artificiality. However, a certain amount of comic relief is provided by the court jester Arlequín, who is apparently roguish, humorous, immodest and cynical. For example, in Act 1 Scene 3, Princess Lesbia tells him: 'y tú, bufón desvergonzado, que eres bueno en el fondo, acalla un momento ese diablillo procaz que rebulle dentro de ti inspirándote burlas y sarcasmos' ('and you, shameless clown, are basically a good person. So silence for a moment that insolent little devil that stirs within you and inspires you to play tricks and be sarcastic') (p.356). In Act 1 Scene 4 Arlequín expresses the following intention: 'yo haré de todo un poema burlesco y me burlaré en él de todo..., hasta del poema' ('I will make a burlesque poem of everything, and in it I will make fun of everything, even the poem') (p.359). In Act 1 Scene 17 his companion Colombina paints his roguishness as a noble virtue:

> Tú me comprendes siempre, ¡pobre bufón de mil colores! Noble y villano, honrado y vicioso, en tus aspectos varios, y en el centro de todos, espíritu crítico, espectador inmutable que ríes o lloras contigo, te aplaudes o te silbas a tí mismo. (p.379)

> You always understand me, you poor, colourful clown! Noble and base, honourable and depraved, in all your many aspects; and at the centre of them all, with your critical turn of mind, you are the unchanging spectator who laughs and cries, applauds or whistles at yourself.

Arlequín, at least on the surface, seems to illustrate well E.González López's view that there are elements in the play which counterbalance the generally lyrical and sentimental tone, and produce a cynical or ironical effect.[10] At first sight, it might appear that in *Cuento de primavera* Benavente is a precursor of Lugones or Valle-Inclán as far as his treatment of the *commedia* is concerned.

However, the above descriptions of Arlequín by Lesbia and Colombina are also, it might be said, basically sentimental and Romantic, and there is too a sadder

side to Arlequín's character, which is typical of the clown. In Act 1 Scene 17, for
example, he declares that love makes him sad on moonlit nights, and although
Colombina tries to shake him out of his sadness with the words 'No, no. El amor
ha de ser todo alegría' ('No, no. Love must be all happiness and joy') (p.379), the
point has been made. The epilogue to the play reinforces the notion of the sad face
behind the clown's mask, as Arlequín reveals that his life has been a constant
struggle with reality. He reveals that he has come to possess the seed of a magic
flower which he feels will transform his existence: 'y tú, maravillosa semilla, vas a
redimirme. Por mí planatada, por mis cuidados floreciente, en la primavera futura
será tu flor el premio del poeta cantor de los amores..., y ese poeta seré yo' ('and
you, marvellous little seed, will save me. You were planted by me, you thrive
because I look after you, and in our future spring your flower will be the love
poet's prize... and I will be that poet') (p.402). Judging by the evidence of *Cuento
de primavera*, Starkie is right to see *Teatro fantástico* as part of the movement
against Naturalist drama.[11] Despite the limited element of roguishness and humour
that he brings to *Cuento de primavera*, Arlequín illustrates the dream and fantasy to
which Ganimedes referred in the prologue. Benavente's *commedia* is sentimental,
belonging firmly to the dream world of the Banvillian 'Arlequin'.

Rubén Darío

The same Banvillian emphasis on escapism through the colour and vitality
of the *commedia* is a feature of the work of the leading *modernista* poet, Rubén
Darío. Darío was an admirer of *Teatro fantástico,* and wrote of its 'Fêtes galantes'
and 'Watteau atmosphere'.[12] The influence of Banville's vision of the *commedia* on
Darío's poetry is clearest in 'Canción de carnaval', from one of the canonical texts
of early *modernismo*, *Prosas profanas* (*Profane Prose*) (1896).

The *commedia* world is part of an escapist *modernista* fantasy in Darío. This is
best illustrated in the poem 'Canción de carnaval' ('Carnival Song'), which is
headed with a quotation from Banville: 'le carnaval s'amuse!/ Viens le chanter, ma

Muse...'. The whole poem is an apostrophe to Talía, the muse of drama, and colour, rhythm and smell dominate:

> Mueve tu espléndido torso
> por las calles pintorescas,
> y juega y adorna el Corso
> con rosas frescas[13]

> Move your splendid torso through the colourful streets, and play and adorn the Corso with fresh roses.

Darío urges us to treat the carnival as an opportunity to forget our worries: 'penas y duelos olvida,/ canta deleites y amores' ('forget your woes and and suffering, sing about joys and loves' (p.562). Melancholy has no part in the carnival: 'lleva un látigo de plata/ para el spleen' ('carry a silver whip to combat spleen') (p.562) . Neither is there any suggestion of sadness beneath the false mask that one finds in other writers, or indeed elsewhere in Darío's work. The emphasis is on surface gaiety:

> Sus gritos y sus canciones,
> sus comparsas y sus trajes,
> sus perlas, tintes y encajes
> y pompones. (p.563)

> Its shouts and its songs, its masquerades and its costumes, its pearls, shades, lace and pom-poms.

There is no time for reflection in the hectic carnival:

> Pirueta, baila, inspira
> versos locos y joviales;
> celebre la alegre lira
> los carnavales. (p.562)

> Pirouette, dance, inspire mad, jovial poetry; let the joyful lyre celebrate the carnivals.

Darío, however, does not attempt to explore the possibilites of carnival in 'Canción de carnaval', being content to describe and convey the colourful atmosphere, into which the masked characters of the *commedia* fit.

Darío gives only brief thumbnail sketches of some of them in the poem, as, for example, when he evokes the diamond-patterned costume of Harlequin and the hump of Pulcinella or Punch:

> Mientras Arlequín revela
> que al prisma sus tintes roba
> y aparece Pulchinela[14]
> con su joroba... (p.561)

> While Arlequín reveals that he steals his colouring from the prism
> and Pulchinella appears with his hump...

There are shades of the Verlaine Colombine in Darío's description of her as 'la bella' ('the belle'), although there are no hints in 'Canción de carnaval' that Colombina is 'méchante' ('evil'). Darío's Pierrot is also reminiscent of the Pierrot who appears in 'Pantomime', the lines: 'y descorcha una botella/ para Pierrot' ('uncork a bottle for Pierrot') (p.561) recalling Verlaine's Pierrot, who 'vide un flacon sans plus attendre,/ Et pratique, entame un pâté'[15] ('empties a bottle without delay, and, ever practical, starts on his pâté'). There are suggestions of the Deburau Pierrot in both these descriptions, as in the following stanza from 'Canción de carnaval', in which Pierrot represents a combination of poetry and mime:

> Que él te cuente cómo rima
> sus amores con la luna
> y te haga un poema en una
> pantomima. (p.562)

> Let him tell you how he rhymes his loves with the moon, and let
> him make you a poem in a mime.

The intimate link between poetry and mime has its parallel in the explicit connection made by both Banville and Benavente between the acrobatic circus clown and poetry. At the same time, Pierrot as poet is, of course, a commonplace in French Symbolist poetry, and is found in another poem from *Prosas profanas*, 'El faisán' ('The Pheasant'). Once again the setting is that of the Shrovetide carnival ('aquella noche de Carnestolendas' [p.565]), but this time the poet/Pierrot, suffering sadness due to unrequited love, is unable to participate in it:

> La careta negra se quitó la niña,
> y tras el preludio de una alegre riña
> apuró mi boca vino de su viña.
>
> Vino de la viña de la boca loca,
> que hace arder el beso, que el mordisco invoca.
> ¡Oh los blancos dientes de la boca loca!
>
> En su boca ardiente yo bebí los vinos,
> y, pinzas rosadas, sus dedos divinos
> me dieron las fresas y los langostinos. (p.565)

> The girl took off her black mask, and, after the prelude of a light-hearted banter, my mouth tasted wine from her vine. Wine from the vine of the crazy mouth, which makes the kiss burn, which begs for the bite. Oh the white teeth of the crazy mouth! I drank the wines from her burning mouth, and like pink pincers, her divine fingers gave me strawberries and prawns.

As the above lines indicate, the atmosphere is extremely decadent, but the frivolity masks the sadness of the poet/Pierrot: 'yo la vestimenta de Pierrot tenía,/ y aunque me alegraba y aunque me reía,/ moraba en mi alma la melancolía' ('I was wearing a Pierrot costume, and although I was joyful and although I laughed, my heart was filled with melancholy') (p.565). These lines are an expression of the surface colour and gaiety of the *commedia* merely masking a melancholy state, an effect which is, of course, heightened by the repeated use of the 'm' sound in the final line. The suffering of the poet/Pierrot is caused by the fact that the girl has a new lover, a 'peregrino pálido de un país distante' ('pale pilgrim from a distant land') (p.566).

The poet mentions to his casual carnival pick-up ('amada de un día') that the moon has been covered by a cloud, which is commented upon by the golden pheasant of the title in the concluding lines of the poem: '«¡Pierrot, ten por cierto/ que tu fiel amada, que la Luna, ha muerto!»' (' "Pierrot, you can be certain that your faithful love, the Moon, is dead!" ') (p.566). Although the moon as the faithful lover of Pierrot is contrasted with the fickle carnival pick-up, Darío's tone seems to be somewhat mocking, perhaps even self-deflating. It is almost as if he is trying to get the decadence into some sort of perspective.

In the two Darío poems so far examined, we have seen a contrasting approach to the *commedia*, particularly Pierrot. Duality is also the characteristic of Darío's clown figure. Darío was particularly fascinated by the English clown Frank Brown, who entertained three generations of Argentinians in the Teatro San Martín in Buenos Aires. Darío devotes a number of pages of his autobiography to Brown, and writes of him: 'hay que tener en cuenta que el arte del «clown» confina, en lo grotesco y en funambulesco, con lo trágico del delirio, con el ensueño y con las vaguedades y explosiones hilarantes de la alienación'[16] ('you have to remember that the art of the clown, in its grotesque and funambulesque aspects, borders on tragic delirium, dream and the vagueness and hilarious explosions of madness'). Darío recognises that the art of the clown combines such seemingly incompatible qualities as the grotesque, tragedy, delirium and dream, although he does not explore the potential of these so-called comic characters for combining sentimentality and the grotesque as, for example, Valle-Inclán does with his *commedia* figures in *La marquesa Rosalinda* (see chapter 5).

Frank Brown makes another appearance in the carnaval of 'Canción de carnaval':

> Unete a la mascarada,
> y mientras muequea un clown
> con la faz pintarrajeada
> como Frank Brown... (p.561)

Join in the masquerade, and while a clown grimaces with his face
daubed like Frank Brown...

Darío is not interested in the tragic side of the clown in this poem, however, in
contrast to another poem entitled simply 'Frank Brown': 'Frank Brown, como los
Hanlon Lee,/ sabe lo trágico de un paso/ de payaso, y es, para mí,/ un buen jinete
de Pegaso' ('Frank Brown, like the Hanlon Lees, knows how tragic a clown's
walk is, and he is, for me, a good horseman of Pegasus') (p.978). Darío's Frank
Brown, like Banville's clown, provides a link between the circus spectator and an
imaginary ideal world. He 'salta del circo hasta el Parnaso./ Banville le hubiera
amado así' ('he leaps from the circus to Parnassus. Banville would have loved him
like this') (p.978), and 'el niño mira a su payaso/ de la gran risa carmesí,/ saltar del
circo al cielo raso' ('the child watches his clown with the big crimson smile leap
from the circus ring to the ceiling') (p.979). As in the Benavente essays on clowns,
Darío's Frank Brown transcends his immediate surroundings and suggests to us an
ideal existence far removed from our own humdrum one.[17]

Similar sentiments are conveyed in Darío's prologue to Martínez Sierra's
Teatro de ensueño (*Dream Theatre*). The prologue is entitled 'Melancólica sinfonía'
('Melancholy Symphony'), and in it Darío presents an unashamedly idealistic
apology for the magical qualities of these art forms:

> Nosotros sabemos lo trágico del clown, lo lírico de una danzarina de
> cuerda, lo ideal del circo; el hechizo oculto de la pantomima.
> Siempre es la influencia de las máscaras la que nos hace rememorar
> o prever una existencia aparte de lo que conocemos por nuestros
> sentidos actuales; de ahí proviene la revelación mallarmeana del
> arcano prestigio del ballet, ciertos aspectos de las fiestas galantes, el
> misterio del Gilles de Watteau, la incomparable magia gráfica del
> enigmático y prodigioso Aubrey Beardsley.[18]

> We know how tragic is the clown, how poetic is a rope dancer, how
> ideal is the circus; we know too the secret magic of mime theatre. It
> is always the influence of the masks which makes us recall or
> foresee an existence separate from the one we know through our

human senses; and from this comes the Mallarmean revelation of the mysterious spell of the ballet, certain aspects of the *Fêtes galantes*, the mystery of Watteau's Gilles, the incomparable graphic magic of the enigmatic and prodigious Aubrey Beardsley.

The passage underlines the symbolic significance of mime, circus, *commedia* and ballet in that they are intermediaries between our world and another one which is beyond our own perception. The key phrases in the above passage are 'ideal', 'the secret magic', 'an existence which is apart from what we know through our human senses', and 'the enigmatic and prodigious Aubrey Beardsley'.[19] These phrases also, of course, underline the *modernista* interest in the occult.[20]

The '"vertical" aspirations' (as defined by King) are once more associated with the Watteau Gilles in a Darío poem entitled 'Balada en loor del "Gilles" de Watteau' ('Ballad in Praise of Watteau's *Gilles*'), which was written in Paris in 1911. In this poem Darío evokes the 'nocturnal melancholy' with which Gilles passes by, and he is linked with a world of mystery and dream:

> Un supraterrestre violín
> en sueño terrestre encantó.
> Y un ensueño he tenido yo,
> pasado, bello, extraordinario:
> en la grupa de un Sagitario,
> raptado, el Gilles de Watteau. (p.1057)

> An other-worldly violin charmed a worldly dream. And I have had a dream, faded, beautiful, extraordinary: on the rump of a Sagittarius, kidnapped, Watteau's Gilles.

The interplay between the human and the mythological, and the worldly and the other-worldly, is typical of Darío. As in French nineteenth-century poetry a *commedia* figure is the intermediary between the two worlds, and the launching-pad for the poet's evocation of a poetic dream-world beyond our prosaic, limited and limiting human existence.[21] He belongs to the familiar *modernista* 'distant land':

> Lejos en un país que adoro,
> vi a Gil, a eco de serenata,
> cortar margaritas de plata
> en unas montañas de oro. (p.1057)
>
> Far away in a land I adore, I saw Gilles, to the echo of a serenade, cutting silver daisies on mountains of gold.

The Gilles of the 'Balada' possesses the spiritual qualities which French poets saw in the Watteau portrayal of this *forain* character: he is 'más espíritu que materia' ('more spirit than matter') (p.1057).

A similar spirituality characterises the Parisian Pierrot evoked by Darío in his Autobiography, where, as in 'El faisán', Pierrot is the typically Symbolist/*modernista* melancholy loner, an externalisation of the poet's soul:

> Luego será un recuerdo galante en el escenario del siempre deseado París. Pierrot, el blanco poeta, encarna el amor lunar, vago y melancólico, de los líricos sensitivos. Es el carnaval. La alegría ruidosa de la gran ciudad se extiende en calles y bulevares. El poeta y su ilusión, encarnada en una fugitiva y harto amorosa parisién, certifica, por la fatalidad de la vida, la tristeza de la desilusión y el desvanecimiento de los mejores encantos.[22]
>
> Later it will be a gallant memory on the stage of the always-longed-for Paris. Pierrot, the white poet, embodies the lunar love, vague and melancholy, of sensitive poets. It's carnival time. The noisy gaiety of the great city spreads through streets and boulevards. The poet and his illusion, embodied in a fugitive, amorous Parisian girl, bears witness, through life's chance, to the sadness of disillusionment and the dissipation of the finest moments of magic.

As in 'Canción de carnaval' and 'El faisán' Pierrot is a 'poet', and the relationship between him and the moon is the stereotyped Romantic one. The atmosphere, as in 'El faisán', is one of vague *modernista* melancholy caused by unrequited love, and Pierrot is the loner who is unable to relate to the hectic carnival atmosphere of which all the *commedia* characters are a part in 'Canción de carnaval'. Disillusionment with love is responsible for the breaking of the illusion, but this theme is treated completely seriously, and without any of the cynical humour that is characteristic of Lugones's portrayal of the *commedia*. Darío's is the stereotyped 'poor' Pierrot.

The Pierrot of Gómez Carrillo

The above passage from Darío's Autobiography is similar in many ways to one from *El teatro de Pierrot* (*Pierrot Theatre*), which is a personal history of the Parisian Pierrot written by another Latin American *modernista*, the Guatemalan poet Enrique Gómez Carrillo:

> Porque Pierrot, en Montmartre, se ha convertido en un muchacho sentimental, tierno, alocado, artista y amoroso. Fuera de Colombina, lo único que le interesa es el Arte - cualquier arte. A veces se hace arquitecto y sueña en edificar altas torres de nieve para encerrarse a llorar. Otras veces la Escultura lo tienta y con el pulgar modela en el espacio formas ondulantes. También le gusta la Poesía a causa del madrigal. Pero lo que más le entusiasma es la Música y la Pintura, que son las artes más adecuadas para la seducción. Cuando no tañe la guitarra bajo el balconcillo florido, escribe esquelas ofreciendo a su amada que va a pintarle su retrato. Y Colombina, ante esta tentadora promesa, acude. Colombina es coqueta, y como conoce la inflexible monotonía de los espejos, desea verse en un lienzo. Pero Colombina, a la larga, no quiere a Pierrot, puesto que Pierrot es pobre y triste.[23]

> For Pierrot, in Montmartre, has become a sentimental lad, tender, crazy, an artist, and in love. Apart from Columbine, all that interests him is Art - any Art. Sometimes he becomes an architect and dreams of building high towers of snow so that he can shut himself up and weep. On other occasions he is tempted by sculpture and draws

undulating shapes in the air with his thumb. He also likes Poetry because of the madrigal. But what excites him most is Music and Painting, which are the art forms most suited to seduction. When he is not strumming his guitar beneath the flower-filled balcony, he is writing love letters offering to paint his beloved's portrait. And Columbine gives in to this tempting promise. Columbine is a coquette, and since she knows all about the inflexible monotony of mirrors, longs to see herself painted on a canvas. But Columbine, in the long run, does not love Pierrot, because Pierrot is poor and sad.

Here Pierrot is painter rather than poet, but the sensitive artistic temperament which leads to his suffering and loneliness is the familiar Symbolist and *modernista* one.[24] The phrase 'Pierrot is poor and sad' sums up the Darío-Gómez Carrillo approach to the figure. It was Gómez Carrillo who introduced Darío to Paris, which was to a large extent the spiritual home of Latin American *modernismo*. To quote Suárez Miramón on Darío's love of Paris, 'París era para él "la ciudad del arte, de la belleza, de la gloria y, sobretodo, la capital del amor, la reina del ensueño" '[25] ('Paris was for him "the city of art, beauty, glory and, above all, the capital of love, the queen of fantasy and illusion" ').

Gómez Carrillo's essay on the Parisian Pierrot reveals the author's fascination with the history of the *commedia* in France, and its links with the great names of Pierrot mime shows like Deburau and Legrand. Gómez Carrillo in particular stresses the complex nature of Pierrot's character: the changes brought about by such actors as Legrand affect more external appearances than inner character:

> Que este complejo representante del alma plebeya llegue a ser el exquisito e intenso personaje que en nuestros días encarna todos los sentimientos, todas las pasiones, todas las penas y todos los anhelos, no es extraño. Entre uno y otro, al fin y al cabo, la única diferencia es la educación, la superficie. El fondo es el mismo. Y bajo el frac que Paul Margueritte le pone a su mudo héroe, las mismas pasiones fuertes, los mismos instintos groseros, los mismos apetitos pasionales, las mismas codicias ciegas palpitan, aunque se expresen de otro modo y se den otros nombres. (p.168)

It is not surprising that this complex representative of the plebeian spirit should be the exquisite and intense character who nowadays embodies all feelings, passions, suffering and desires. After all, the only difference between the one and the other is education, the surface. The basic nature is the same. And beneath the dress coat that Paul Margueritte puts on his silent hero beat the same powerful passions, the same coarse instincts, the same passionate desires, the same blind greed, even though they may be expressed in a different way and be given different names.

Pierrot is not only a complex character, but becomes a symbol of mankind for Gómez Carrillo: 'un ser universal en sus pasiones' ('an universal being in his passions') (p.169); '[el] buen Pierrot, que en realidad no es sino un hombre: el hombre' ('the good Pierrot, who in reality is only a man: mankind') (p.170); 'aquel lunático muchacho que se ha convertido en un hombre complejo' ('that lunatic lad who has become a complex man') (p.241). While Harlequin was for Rivas Cherif an example of a universal comic type, so for Gómez Carrillo Pierrot is a kind of passionate, but complex Everyman: 'hoy los poetas, aun los poetas que ayer sólo pensaban en hacerlo gemir bajo los balcones, todos los poetas funambulescos, vuelven a dar al enharinado su compleja personalidad de gran instintivo' ('today poets, even those poets who only yesterday thought of no more than making him groan beneath the balconies, all the *funambulesque* poets, once more give to the white-faced figure the complex personality of a man of great sensitivity') (p.170).

The most modern *commedia* mime discussed by Gómez Carrillo is Jean Cocteau's *Boeuf sur le toit,* which the Guatemalan author sees as revolutionary. He quotes from what purports to be Cocteau's prologue:[26]

Desde los tiempos más clásicos, la farsa no se pone sino los trajes de la comedia italiana. Yo creo que eso no es necesario. Yo me he sentido libre, cual en pleno carnaval, y he aprovechado esa independencia para rejuvenecer las máscaras antiguas.

Since Classical times farce has put on only the costumes of Italian comedy. I think that this is unnecessary. I have felt free, just as in carnival time, and I have used this independence to revitalise the old masks.[27]

Gómez Carrillo is clearly uneasy with the Cocteau mime; having described its plot, he asks his readers: '¿Os choca todo esto?... A mí también' ('Does this shock you?...It shocks me too') (p.246). According to its author, it is supposed to be a circus farce, 'un juego bufo y cruel hecho para satisfacer el instinto sanguinario de los niños' ('a farcical, cruel game invented to satisfy the bloody instinct of children'), but Gómez Carrillo shrewdly suggests an inconsistency on the French author's part:

> Lo único malo es que el poeta no quiere que sean los niños los que aplauden su obra. «Para ellos - parece decir - ahí están las puerilidades de Bernstein y de Henri Bataille». Su *Boeuf sur le toit* es para gente seria, para filósofos capaces de meditar, para artistas que comprenden los arcanos de la risa y del silencio. (p.246)

> The only bad thing is that the poet does not want the children to be the ones to applaud his work. He seems to be saying: 'the puerile works of Bernstein and Henri Bataille are for them'. His *Boeuf sur le toit* is for serious people, for philosphers who are capable of meditation, for artists who can understand the mysteries of laughter and silence.

The 'simple' element in the audience, perhaps expecting a traditional mime show, feels ridiculed:

> Los hombres sencillos murmuran al final del espectáculo...
> - Este señor se burla de nosotros.
> Y puede que no se equivoquen. Se burla de nosotros probablemente... Pero también se burla de sí mismo... (p.246)

> Simple people mutter at the end of the show...
> - This man is making fun of us.
> And perhaps they are right. He is probably making fun of us... But he is also making fun of himself.

One feels that the sympathies of Gómez Carrillo are more with the ordinary people than with the intellectuals.[28]

The comments on the Cocteau work come right at the end of *El teatro de Pierrot,* and seem to point away from nineteenth-century to twentieth-century *commedia*. Gómez Carrillo perceptively detects the shift from sentimental melancholy to a much sharper portrayal of the *commedia* in the early twentieth century, in which the grotesque is emphasised, the characters become more disturbing, and the relationship between actors and audience is explored. These elements will form the basis of the discussions in chapters 5 and 6. However, it is the nineteenth-century Pierrot mime which excites Gómez Carrillo more than the work of Cocteau.

Gómez Carrillo's fascination with Pierrot mime is central to his 1899 novel, *Bohemia sentimental (Sentimental Bohemia)*. It is characterised by a sentimental portrayal of Bohemian values and love, typical of Decadentism. It deals with a young impoverished man called Luciano who is trying to forge a literary career in Paris. He collaborates with a certain Durán, a pretentious Bohemian for whom money is more important than art. Luciano has written a play about a woman who divorces her husband in a fit of anger, marries an elegant man, but, unable to choose between the two, maintains a relationship with the first husband. Luciano's real-life situation parallels that of his play, as an unspoken love grows between him and Durán's mistress, Violeta. She wants to work in the theatre, and sees Durán's money and influence as the means to achieve her goal, while at the same time she considers him to be a vain bourgeois. At the end of the novel, true love triumphs over false values, as Luciano and Violeta openly declare their feelings to each other.

The interplay between 'real' life and acting, inherent in the portrayal of the theatre, is heightened in the mime scenes which punctuate the novel. Luciano's friend Luis dreams of writing *commedia* mimes which are very much in the Symbolist/Decadent tradition:

Quería hacer pantomimas trágicas, pantomimas psicológicas, pantomimas profundas. Deseaba compendiar todas las pasiones de la humanidad, todas las ideas de los hombres, todas las sensibilidades de las mujeres, en dramas mudos y evocadores, representados por Pierrot y Colombina.[29]

I wanted to write tragic mimes, psychological mimes, profound mimes. I wanted to summarise all human passions, all the ideas of men, all the artistic feelings of women, in silent, evocative dramas, performed by Pierrot and Columbine.

Gómez Carrillo was presumably influenced in writing this by his knowledge of the development of the *commedia* in France and by the many Parisian Pierrot mime shows he had seen. The mime Luis wishes to write is of the kind evoked in *El teatro de Pierrot.*

Eventually a mime written by Luis is performed, in which he himself plays the part of Pierrot. Luis's affirmation that mime is the antithesis of 'bourgeois' drama suggests a comparison with some of the authors who were discussed in chapter 3, but the types of work we are talking about are quite dissimilar in content and tone. Luis explains his work to Luciano: it is very different, he says, to the sort of mime to which Luciano is accustomed: 'para ti la pantomima es un arte de circo' ('for you mime is a circus art') (p.112) in which the same stereotyped situation is constantly repeated. This stock circus mime, claims Luis, always contains a Punch figure, an old husband with his white wig, a young bride, etc: 'los ademanes son enormes. El perro se lo come todo, el polichinela se lleva a la novia y la suegra recibe los bastonazos que el marido destinaba al raptor' ('the gestures are huge. The dog eats up everything, the Punch carries off the bride and the mother-in-law gets the blows which the husband intended for the abductor') (p.113).

The circus mime is anonymous and designed to make audiences laugh. This is in complete contrast to those of Luis (it turns that out he has written several), which are essentially tragic and sentimental:

El héroe es Pierrot y la protagonista Colombina. Ambos se adoran, pero el amor que los atrae y que los une no es nunca un amor sencillo.
      Colombina aparece en traje de baile, pintada, teñida. A su lado viene el marqués... son las doce de la noche... a lo lejos la silueta de Pierrot surge. Vestido de frac, va corriendo tras su querida... Ya llega... ya se acerca... va a encontrarla... Colombina está vestida de novia y Pierrot de novio. Van a la Iglesia, van a casarse... A lo lejos las campanas repican alegremente. Es el día de las bodas. De pronto - en pleno día - baja la Luna a quejarse del olvido de Pierrot... Baja la Luna. Y Colombina, tristemente, se echa a llorar y sus lágrimas forman un lago en el cual se refleja la imagen de su rival... ¡Pobre novia! - dice el cortejo. Pero no... la novia es dichosa porque acaba de ver reflejarse en el lago de lágrimas, la imagen de Pierrot que llora también en el palacio de la Luna. (pp.114-16)

The hero is Pierrot and the leading lady Columbine. They adore each other, but the love which attracts and unites them is never a simple one.
      Columbine appears in a ball gown, made up, her hair dyed. At her side is the marquis ... it is midnight... in the distance the figure of Pierrot appears. Wearing a dress-coat, he goes running after his loved one....He is getting close, he is going to meet her... Columbine is dressed as a bride, and Pierrot as a groom... They are going to the Church, they are going to be married... In the distance the church bells ring joyfully. It is the wedding day... Suddenly, in broad daylight, the Moon comes down to complain about Pierrot's having forgotten her. The Moon comes down. And Columbine, sadly, begins to weep and her tears form a lake in which her rival is reflected... Poor bride! - says the entourage. But no,... the bride is happy because in the lake of tears she has just seen reflected the image of Pierrot who is also weeping in the palace of the Moon.

Gómez Carrillo has used the situation of an unconsummated *ménage à trois* of sorts to parallel the Luciano-Violeta-Durán situation. The Pierrot of Luis's mime belongs firmly to the line of the 'poor' Pierrot tradition, both materially and in terms of his frustration. Colombina, interestingly, is like Pierrot a sad victim of unrequited love, and not the coquettish deceiver she is in many farces. The mime is a sentimental tearjerker, clearly very diferent from the Cocteau work described in *El teatro de Pierrot*.

One of Luis's mimes takes Paris by storm. Violeta and Luciano attend a performance together, and Gómez Carrillo subtly establishes an interplay between what happens on stage and the latent but as yet undeveloped feelings of attraction between the two protagonists. The following extract will serve as an example of the interplay, as well as pointing up Violeta's basically honest and sentimental character, similar to that of Luciano and different from the hard-bitten cyncism of Durán. I quote it at length, as its content and tone epitomise the sickly sentimentality that characterises the presentation of *commedia* in some of the works which are analysed in this chapter. This sentimentality is combined with an equally sickly religiosity in a passage which provides an excellent illustration of some of the worst excesses of *modernismo*. It also demonstrates the frustration and jealousy of the almost whiter-than-white, tragic Pierrot as he overhears a love scene between Colombina and the marquis:

> El telón se levantó de nuevo... Y Pierrot, más blanco todavía, blanco con la blancura cadavérica de los celos, blanco como la hostia de la comunión de los agonizantes, blanco, cual un muerto, en su túnica color de sudario, apareció tras una puerta. Sus ojos brillaban, en la máscara de yeso, con resplandores lamentables de cirio. La contracción de sus labios, tenía algo de macabro... Oía...
> ... ¡Pobre Pierrot!... Pegando el rostro contra la puerta cerrada, oía lo que pasaba en la alcoba... Oía los suspiros de Colombina; y oía las palabras del marqués... Su frente, su boca, sus manos, todo su ser, en fin, iba indicando las impresiones que producían en su alma doliente las escenas de la traición...
> Cuando un beso sonaba adentro, Pierrot sentía el beso... cuando una risa llegaba hasta él, Pierrot reía... cuando las manos de Colombina estrechaban las manos del marqués, Pierrot unía sus manos... Y ese simulacro de amor, indicando el amor de la mujer amada y del hombre aborrecido, tenía, en su elocuencia silenciosa, un aspecto trágico y alucinante.
> Los ojos de Violeta estaban húmedos de lágrimas. Luciano se acercó a ella y sin decirle una palabra, impulsado por la pasión que flotaba en la atmósfera, la cogió una mano y la acarició largo rato entre las suyas. Sus ojos se encontraron tiernamente...(pp.182-83)

The curtain went up again... And Pierrot, whiter still, white with the deathly whiteness of jealousy, white as the communion host of the dying, white, like a dead man, in his shroud-coloured tunic, appeared behind a door. His eyes were shining, in his plaster mask, with the pitiful brightness of a candle. There was something macabre about his wasting lips... He could hear...

Poor Pierrot! ... Pressing his face against the closed door, he could hear what was going on in the bedroom... He could hear Columbine's sighs; and he could hear the words of the marquis... His forehead, his mouth, his hands, his whole being, in short, betrayed the impressions produced in his suffering soul by the scenes of betrayal.

When the sound of a kiss was heard within, Pierrot heard the kiss... when the sound of laughter reached him, Pierrot laughed too... when Columbine's hands held the marquis's hands, Pierrot pressed his own hands together... And this mock love scene, which showed the love of the beloved woman and the rejected man, possessed in its silent eloquence, a tragic and beguiling appearance.

Violeta's eyes were damp. Luciano moved close to her and, without uttering a word, driven on by the passion that floated in the atmosphere, took her hand and caressed it for a long while in his. Their eyes met tenderly....

Practically all the instances of Pierrot mime in *Bohemia sentimental* are serious or tragic. The ending of the mime attended by Luciano and Violeta is even melodramatic, as Pierrot, mortally wounded in a duel with the Marqués, dies in the repentant Colombina's arms, 'ofreciéndola aún sus labios ya muertos pero llenos aun de besos funerales' ('still offering her his lips which are now dead, but still filled with funereal kisses' (p.187). This scene oozes with decadent morbidity, and Pierrot is a rather extreme example of the *fin-de-siècle* character discussed in chapter 1.

The tragic Pierrot: Mota and Zamacois

A number of other early twentieth-century Spanish works present a similarly tragic picture of the Pierrot. Fernando Mota's *Colombina se casa* (*Colombina Gets Married*), for instance, uses the carnival setting to highlight the question of false and true love.[30] The two young lovers (Leandro and Roxana), who are not allowed to marry because the girl's father (the materialistic Polichinela) wishes to marry her to a rich suitor, disguise themselves as Pierrot and Colombina. The sentimentality of the 'poor' Pierrot theme is shown in Colombina's words: '¡Pobre Pierrot mío, mi blanco poeta! ¡Qué triste será su canto de melancolía esta noche en la que unas manos crueles y egoístas van a destruir el mágico ensueño de nuestro amor' ('Poor Pierrot, my white poet! How sad will be his melancholy song tonight when cruel and egotistical hands destroy the magical dream of our love!'). Here is the other side of the escapist coin, as the magical world of dream is destroyed. But the point is that whether it is the dream or its destruction which is being evoked, the tone is sentimental, and the work lacks any of the irony which is so important to Lugones and Valle-Inclán. *Colombina se casa* duly ends in tragedy as Leandro-Pierrot's mortally-wounded body is discovered, an event commented on in a detached fashion by the cynical Arlequín.

A similar situation pertains in a short story by Eduardo Zamacois, *Noche de máscaras* (*Night of Masquerade*), which was published in *Por esos mundos* in February 1906. This time it is a brother rather than a father who refuses to allow the girl to marry the man she loves. The lover, dressed as Pierrot for a masked ball, challenges the brother to a duel, loses it and is killed. The death is evoked in melodramatic fashion:

> Sin perder momento Anselmo se agachó y recogió un puñado de polvo y de arena que lanzó a los ojos de su víctima. Fernando, cegado, bajó la cabeza. Aprovechando cobardemente aquel momento de abandono, Anselmo volvió a acometerle, dejando ir todo su

cuerpo tras su brazo iracundo, abriendo con este golpe terrible un camino seguro a la muerte.

En tal instante las nubes se desgarraron y la luna apareció, lanzando sobre la pared del cementerio las dos siluetas del trágico grupo: a *Pierrot* reculando, con el busto caído hacia atrás, las manos sobre el vientre y las piernas dobladas en un estertor de agonía; y a Anselmo delante de él, con su diestra extendida, el ademán hostil y la salvaje cabezada coronada de plumas. (p.116)

Without wasting a moment, Anselmo bent over and picked up a handful of dust and sand and threw it into his victim's eyes. Blinded, Fernando lowered his head. Taking advantage in a cowardly fashion of this momentary lowering of his guard, Anselmo attacked him again, throwing the whole weight of his body behind his furious arm, opening with this terrible blow a sure path to death.

At that very moment the clouds broke up and the moon appeared, and threw against the cemetery wall the shadows of the tragic group: Pierrot reeling backwards, his hands clutching his stomach and his legs bent in his death throes; and Anselmo in front of him, his right hand held out, his gesture hostile and his savage head crowned with feathers.[31]

Felipe Sassone

Pierrot does not always lose out in Spanish plays of the early twentieth century. In Felipe Sassone's *La canción de Pierrot* (*Pierrot's Song*), published in *Por esos mundos* in December 1914, he overcomes the handicap of his 'poor' reputation to win Colombina's love in the end. She is captivated by his lyricism (the 'Song' of the title), which proves more attractive to her than the Abbot's money and Arlequín's wit and boldness. Of course this outcome is as sentimental in its own way as those of *Colombina se casa* and *Noche de máscaras*, but there are elements of *La canción de Pierrot* which at least bear some resemblance to the theatricality and the humour of a work like *La marquesa Rosalinda*.

Gómez Carrillo's *Bohemia sentimental* also contains one example of a comic grotesque Colombina-Pierrot scene in the novel. It occurs when Luis, in a drunken state, recites a poem:

Colombina, Colombina
Mi divina
¿Dónde estás quién lo adivina
Colombina,
Si eres más fluida y más fina
Que la misma Melusina?
¿No me esperas en la esquina?
Dilo pronto, Colombina
Dilo pronto, que se arruina
Mi alma débil y mezquina
Por buscarte como mina
De diamantes de la China;
Colombina,
Mi cochina,
Mi adorada Colombina...
¿No oyes ya mi mandolina
Colombina?
¡Colombina, Colombina!
Una carcajada estridente remató su loca improvisación.. (p.258)

Colombina, my divine Colombina. Who can guess where you are,
Colombina? You are more free-flowing and finer than Melusina.
Won't you wait for me on the corner? Tell me soon Colombina, for
my weak, mean soul is destroying itself as it searches for you like a
diamond mine from China; Colombina, my rotten Colombina, my
adorable Colombina... Can't you hear my mandolin, Colombina?
Colombina, Colombina!
Harsh laughter cuts short his improvisation..

The style and tone of this extract is more in keeping with some of the works which
will be discussed in chapter 5, such as the poetry of Manuel Machado and Lugones,
and Valle-Inclán's *La marquesa Rosalinda*. The verse recited by Luis perhaps
reinforces the following comment from *El teatro de Pierrot*, 'la verdad es que para
la pantomima, tal cual la comprendemos ahora, una prosa expresiva y pintoresca es
más propia que un verso sonoro' ('the truth is that expressive and colourful prose is
more appropriate than resonant verse to the mime theatre form as it is understood
now') (p.205).

Carrere and the Bohemian Pierrot

Pierrot, in all his *fin-de-siècle* sentimentality, encapsulates the positive side of Bohemian Decadentism admired by Gómez Carrillo. In *Bohemia sentimental* he distinguishes between two types of Bohemianism: the pure, true variety exemplified by Luciano, and the corrupt, false version of Durán. A similar distinction is drawn by Emilio Carrere in his collection of essays *Retablo grotesco y sentimental* (*Grotesquely Sentimental 'Retablo'*). The true Bohemian, whom he much admires, is summed up in 'Divagación acerca de la señorita bohemia' ('Digression on Miss Bohemia'):

> Es una forma espiritual de aristocracia, de protesta contra la ramplonería estatuida. Es un anhelo ideal de un arte más alto, de una vida mejor; y por eso la situación de un bohemio es mucho más amarga, en la vida de relación, de lo que se creen los que se figuran que la bohemia está en el vestido o en las melenas descuidadas.
>
> El bohemio es, pues, un espíritu exquisito de artista que odia toda vulgaridad; un bohemio se asfixia en una oficina, porque la oficina es la cristalización espiritual, la fosilización del individuo.[32]

> It is a spiritual form of aristocracy, of protest against established coarseness. It is an ideal longing for a higher art, for a better life, and it is for this reason that the situation of a Bohemian is much more bitter as far as human relationships are concerned than is believed by those who think that Bohemianism is all about dress and unkempt hair.
>
> The Bohemian is, then, a refined spirit of an artist who hates all vulgarity; a Bohemian is stifled in an office, because the office is human crystallisation, the fossilisation of the individual.

In another essay from *Retablo grotesco y sentimental*, 'Los jardines del crepúsculo' ('Twilight Gardens'), Carrere expresses a preference for the melancholy of Pierrot over the boisterous and noisy Harlequin: 'amo más la ideal tristeza de Pierrot, el triste juglar de la leyenda blanca, que el cascabeleo funambulesco y la bullanga estrepitosa de Arlequín, el bellaco' ('I love more the ideal sadness of Pierrot, the melancholy minstrel of the white legend, than the grotesque jingling and boisterous rowdiness of Harlequin, the rogue') (p.64). Here is a juxtaposition between nineteenth-century *commedia* spirit as personified by Pierrot and the more earthy, roguish characteristics associated with Harlequin.

Carrere's distaste for Harlequin is again demonstrated in 'Divagación acerca de la señorita bohemia', in which the author distinguishes between three different types of Bohemian, *pintoresco*, *tabernario* and *lúgubre* (meaning 'picturesque', 'coarse' and 'mournful' respectively): 'la bohemia pintoresca es la más dolorosa, es la tragedicomedia cotidiana en que la Miseria le pone una cascabalera caperuza de Arlequín' ('picturesque Bohemianism is the most painful sort, it is everyday tragedy in which Misery puts on the jingling hood of Harlequin') (p.10). The most pitiful of all the Bohemians are the *tabernarios*, who are described as failures looking for inspiration at the bottom of a glass. A typical example is Pedro Barrantes, whom Carrere evokes using the image of a Punch-like puppet: 'un temperamento hondo de poeta, fue como un polichinela macabro, con su calva reluciente y su perfil de garduña' ('a deep poetic temperament, he was like a macabre puppet, with his shining bald head and his marten profile') (p.10).

Pierrot and Catalan *modernisme*

Both Gómez Carrillo and Carrere associate 'true' Bohemianism with a melancholy, but somehow pure, decadence. With his innocence, loneliness and suffering, Pierrot encapsulates their vision of the Bohemian. They distinguish between this and what they would consider to be a corrupted version of it.[33] Pierrot as symbol of idealism, purity and innocence is also a feature of Catalan drama of the early twentieth century. Here he is a part of the debate between *modernisme* and *noucentisme*, where the *commedia*, and more specifically Pierrot, is identified with *modernisme*, under threat from *noucentisme*. To quote Fàbregas:

> El noucentisme és disciplinat, aixi com era anàrquic el modernisme; refusa les superfícies aspres i escull les llises, prefereix la llum artificial de la ciutat, de les oficines, dels despatxos dels dirigents,

enlloc del sol del camp, del traqueteig de les màquines a les naus fabrils; imposa el coll dur i la corbata i prescriu la brusa; li escauen més els perfums de les dames, les joies, els sonets, que no pas la suor popular, la faixa i la barretina, els poemes monumentals. El noucentisme pretén d'ésser modern, eficient, burgès i pragmàtic.[34]

Noucentisme is disciplined, just as *modernisme* was anarchical; it rejects harsh surfaces and chooses smooth ones, it prefers the artificial light of the city, of offices, of bosses' rooms, to the sun of the countryside, the rattling of factory machinery; it imposes the stiff collar and the tie and prescribes the overall; it is fonder of lady's perfume, jewellery and sonnets than the sweat of the common people, the sash and the countryman's cap, and monumental poetry. *Noucentisme* claims to be modern, efficient, bourgeois, pragmatic.

The stereotyped vision of Pierrot as lonely and frustrated outsider coincides with the *modernista* topos of the *marginat* (outsider). To quote Joan-Lluis Marfany, 'els modernistes idealitzen el solitari, el marginat'[35] ('the *modernistes* idealise the loner, the outsider'). Marfany also highlights another *modernista*, indeed a more general Romantic and post-Romantic topos, that of the artist as separate from and superior to the common herd: 'els autèntics herois de l'època - cal dir-ho? -, [...] són els caps privilegiats, els intel.lectuals i artistes que somien en un món millor i lluiten per la bellesa i contra la incomprensió de les masses'[36] ('it goes without saying that the real heroes of the period [...] are the exceptional people, the intellectuals and artists who dream of a better world and fight for beauty against the uncomprehending masses').

The aspect of the battle between *modernisme* and *noucentisme* that interests us here is the heart-head conflict, in particular in two plays: Rusiñol's *La cançó de sempre* (*The Same Old Song*) (1906) and Mestres's *Els sense cor* (*The Heartless Ones*) (1909).

The former is a one-act dialogue between Pierrot and Colombina, dominated by Pierrot, with Colombina acting as devil's advocate as he puts forward his pro-*modernista* arguments. Pierrot's central thesis is that reason kills sentiment, and that material progress destroys the spirit. He rejects prudence, claiming that it is an 'excusa dels covards'[37] ('a coward's excuse'). He is a staunch defender of freedom as opposed to order, displaying a particularly scornful attitude to the latter: 'qui ens ho havia de dir, que fins tu, Colombina, havies d'enfangar-te en aquest estany de l'ordre' ('who would have said, Colombina, that even you would muddy yourself in the pool of order') (p.1236). In reply to Colombina's question 'i de què viuràs?' ('and what will you live on?'), he declares:

> De les molles de pa que siguin, de la fruita que espolsin els arbres, de la claror del capvespre, de la llum, de la llibertat, de la remor del bosc, de la fam, de lo que siga. De tot, menos de tenir ordre. (p.1236)

> On scraps of bread, on the fruit that falls from the trees, on the evening brightness, on light, liberty, the noise of the forest, hunger, whatever. On anything but order.

When Colombina the foil tries to make a case for the work ethic, Pierrot scornfully dismisses her as a bourgeois (p.1236).

Pierrot sees himself as part of a race that embodies an anti-order, anti-work ethic. He claims that if the current climate dictates a machine-dominated society, it is the duty, even the destiny, of the race of Pierrots to counteract it by using the Romantic arms of poetry and song:

> PIERROT Que no veus que fins a nosaltres els pierrots ens voldrien junyir a una màquina i fer-nos màquina, i posar-nos transmissions per nervis, i caldera per cor, i de lo que en dèiem esperit fer-ne un rellotge automàtic?
> COLOMBINA És veritat.
> PIERROT Doncs això no pot ser, Colombina. Si hi ha homes negres que treballen, hi ha d'haver pierrots blancs que els deslliurin, ermitans de l'alegria, predicadors del desordre, saions del sentit comú, jardiners de l'ideal, que enmig de tants horts de verdura cuidin les flors de la poesia. (p.1237)

> PIERROT Can't you see that they even want to tie us Pierrots to machines and turn us into machines, and to replace our nerves with

transmissions, put a boiler in place of our hearts and turn what we call the soul into an automatic clock?
COLOMBINA It's true.
PIERROT Well this cannot be allowed, Colombina. If there are black men who work, there have to be white pierrots to free them, hermits of joy, preachers of disorder, fields of common sense, gardeners of idealism, who in the midst of so many vegetable plots tend the flowers of poetry.

The above passage is almost embarrassing in its sentimentality. Pierrot also believes that the role of the race of Pierrots is to bring laughter and music to brighten up the lives of sad people:

PIERROT No em creuries. Els pierrots, si donen consells, fan riure.
COLOMBINA Jo no em ric mai de tu, Pierrot.
PIERROT Doncs, canta amb mi; fes cançons.
COLOMBINA Per qui?
PIERROT Per als que treballen i pateixen; per als que estan tristos en la terra per falta de cors que els alegrin. (1237)

PIERROT You wouldn't believe me. When pierrots give advice, they make people laugh.
COLOMBINA I never laugh at you, Pierrot.
PIERROT Then sing with me; make songs.
COLOMBINA For whom?
PIERROT For those who work and suffer; for those who are sad due to a lack of choirs to make them happy.

Laughter and brightness are important components of Pierrot's *modernista* philosophy. The word 'philosophy' is used advisedly, since what is merely implied in Gual's *La serenata* is for Rusiñol in *La cançó de sempre* a polemical approach to life. *La cançó de sempre* also contains the poetry/prose dichotomy that underpins another and better-known one-act Rusiñol dialogue, *Cigales i formigues* (*Cicadas and Ants*) (1901), in which the prosaic, hard-working, materialistic ants are juxtaposed to the poetic dreamers, the cicadas. The uniformity of the worthy but dull ants has its parallel in Pierrot's depiction of the common people in *La cançó de sempre* as 'la tristor en ramat dels tristos' ('the herd-like sadness of the miserable') (p.1238). Rusiñol uses colour contrasts once more to juxtapose workers and dreamers:

> PIERROT I què hi veus entre aquesta negror, allà al fons?
> COLOMBINA Una ratlla blava.
> PIERROT Aquesta ratlla són homes que pleguen, que pleguen del treball. En veus cap se separi dels altres?
> COLOMBINA Tots són iguals. (p.1238)

> PIERROT And what can you see there in the distance, in the middle of all that blackness?
> COLOMBINA A blue line.
> PIERROT That's a line of men finishing work. Can you see one who stands out from the others?
> COLOMBINA They're all the same.

The blue of the workers' uniforms undoubtedly symbolises the mased society of industry in opposition to the individuality of the white-costumed Pierrots. The blue anonymity of modern industrial society embodies a threat to the timeless world of the *commedia dell'arte*.[38] Pierrot's sense of his superiority over the 'blue masses' illustrates Marfany's description of the 'exceptional people' quoted above.

Another of Rusiñol's well-known plays, *L'alegria que passa* (*Fleeting Joy*) (1898), is also of relevance here. The clown (who historically shares many of Pierrot's characteristics) encapsulates the play's message, in words which carry an echo of Pierrot's sentiments in *La cançó de sempre*: 'Que se'ns endona el teu diner! Aquí el tens! Poble pastaurant terrossos! No en tastareu de poesia! Us condemno a prosa eterna, us condemno a tristesa perdurable! (*Rient i tocant el bombo*). Visca la bohèmia! Visca la santa alegria!'[39] (What do we care about your money! Take it! People chewing soil! You'll not taste poetry! I condemn you to eternal prose, I condemn you to eternal sadness! (*Laughing and playing the drum*) Long live Bohemianism! Long live blessed happiness!').

The travelling players have been drummed out of town by the Philistine townsfolk, and yet the clown's defiant words represent a victory of sorts. Similarly, the Pierrot of *La cançó de sempre*, despite feeling threatened by prose, retains his dream that poetry will be triumphant:

> COLOMBINA I quins somnis vols seguir?
> PIERROT El de posar la vida en vers, mentres em sitia la prosa.
> (p.1236)
>
> COLOMBINA And what dreams will you pursue?
> PIERROT The dream of putting life to poetry, while I am besieged by prose.

Just before the end of the playlet the sound of a chorus singing that freedom will be achieved by a combination of work and song gladdens Pierrot's heart, and gives him hope for the future. In brief, *La cançó de sempre* is a short, polemical playlet which expresses its author's opposition to the growing presence of *noucentisme* and its values in Catalonia.

Mestres's *Els sense cor* is a full-length play on the same topic, with Pierrot once again illustrating *modernisme* under threat from *noucentisme*. The plot of the play revolves around the contrast between the sentimental Pierrot and the majority of the other characters, whose hearts have been removed by Doctor Gras. One such character is Pierrot's former friend Pep, who has changed his name to Arnau, since this is more appropriate to his new status as a poet. Pep/ Arnau is portrayed by Mestres as a poet of the *noucentista* variety:

> ARNAU Ja comprendràs tu mateix que, decentment, un poeta no pot dir-se Josep Torrabadella.
> PIERROT Vols dir que pot influir?
> ARNAU (*heroic*) O poeta o Torrabadella, *o tempora... o mores*!
> PIERROT (*tímidament*) I, no obstant... era el nom del teu pare...
> ARNAU (*amb desdeny*) El pare, el pare!... El pare *perteneixia* a una generació *atrassada* que no sabia res d'estetisme ni psiquisme ni civilitat.[40]

ARNAU You yourself will realise that a poet can't decently call himself Josep Torrabadella.
PIERROT Do you mean to say that that can affect things?
ARNAU Oh Poet oh Torrabadella, *o tempora... o mores*!
PIERROT (*timidly*) And yet it was your father's name.
ARNAU (*disdainfully*) My father, my father! My father belonged to a backward generation who knew nothing about aestheticism, psychism nor civility.

Arnau is scornful of Pierrot's innocence and naivety, and the latter feels ill-at-ease in the company of the former and his associates. Pierrot fulfils his Romantic and Symbolist function as an alienated outsider, tricked and misunderstood by the rest of society. He does not belong to the respectable world of Arnau and company, whose empty ritual and frivolity are satirised by Mestres. His heart is shown to be preferable to their so-called reason, which is shallow and lacking in true sentiment. This point will be underlined by a brief examination of various characters' treatment of the widow and her children in Act 2.

Pierrot's reaction to their wretched state is spontaneous and sentimental, typical of a man with a heart. However, as with Deburau, sentimentality is combined with practicality as Pierrot sees the absurdity of the other characters' proposal to organise a charity ball for the benefit of the widow and her family (*kermesse*). As they warm to their task, Pierrot stands gaping, unable to understand their fanciful ramblings, until Doctor Gras (Fat Doctor) provides the explanation to dispel Pierrot's perplexity:

DOCTOR Aquesta gent, qui més qui menys, es trobaven en el mateix estat de vostè, abans de la meva intervenció quirúrgica; i ara... (*Grans riallades i picaments de mans a dintre*) i ara ja els veu, tan feliços!
PIERROT Vol dir, que són feliços?
DOCTOR Què els falta per ser ho?
PIERROT No sé... trobo a faltar hi alguna cosa... El cor.

DOCTOR (*paternalment*) Desenganyi's, jove: el cor és una entranya no tan sols inútil, sinó molesta, que no hi ha més remei que suprimir-la.
PIERROT Començo a sospitar que té raó.
DOCTOR I acabará per convence's. Per tant, ja ho sap: quan se senti decidit... estic a les seves ordres. (p.79).

DOCTOR These people were more or less in the same state as you, before I performed surgery on them; and now... (*Great peals of laughter and clapping of hands offstage*) and now look at them, so happy!
PIERROT Do you mean to say they're happy?
DOCTOR What more do they need?
PIERROT I don't know... something seems to be missing... The heart.
DOCTOR (*paternalistically*) Wake up, young man: the heart is an organ that is not just useless but a nuisance. So it has to be removed.
PIERROT I'm starting to believe that you are right.
DOCTOR And you'll be convinced in the end. So, when you're ready, I'm at your service.

Pierrot, however, resists the temptation to follow the good doctor's advice, and sticks to his traditional guns by entrusting everything to his heart, despite the pain that this sometimes causes. As in *La cançó de sempre*, sentiment triumphs over reason, as the values of *modernisme* prove superior to those of *noucentisme*. And yet the authors' sense of unease is evident, as the new world of logic and scientific rationalism replaces the old one of spontaneity and poetry. Pierrot is equated with the disappearing world, a relic from the past in a brave new one in which Rusiñol and Mestres felt ill-at-ease.

A very different vision of the *commedia* has emerged from this chapter compared with the previous one. Whereas writers such as Pérez de Ayala, Gual and Rivas Cherif saw in this historically significant genre a path for a reform of the contemporary Spanish theatre, the view of *modernistas* and *modernistes* like Darío and Rusiñol is basically rooted in the nineteenth century. While Gómez Carrillo in particular shares with Pérez de Ayala and Gual an interest in the history of the *commedia*, he and other writers are concerned not so much with Harlequin as with

Pierrot, the *commedia* character who is most associated with nineteenth-century sensibility. He is the stereotyped 'poor' Pierrot, unlucky in love. If he is not rejected by the lady who is the object of his desires, then social forces combine to thwart him. He is a Romantic cliché in that he is an outsider who is considered by the writer to be superior to the common herd. This theory is most clearly spelt out by Rusiñol, while for Carrere the sad Pierrot is superior to the noisy, coarse Harlequin.

The dominant mood of the writings analysed is one of melancholy and sentimentality, and nostalgia occasionally develops into melodrama. No writer seems able or willing to step back and view Pierrot and what he signifies with detachment, and thereby establish an aesthetic distance between the creator and his creation. There is sometimes disillusionment with the magic of the dream, but this is never with the *commedia* itself. There is no equivalent character to Crispín in Benavente's *Los intereses creados*, whose view of life, like that of the author's, is one of cynicism and disillusionment. An attitude of detachment and cynicism, particularly to Pierrot, but dealt with in a much more Modernist way than by Benavente, is to be found in a whole range of authors to be discussed in chapter 5.

1 Jesús Rubio's words on the element of dream (*ensueño*) in *modernista* drama come to mind here: 'el ensueño tiene un carácter compensador del prosaísmo cotidiano' ('fantasy compensates for the prosaic nature of everyday life') (Jesús Rubio Jiménez, 'Perspectivas críticas: horizontes infinitos. Modernismo y teatro de ensueño', *ALEC*, 14 [1989], 199-222 [p.209]).
2 Ramón Gómez de la Serna, *Nuevos retratos contemporáneos* (Buenos Aires: Sudamericana, 1945), p.93.
3 See for example Federico de Onís, *Jacinto Benavente* (New York: Instituto de las Españas en los Estados Unidos, 1923), p. 12. Marcia Simpson Lewis, 'The *Modernismo* of Jacinto Benavente' (unpublished doctoral thesis, University of Illinois, 1967), p.97, considers that Benavente never provided sufficient evidence to suggest that this was the case.
4 See *Obras completas*, 11 vols (Madrid: Aguilar, 1940-1958), X (1956), 795.
5 All these essays can be read in *Obras completas*: 'El circo' in XI (1958), 64-66; 'Los payasos del circo', which is part of *Pan y letras*, in VI (5th. ed., 1963), 687-88; 'Los "clowns" ' and 'El poema del carnaval', which are part of *Vilanos* (1905), in VI, 525-27 and 551-53 respectively; and 'Carnaval' in XI, 99-102. It has been possible to date only *Vilanos*, but the themes and style of the others suggest that they belong roughly to the same period. Page references to these essays given in the text are to the appropriate volume of *Obras completas*.
6 From 'Los payasos del circo', in *Obras completas*, VI, 687.
7 In *Critiques*, p.422.
8 In *Obras completas*, VI, 349. Further quotations from the work are taken from this edition, and the corresponding page references are given in the body of the text.

104

9 Once more Crispín's prologue to *Los intereses creados* comes to mind.
10 'El teatro de fantasía de Benavente', *Cuadernos Hispanoamericanos*, 320-1 (1977), 308-26 (p.320).
11 Walter Starkie, *Jacinto Benavente* (London: Humphrey Milford, 1924), pp.26-27.
12 Rubén Darío, 'La joven literatura', in *España contemporánea, Obras completas*, 21 vols (Madrid: Biblioteca Rubén Darío, 1923-29), XXI (1929), 88-100 (p.94).
13 Rubén Darío, *Obras completas*, 11th edn (Madrid: Aguilar, 1968), p.562. Further quotations from Darío's poetry are taken from this edition, and the corresponding page references are given in the body of the text.
14 Darío uses this Italianised form rather than the usual Spanish form Polichinela.
15 Paul Verlaine, *Œuvres poétiques complètes*, p.107.
16 *La vida de Rubén Darío escrita por él mismo* (Barcelona: Maucci, 1915), p.207.
17 See Russell King's point about 'vertical aspirations' quoted in chapter 1. Starobinski's explanation of the clown's acrobatics are also apposite here: 'par sa virtuosité même, la provesse acrobatique se sépare de la vie de ceux d'en bas: le poète, s'il en fait à lui-même l'application allégorique, se donne pour vocation d'affirmer sa liberté en un jeu supérieur et gratuit, tout en faisant le grimace aux bourgeois, aux "assis" ' ('because of their very virtuosity acrobatic feats are separate from life here on earth: the poet, if he applies the allegory to himself, takes as his vocation the affirmation of his liberty in a superior and gratuitous game, while cocking a snook at the bourgeois, the "seated ones" ') (*Portrait de l'artiste en saltimbanque*, p.22).
18 G.Martínez Sierra, *Teatro de ensueño*, 3rd edn (Madrid: Renacimiento, 1911), p.14.
19 Starobinski highlights the attractiveness of the escapist possibilities of the circus and fair culture in the context of a society in the process of industrialisation: 'le monde du cirque et de la fête foraine représentait, dans l'atmosphère charbonneuse d'une société en voie d'industrialisation, un îlot chatoyant de merveilleux, un morceau demeuré intact du pays d'enfance, un domaine où la spontanéité vitale, l'illusion, les prodiges simples de l'adresse ou de la maladresse mêlaient leurs séductions pour le spectateur lassé de la monotonie des tâches de la vie sérieuse' ('in the carbonaceous atmosphere of a society that was undergoing an industrial revolution, the world of the circus and the fair spectacles represented an oasis shimmering with wonder, a piece of childhood that was still intact, a domain where vital spontaneity, illusion, the simple wonders of dexterity and clumsiness blended their seduction for the spectator who was tired of the daily round of serious life') (*Portrait de l'artiste en saltimbanque*, p.8).
20 See for example Cathy Login Jrade, *Rubén Darío and the Romantic Search for Unity* (Austin: University of Texas Press, 1983).
21 See for example Russell S. King, 'The Poet as Clown'.
22 *La vida de Rubén Darío escrita por él mismo*, pp.182-83
23 *La mujer y la moda. El teatro de Pierrot* , which is vol. 12 of *Obras completas*, 12 vols (Madrid: Mundo Latino, n.d.), 224-25. Further quotations from the work are taken from this edition, and the corresponding page references are given in the body of the text.
24 See for example Ana Suárez Miramón, *Modernismo y 98* (Madrid: Cincel, 1980), p.31.
25 *Ibid.*, p.57. She does not quote her source. The fascination with Paris clearly reflects the topos of Bohemia.
26 I have consulted the original text of the play, but have not discovered the source of what Gómez Carrillo quotes. On the genesis and performances of the play see Francis Steegmuller, *Cocteau: A Biography* (London: Macmillan, 1970), pp. 238-45.
27 Similarities will be noted with writers discussed in chapter 3.
28 In a study of the *commedia* in early twentieth-century French music, Gabriel Jacobs makes a related point about composers' adaptation of the 'popular' models: '*Pierrot lunaire* and *Petrushka* are supreme masterpieces which have deeply influenced the course of twentieth-century music not because they attempted a fusion of popular art and its intellectualization, but almost despite that attempt' ('The *Commedia dell'arte* in Early Twentieth-century Music: Schoenberg, Stravinsky,

Busoni et Les Six', in *Studies in the Commedia dell'Arte*, ed. by David J.George and Christopher J.Gossip, pp.227-45 [p.243]).

29 E.Gómez Carrillo, *Bohemia sentimental* (Paris: La Campaña, 1899), p.69. Further quotations from the work are taken from this edition, and the corresponding page references are given in the body of the text.

30 This work was consulted at the Theatre Institute in Barcelona; in the edition used, there are no details of publisher or date, and it has not been possible to trace these.

31 For illustrations of this short story see figs. 10 and 11.

32 Emilio Carrere, *Retablo grotesco y sentimental* (Madrid: Mundo Latino, n.d.), p.7. Further quotations from the work are taken from this edition, and the corresponding page references are given in the body of the text.

33 However, the common perception of contemporaries was that the corrupted version was the only one. This was the case with the critic Antonio de Zayas, who in one of a series of absurdly pompous essays entitled *Ensayos de crítica histórica y literaria* criticises frivolous *modernistas* for what he alleges is their abandonment of 'traditional' Spanish values in favour of inferior foreign ones. He uses the example of the *commedia dell'arte* to illustrate his point: 'no resiste casi ninguno de nuestros jóvenes poetas la tentación de caer en ese lazo y suelen dejarse seducir por la frivolidad de los personajes de la comedia italiana, los cuales trasplantan al fértil campo de la literatura española, en el que, como plantas exóticas, no pueden prosperar con lozanía' ('hardly any of our young poets can resist the temptation of falling into this trap, and they allow themselves to be seduced by the frivolity of the characters of Italian Comedy, which they transplant to the fertile field of Spanish literature, in which, like exotic plants, they are unable to flourish with vigour') ('El modernismo', in *Ensayos de crítica histórica y literaria* [Madrid: A. Marzo, 1907], pp.387-420 [p.410]).

34 Xavier Fàbregas, *Història del teatre català*, pp.206-07.

35 *Aspectes del modernisme*, 5th edn (Barcelona: Curial, 1982), p.195.

36 *Ibid.*, p.225.

37 Santiago Rusiñol, *La cançó de sempre*, in *Obres completes* (Barcelona: Selecta, 1947)), p.1236. Further quotations from the work are taken from this edition, and the corresponding page references are given in the body of the text.

38 The Starobinski comment on the attractiveness of the escapist possibilities of the circus and fair culture in the context of a society in the process of industrialisation is apposite here.

39 Santiago Rusiñol, *L'alegria que passa*, in *Teatre* (Barcelona: Edicions 62, 1981), p.38.

40 Apel.les Mestres, *Gaziel/ Els sense cor* (Barcelona: Edicions 62, 1969), p.50.

Fig. 1 *Juego de Bolos*, Madrid carnival float.

Fig. 2 Masked ball at carnival time in Madrid.

Nada temas Colombina:
tus neuralgias singulares,
to jaqueca y malestares
se van con Sanatorina.

En Farmacias y Droguerías al por maytor: Pérez Martín y Cia, Alcalá 9
Concesonario Exclusivo. J. Burgos de Orellana, Puerta del Sol 2

Fig. 3 Advertisement for headache tablets.

PIERROT: ¡Bellísima Luna, tu palidez la haré brillar limpiándote con LUXOL!

Fig. 4 Advertisement for cleaning fluid

Fig. 5 Madrid carnival float (1906)

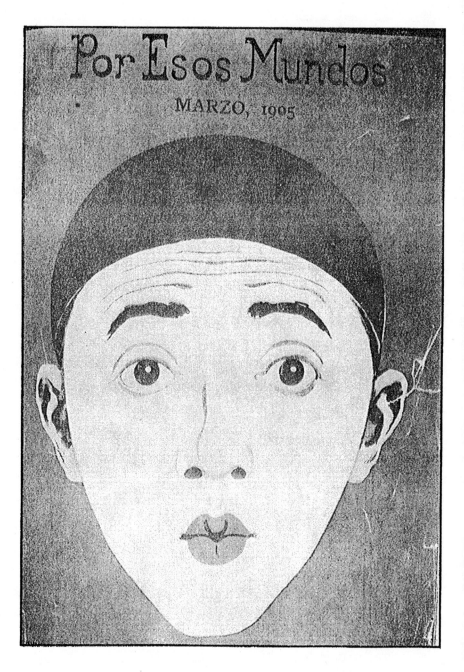

Fig. 6 *Arlequín*, front cover of *Por esos mundos* (March 1905).

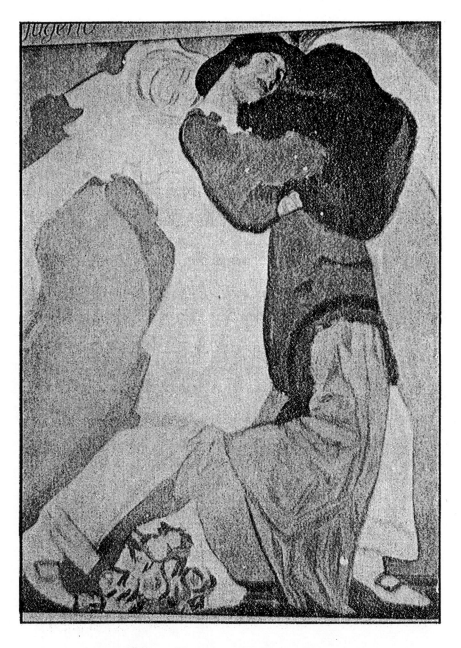

Fig. 7 *Pierrette Pariense*, illustration of Manuel Abril's article, 'El ideal carnavalesco', in *Por esos mundos* (March 1915).

Fig. 8 An illustration of E. Ramírez Angel's *Drama en un bazar*, in *Por esos mundos* (December 1911).

Fig. 9 An illustration of E. Ramírez Angel's *Drama en un bazar*, in *Por esos mundos* (December 1911).

—¿Eres tú?—Sí, yo, vámonos..

Fig. 10 An illustration of Eduardo Zamacois' *Noche de máscaras*, in
Por esos mundos (February 1906).

...Pierrot, reculando, con el busto caído hacia atrás, las manos sobre el vientro,...

Fig. 11 An illustration of Eduardo Zamacois' *Noche de máscaras*, in
Por esos mundos (February 1906).

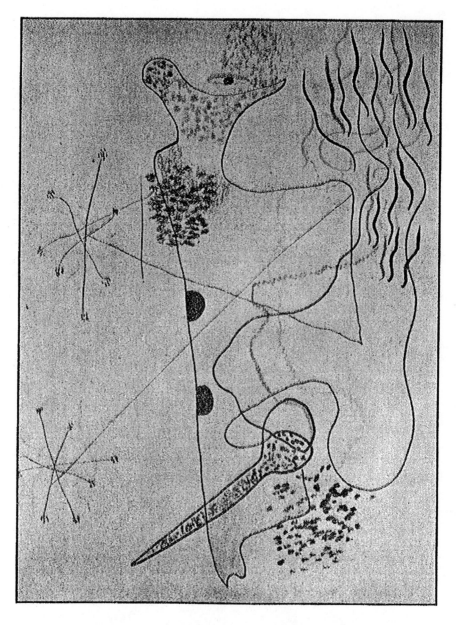

Fig. 12 Federico García Lorca, *Pierrot priápico* (1932-36).

Fig. 13 Federico García Lorca, *Arlequín desdoblado* (1927).

Fig. 14 Federico García Lorca, *Cabeza de Pierrot* (1931)

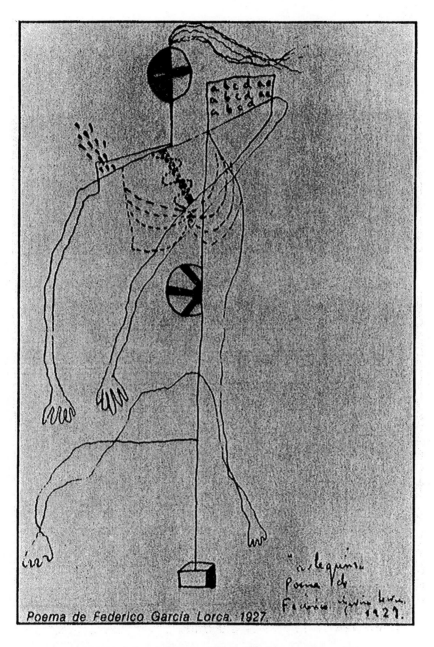

Fig. 15 Federico García Lorca, *Arlequin. Poema* (1927).

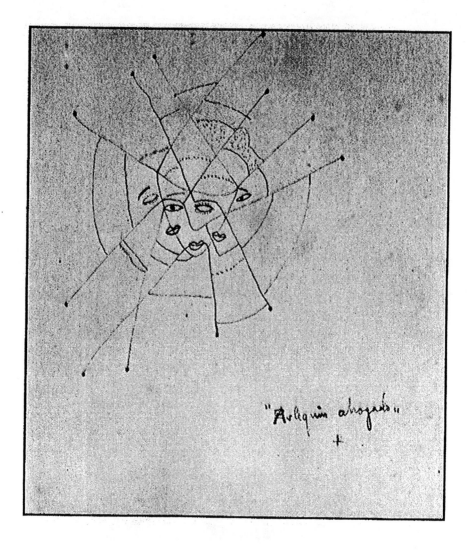

Fig. 16 Federico García Lorca, *Arlequín ahogado* (1927-28)
(also used as frontispiece).

Chapter 5

The Destruction of the Illusion

A very different attitude and perspective are revealed by the authors to whom I now turn. The magical dream is disrupted as writers approach their *commedia* subjects either ironically or with a sense of disillusionment. The stereotyped 'poor' Pierrot myth is destroyed either through bitter sarcasm or humorous yet wounding irony. In these authors Pierrot is often a pathetic figure and the subject of scorn or ridicule rather than sympathy. Language, in particular metaphor, becomes a tool not of transposition to a world of colour and imagination but of the destruction of the very myth *modernistas* such as Darío and Gómez Carrillo sought to create. A poetic ideal is juxtaposed to prosaic reality. Here poetry does not enjoy an unquestioned superiority over prose as was the case with Rusiñol, but instead the everyday and the commonplace are set against the fantastic, undermining the latter. The escapist settings of idealised country *fêtes galantes* are contrasted with a squalid urban environment, which now takes the place of what are seen as the outdated conventions of the Watteau-inspired setting.

Most of the works discussed in this chapter belong to the period 1909 to 1916, one in which many of the tenets and myths of early *modernismo* were being challenged and replaced. The critic José Olivio Jiménez sums up the change, characterising early *modernismo* in the following way:

> El respeto a la belleza; la búsqueda de una palabra armoniosa y pura, que reflejara la armonía secreta de la creación tan añorada por el artista de la época ...la confianza en el poder salvador y por ello sagrado del arte...fe en la palabra artística, conciencia de arte...se aventuraron por los ámbitos de lo que no tenían: el lujo y el placer,

108

siempre asociados en el decadente al dolor y a la muerte. O se evadieron a realidades igualmente lejanas: al brillo cosmopolita de París o al refinamiento de la Francia del siglo XVIII, al repertorio rutilante y prestigioso de las mitologías (clásica y nórdica), a países exóticos como la China y el Japón.[1]

Respect for beauty; the search for the harmonious, pure word, which would reflect the secret harmony of creation for which the artist at that period so yearned...the confidence in the saving and therefore the sacred power of art...faith in the artistic word, consciousness of art...they set out in search of what they did not have: luxury and pleasure, always associated in the case of the Decadent writer with pain and death. Or they escaped to equally distant realities: to the cosmopolitan glitter of Paris or to the refinement of eighteenth-century France, to the shining, prestigious repertoire of mythology (be it classical or Nordic), to exotic countries like China and Japan.

Later *modernismo,* explains Olivio Jiménez, turns against its own clichés:

Por los caminos de la ironía y la distancia crítica, prepararán al cabo esa negación del modernismo... usarán sin embargo el lenguaje como un ya acerado instrumento de esa actitud irónica que les sostiene. Y de aquí los resultados expresivos esperables: el humor, el socavamiento paródico, la burla, y hasta la caricatura de aquellas entidades supremas de la belleza que sus antecesores profesaban como artículo de fe.[2]

Through the paths of irony and critical distance they [i.e. later *modernistas*] were to prepare finally a negation of *modernismo* ... nevertheless, they were to use language as a by now sharp instrument of that ironical attitude which sustained them. And this gave rise, predictably, to humour, parodic undermining, joking, and even caricature of those supreme entities of beauty which their predecessors professed as an article of faith.

Broadly speaking, the authors considered in this chapter belong to the second of Olivio's categories, in contrast to those discussed in chapter 4, who belong to the first. Historically, of course, the change between one cultural era and the next is rarely clearcut and often messy, which is also the case with the development of the *commedia* in early twentieth-century Hispanic literature. Four authors will be considered: Manuel Machado and Benavente, whose attitude to the *commedia* is essentially bitter and dismissive, and Lugones and Valle-Inclán, whose work is characterised more by humour and brilliance of metaphor, and contains a certain ambiguity. Firstly, I consider Machado and Benavente, and then analyse the strikingly inventive approach to the subject which is evinced in Lugones' *Lunario sentimental* (1909) and Valle-Inclán's *La marquesa Rosalinda* (1912).

The lonely and desolate *commedia* figures of Manuel Machado

Like most of the *modernistas*, Manuel Machado spent the obligatory apprenticeship period in Paris under the habitual guidance of Gómez Carrillo, where he participated eagerly in the Bohemian world, and discovered such artists and writers as Paul Fort and Aubrey Beardsley. His portrayal of Pierrot in *Alma* (*Soul*) (1898-1900) is obviously influenced by the same French sources as Darío *at al*, but Machado's poems display little of the surface gaiety that is evident in at least some of Darío's poetry. An examination of two poems from *Alma*, 'La noche blanca' and 'Copo de nieve', highlight this point.

The Pierrot of 'La noche blanca' ('The White Night') symbolises sexual frustration and despair. The poem evokes a deserted, snow-covered Paris in which 'sólo están en vela/ la nieve, la Luna y Pierrot'[3] ('only the snow, the Moon and Pierrot are awake'). The object of his frustrated love, Colombina:

> En brazos
> del marqués
> se entrega
> por una pulsera de oro
> y un collar de perlas. (p.35)

surrenders herself to the marquis for a gold bracelet and a pearl necklace.

110

As she lies passively in his arms like a prostitute, her fantasies turn to Pierrot, whose naked arm and neck she would like to see adorned with her jewels as a kind of homage of her love and an indication of the high price her body has been able to command. Pierrot, meanwhile, in his despair, frustration and jealousy, turns to the moon, his traditional confidante, but here more like the cold, aloof moon-goddess of mythology. He calls in vain for her aid and scolds her for her unresponsiveness. There is also the implication that he knows nothing of Colombina's secret dreams and thinks that she has merely abandoned him for material gain. There is a strong erotic element in the poem, but it is essentially frustrated eroticism, heightened by a feeling of coldness and loneliness. The point is that all lovers are fools; Pierrot, in a poem such as 'La noche blanca', is ideally suited to expressing the futility of love.

In a sense, 'La noche blanca' is atypical of Machado's presentation of the *commedia* in that it is characterised by none of the bitter frivolity with which he normally evokes the Pierrot figure. Another poem from *Alma*, 'Copo de nieve', with its light, mocking irony, is more typical:

> Colombina llora,
> Colombina ríe,
> Colombina quiere
> morir, y no sabe
> por qué...
>
> Pierrot, todo blanco,
> de hinojos la implora,
> la besa y le pide
> perdón, y no sabe
> de qué... (p.36)

Colombina weeps, Colombina laughs, Colombina wants to die and does not know why. Pierrot, all in white, begs her on bended knees, kisses her and begs her forgiveness, and does not know for what...[4].

The utter pointlesness of the whole Pierrot-Moon-Colombina ritual, evident in the above, is even more apparent in the nihilistic final three lines: 'y nadie ha sabido,/ ni sabrá, ni sabe/ por qué...' ('and no-one knew, will know or knows why') (p.36).

The frivolity and the sheer pointlesness of the *commedia* is the dominant theme of three poems from *Caprichos* (*Caprices*) (1900-05). In 'Pierrot y Arlequín', for instance, the *commedia* figures of the title ask each other the names of their respective girlfriends:

> «Y sepa yo, al fin,
> tu novia, Arlequín...»
> «Ninguna.
> Mas dime, a tu vez,
> la tuya.»
> > «Pardiez!...
> > ¡La Luna!». (p.37)

'And I must know who your girlfriend is, Arlequín'. 'I haven't got one, but tell me the name of yours. By gad, the Moon'.

Two other poems from *Caprichos*, 'Pantomima' and 'Escena última' ('Final Scene'), treat the theme of frivolity in a more bitter manner than 'Pierrot y Arlequín'. The rhythm of 'Pantomima' enhances the mood. As Brotherston puts it:

> Groups of 3-syllable units alternate brusquely with groups of 4-syllable ones, creating the savage syncopated rhythm Machado wanted for his description of the farcical jerky movements of his characters Pierrot and Margot.[5]

With its theatricality and grotesque, puppet-like characters, 'Pantomima' seems to anticipate Valle-Inclán's *La marquesa Rosalinda*. The following two examples are indicative:

Se escucha un grito grotesco
y cae en escena Pierrot
de un salto funambulesco.
¿Por qué no ríe Margot?... (p.39)

A grotesque sound is heard, and Pierrot leaps comically onto the
stage. Why does Margot not laugh?

and

Margot, como una muñeca
destrozada,
se desploma en un rincón,
desmayada... (p.40)

Like a broken doll, Margot collapses in a corner, in a faint.

The dominant mood of the poem is summed up in the first three lines of the second
verse: '¡Nada importa./ ¡Alegre es la vida y corta, /pura farsa!' ('Nothing matters.
Life is joyful and brief, pure farce!'). In 'Pantomima' Machado probes beneath the
mask, and exposes the falseness of carnival:

Siguen bandas, serenatas
de quimérica, de histérica armonía...
Salta como rota cuerda
la alegría.
Y fatigan los disfraces,
y ahogan los antifaces
a su dueño...
Pasa el sueño...
Rostros pálidos se ven. (p.40)

Bands play on, serenades of fanciful, hysterical harmony... Joy
leaps like a broken cord. And the disguises grow tiresome, and the
masks stifle their owner. The dream passes. Pale faces can be seen.

These lines are an excellent evocation of the vanity of the whole carnival/ mime scene with its pathetic pierrots and masked characters playing silly games. The underlying bitterness is encapsulated in 'hysterical' and in the broken chord image, while the line 'the dream passes by' embodies the disillusionment caused by the ending of the dream.[6] This sentiment is also conveyed in 'Escena última', in which Pierrot symbolises a carnival that has died:

> Y ante mí, aterido,
> blanca la faz de harina
> y las manos exangües, ha caído
> muerto el pobre Pierrot. (p.41)

> And before me, stiff with cold, his face white with flour and his hands lifeless, poor Pierrot has fallen dead.

Although *Caprichos* was dedicated to Machado's close friend Rubén Darío, the former's depiction of carnival is a long way from that found, for instance, in the latter's 'Canción de carnaval', and illustrates perfectly the way the inflated world of dream inhabited by *commedia* characters and masked figures of carnival has been deflated, although Machado's deflation does not contain the humorous irony and brilliant imagery that are employed by Lugones and Valle-Inclán.

Machado's depiction of the *commedia* in *Caprichos* is indicative of a significant shift in his attitude towards *modernismo* after *Alma*. He was beginning to reject Parisian Bohemianism in favour of the Spanish Catholic tradition which was to turn him into a reactionary later in his life. He explains his loss of interest in Paris in a poem from *Caprichos* entitled 'Despedida a la luna' ('Farewell to the Moon'), in which the figure of Harlequin symbolises the life-style and the attitudes he is in the process of jettisoning:

> Volví de París, en fin,
> donde nos hemos querido,
> y he puesto ya en el olvido

114

mis aventuras de Arlequín. (p.61)

I finally returned from Paris where we loved each other, and I have forgotten about my Harlequin adventures.

Brotherston explains the tensions involved in Machado's working out his rejection of *modernismo*:

> The Bohemian and anarchic view of life which Machado held as a Modernist[7] was, then, being compromised both by an admission that he had nothing new or challenging to say for the moment, and by fascination for a Spanish tradition he had declared stultifying. But he was goaded on, almost despite himself, during the next few years, to live out to the end, as few of his companions did, the 'tragedia ridícula de la bohemia'. [8]

Machado's artistic anguish coupled with his precarious financial circumstances are reflected in *El mal poema* (*The Bad Poem*) (1909), for example in 'Carnavalina' ('Little carnival'), in which for Machado the carnival expresses the futility and frustration of love. Pierrot is the foolish lover who, now unmasked, vainly pursues Colombina, the cruel *belle dame sans merci* who deceives him with her beauty: 'la divina, la traidora,/ la que ríe cuando él llora...' ('the divine traitress, the woman who laughs when he cries') (p.99). He is the dreamer who searches for the 'oscuro logaritmo/ imposible del amor' ('the impossible dark logarithm of love') (p.100). Machado, one feels, does sympathise with Pierrot to a certain extent, and even identifies with him. The last verse (which, significantly, is the last verse of *El mal poema*) reveals that Pierrot, denied sexual fulfilment with Colombina, looks for what is untimately sterile solace in his old companion, the moon:

Y, el rostro lleno de harina,
grita aún el sin fortuna:
«¡Colombina! ¡Colombina!»

Y su alma se va a la luna
como una carnavalina.

And with his face covered with flour, the luckless one still cries:
'Colombina! Colombina!' And his soul goes to the moon like a little
carnival.

Pierrot appears again in a Machado sonnet entitled simply 'Pierrot', which
is one of two poems from the collection *Apolo* (1910) that appear to be inspired by
Watteau's paintings (probably *Gilles*). Once more Machado emphasises his
character's whiteness. He is 'el blanco personaje.../ que todos conocéis' ('the white
character you all know') (p.119), and

De blanco viste
como la luna.
Y cual la luna, es triste,
blanco, más blanco que su blanca veste. (p.119)

He dresses in white like the moon. And like the moon he is sad,
white, whiter than his white costume.

It is as if the white moon, costume and face of Pierrot reflect each other, and the
'impossible' love of Pierrot is essentially narcissistic.[9] In verse 3 Pierrot 'juega a
juegos de amor con Colombina' ('plays love games with Colombina'), who is 'ya
no cabe duda, una traidora' ('without doubt a traitress'), just like 'un niño con una
golosina' ('a child with a sweet') (p.119). In the final tercet Machado sums up the
pathetically sad figure cut by the Watteau Pierrot: 'porque, cuando Watteau lo ha
retratado,/ en medio del paisaje recortado,/ el personaje blanco llora y ora' ('for
when Watteau painted him in the middle of the rugged landscape, the white
character weeps and prays') (p.119). He is very different from the Darío version of
'Balada en loor del "Gilles" de Watteau', who is 'más espíritu que materia' ('more
spirit than matter'), and who 'en melancolía nocturna/ pasaba' ('passed by in
nocturnal melancholy').[10]

Benavente: *La ciudad alegre y confiada*

If personal and artistic motives shape Machado's version of the *commedia*, then the striking difference between *La ciudad alegre y confiada* (*The Happy, Confident City*) (1916) and Benavente's earlier *commedia* plays owes more to political than to aesthetic circumstances. The play is an expression of its author's opposition to the majority of Spanish intellectuals, who were on the side of the Allies during the First World War. The play expounds the view that the City (which clearly refers to Madrid) is being sacrificed by its leaders for their own interests, against the will of the ordinary people. Despite its failure to find favour with the critics, the play was a huge popular success.

The differences between *Los intereses creados* and *La ciudad alegre y confiada* are apparent in their prologues. Although in *Los intereses creados* Crispín does attempt to play down the importance of the work by telling the audience that they should not expect anything so fine as the comedies of the past and that the characters are puppets, nevertheless he tries to stir their interest in what they are about to see. No such attempt is made in the prologue to *La ciudad alegre y confiada*, which is spoken by The Exile (El Desterrado), generally believed to symbolise the exiled Spanish conservative politician Antonio Maura, whom Benavente admired greatly. Its theme is that the travelling troupe (*farándula*) is an insult in the present sad and difficult times because its members attempt to make people laugh: 'todo el mundo es teatro de tragedia, y si el Arte mismo no puede ser hoy serenidad, si no quiere parecer inhumano, ¿cómo puede ser bufonada sin parecernos un insulto al dolor y a la muerte?'[11] ('the whole world is a tragic stage, and if Art itself cannot today be serene, if it does not want to appear to be lacking in humanity, how can it be linked with buffoonery without seeming to be an insult to suffering and death?'). These sentiments are a long way from those expressed by Benavente in his circus essays on the question of clowning, and those on the role of the theatre in the prologues to *Cuento de primavera* and *Los intereses creados*. Although, as we saw in chapter 3, in the latter Benavente seems to be questioning, even satirizing, *modernista* nostalgia for the past, he does so with elegance and humour. *La ciudad alegre y confiada* is a much more serious play than *Los intereses creados* and lacks its subtlety. Julia Ortiz Griffin underlines Benavente's fundamental change of attitude to drama by the time of World War I, quoting from the prologue to *La ciudad alegre y confiada* in order to illustrate her point. She writes:

> Pues el dramaturgo cree que la crisis que atraviesa la humanidad requiere otra actitud y otra clase de drama. El observa que la humanidad se encuentra perpleja, dudosa y perdida, y decide que, como daramaturgo o como artista, tiene el deber de sacarla de esta situación.[12]

> For the dramatist believes that the crisis mankind is going through needs a new attitude and a different type of drama. He observes that mankind is bewildered, confused and lost, and decides that, as a dramatist or as an artist, it is his duty to help it out of this situation.

The masked characters of the *commedia dell'arte* symbolise decadence in *La ciudad alegre y confiada,* and are disgusting and superfluous in a society with grave social problems. Pantalón and Polichinela are even more obsessed with money than were their namesakes in *Los intereses creados*. They epitomize opportunism, and are prepared to sell the city for their own mercenary self-interest. Crispín's master Leandro has fallen out of love with Silvia, who is now his wife, and Crispín himself is no longer the independent rogue of *Los intereses creados*, having allowed the powerful position he has achieved within the City to corrupt him. However, he is ultimately disposed to sacrifice himself, and emerges by the end of the play as the conscience of the City.

The change that has taken place in Benavente's vision of the *commedia* between the 1890s and the First World War will be highlighted by an examination of his portrayal of Arlequín. In *Cuento de primavera* he belongs to the *modernista* world of fantasy and escapism. His role as a schemer and comic servant is taken over by Crispín in *Los intereses creados*, and Arlequín has less relevance to the action than he did in *Cuento de primavera*. However, Benavente depicts him with a certain amount of humour, and the suggestion that he is an anachronism is made

118

gently and without bitterness. In *La ciudad alegre y confiada* this last point is no longer a mere suggestion, and Benavente displays considerable acrimony in his presentation of Arlequín. The erstwhile clown and love poet is now Poet Laureate, and a complete degenerate into the bargain. He dedicates poetry to the dancer Girasol, another frivolous character. He is cynical, a point made by Silvia in the first act when, in a clear reference to *Los intereses creados*, she contrasts the present-day Arlequín with the Romantic poet of the past:

> Esta noche, esta fiesta, una vez más traen a mi corazón el recuerdo de otra noche, de otra fiesta en que por primera vez nos encontramos. Una canción de Arlequín, cuando Arlequín no era el cínico poeta de ahora, cuando cantaba al amor y a la vida. (p.1158)

> Tonight's party reminds me once more of another night, another party, when we first met. A song from Arlequín, when he was not the cynical poet he is today, but sang to love and life.

The whole point is that such *fêtes galantes*, like the people who attend them, are an insult to a society faced with problems like those besetting the City. As Polichinela says in Act 1, 'el pueblo tiene hambre y se indigna contra nosotros porque estamos de fiesta' ('the people are hungry and are angry with us because we are enjoying ourselves') (p.1163). Arlequín, as one would expect, has no time for patriotism: he despises his own culture and longs for a foreign one to be imposed: 'yo me sentiré siempre más compatriota de un poeta turco que de uno de nuestros soldados, que por su parte en nada se diferencia de un soldadote veneciano' ('I will always feel closer to a Turkish poet than to one of our soldiers, who is really no different from the Venetian soldiers') (p.1199). His attitude is typical of that of the decadent older generation, and the contrast between them and the vigorous young people is drawn by Crispín in Act 2: 'cuento con sus soldados y cuento con su juventud, que no toda es como el señor Arlequín y sus desmedrados poetas ('I am counting on the soldiers and the youth of the City, for they are not all like Arlequín and his degenerate poets') (p.1185). Youthfulness has taken on a new meaning here: no longer is it part of an idealised past, but instead points the way to a purer and more heroic future society.

La ciudad alegre y confiada is interesting in that it subverts the colourful, escapist vision of the *commedia*, which here encapsulates a sense of disillusionment on the part of its author not only with the attitude of Spanish intellectuals to World War I but also more generally with the notion of art for art's sake, which is central to *modernismo*. However, it does it in an obvious and unsubtle way, and as far as the use of language is concerned, the play is unexciting. This is true neither of Lugones's *Lunario sentimental*, with its humorous verbal pyrotechnics, nor of Valle-Inclán's *La marquesa Rosalinda*, with its rich fusion of humour, stylised sentimentality and theatricality.

Lugones: *Lunario sentimental*

There are parallels between Manuel Machado's *El mal poema* and *Lunario sentimental* (which could be translated either as *Sentimental Calendar* [lit. *Lunar Calendar*] or as *Crazy Sentimentalist*), namely the date of publication and a therapeutic exteriorisation of personal suffering through the figure of Pierrot. Also, both poets subvert *modernista* language through their use of urban dialogue. In Brotherston's view, in *El mal poema* Machado 'was making one of the first attempts in his language to create poetry out of that sordid city life by means of slang, sarcasm and deliberate prosaism'.[13]   This description could be even more appropriately applied to *Lunario sentimental*, especially as regards the vision of the *commedia*. Lugones, albeit influenced by Laforgue, makes a much more original, dynamic and strikingly modern contribution to the *commedia* than Machado, particularly through his use of imagery.

Instances of both sentimentality and cynical detachment will be observed in Lugones, although it is clearly the latter which predominates. We shall, however, begin with an untypical example, in which, although familiar Lugones humour is present, the sentimental eventually triumphs over the grotesque. This is 'El Pierrot negro' ('The Black Pierrot'), a mime play in four scenes, or *cuadros*, based on the traditional cuckolding of Pierrot by Columbine with Harlequin, and Pierrot's subsequent frustration and anger. This is clearly conceived by Lugones as a set-piece situation, as for instance in the following description of Pierrot in Scene 1: 'a esa hora llorará furioso el nuevo desvío de Colombina' [14] ('at this moment he will be lamenting furiously Colombina's latest rebuff'): the future tense in the Spanish is here a future of probability, or inevitability, and has the effect in this context of highlighting the ritualistic nature of the action. The first sign that Pierrot's frustration is, at least in part, to be comically treated comes when the 'white character' falls into a bowl of black dye having heard Colombina's mocking laughter from the street, and turns completely black. The rest of the mime play revolves around Pierrot's attempts to return to his state of whiteness, through various magic devices, and a trip to the moon, that home of whiteness!

One of the most striking features of 'El Pierrot negro' is the way in which Lugones satirises *modernista* commonplaces through his use of incongruous settings. In the first scene, for instance, which takes place in a dyer's, the twilight atmosphere is conveyed through typically *modernista* impressionism, but this seems out of place in a modern urban environment where nature is dehumanised: 'a los fondos de una tintorería, en el crepúsculo. Vagas construcciones de arrabal. Barracas, viviendas de tabla, dos o tres árboles raquíticos. Todo ello fundido en la suave tinta violeta de la hora' ('at the back of a dyer's, at twilight. Unclear lines of buildings on the outskirts of the town. Huts, shacks, two or three stunted trees. The whole scene is blended into the soft violet light of the hour') (p.303).[15]

Another *modernista* cliché which is satirized in this mime is the interest in the occult and magic. Scene 2 is set in an alchemist's, and the owner unsuccessfully tries various magic tricks in order to help Pierrot regain his whiteness. These include conjuring up mermaids and land nymphs to perform ritualistic dances around Pierrot and offer him precious metals. When these devices fail, Pierrot insists on his trip to the moon, and once more Lugones uses juxtaposition to turn a serious situation (Pierrot's frustration) into a comic one. The alchemist gives Pierrot a broomstick, but refuses to provide him with the talisman until he has been paid. The Romantic association of Pierrot with the moon is thereby made prosaic, and the urgent soul-baring of Pierrot, so familiar in Romantic and Symbolist poetry, is the butt of humour. Likewise, all the magic (including the trip to the moon) fails to remove Pierrot's blackness: this is achieved by his passing through a common or garden raincloud on his return to earth. It is as if Lugones is parodying the 'vertical aspirations' of the Banville-Darío poet-clown, as Pierrot ascends to the moon in search of happiness, but finds it only when he comes back down to earth with a bump.

However, unlike some of the poems in the *Taburete de máscaras* section of *Lunario sentimental,* in 'El Pierrot negro' Lugones's attitude to the frustrated Pierrot is by no means completely cynical. There are moments when he seems to be genuinely tragic, in particular when the mermaids dance around him: 'danzan en torno de Pierrot, ofreciéndole los dones acuáticos que las adornan: sartas de corales y de perlas; nácares, madréporas, pececillos de colores, algas extrañas. Pierrot permanece inmóvil y mudo' ('they dance around Pierrot, offering him the aquatic gifts with which they are adorned: strings of corals and pearls; mother-of-pearl, coloured little fish, strange seaweed. Pierrot remains motionless and dumb') (p.306). This 'motionless and dumb' Pierrot has a clear antecedent in the Watteau *Gilles*. Through movement and gesture Lugones conveys the Symbolist/ *modernista* theme of the lonely Pierrot, but, in contrast to Machado's 'Pierrot', there is no suggestion that the scene is comic or grotesque.

The same applies to the following description at the end of Scene 1: '¡Un viaje a la luna! Pierrot, desesperado, implora al astro, mientras Polichinela se mofa de él a su espalda; hasta que, convencido de su impotencia y de su irreparable destino, el triste amante estalla en lágrimas' ('A trip to the moon! Pierrot in desperation begs the star, while Polichinela mocks him behind his back; until, convinced of his impotence and his irreparable destiny, the sad lover bursts into tears') (p.305) . Here as elsewhere in this mime play the serious Pierrot is contrasted with the other *commedia* characters who are mocking and cynical.

However, mocking cynicism does not prevail in 'El Pierrot negro'. On the contrary, it is love that triumphs over materialism at the end of the play. The only proof Pierrot has of his trip to the moon is a handful of stones in his pocket. They turn out to be precious, he hands them to Colombina, but she flings them behind her, and while the onlookers hurl themselves at the treasure, she amorously searches out Pierrot's lips ('busca amorosa los labios de Pierrot') (p.311). Pierrot has won over the unfaithful Colombina, who sees that however serious a character he may be, he is preferable to the cowardly and cynical Arlequín and Polichinela.

Pierrot's impotence leading to frustration is at the heart of one of the poems from *Taburete de máscaras,* 'Cantilena a Pierrot' ('Ballad to Pierrot'). However, this time, the frustration is absurd, and Lugones applies the irony that is the hallmark of his portrayal of the figure. Several striking images are employed to convey Pierrot's impotence and frustration in the poem.[16] He is like the bad bell-ringer who cannot reach the clapper ('como mal campanero/ que no alcanza la badaja' - p.172), and the fox who never catches the ripe grapes ('como el zorro en la viña/ jamás la ve madura' - p.172).

It is through his depiction of the Pierrot-Moon relationship that Lugones most fully illustrates his point. Allen W. Phillips, for example, analyses how Lugones converts the Romantic and Symbolist moon into an essentially prosaic symbol, and treats it with familiar mocking humour.[17] This point is well illustrated in 'Cantilena a Pierrot'. The moon mocks Pierrot by failing to turn up for an assignation because of her high orbit; Pierrot's patience in waiting for her is likened to a fisherman waiting for his catch, only to be given the slip by his target. Lugones uses an extremely complicated image of a game of billiards to suggest the moon playing with Pierrot: 'cual si armara a tu flaco/ desgaire de palote,/ su disco mondo el bote/ que junta al mingo el taco ('as if she were arming your skinny stick-like awkwardness, her plain, bare disc is the thrust which joins the cue ball to the cue') (p.171) ('bote' is very hard to translate: it could mean 'thrust' or 'bounce', but 'la tonta del bote' means 'prize idiot').

The final two stanzas of the poem suggest a futile remedy should his frustrations continue and should the moon prolong his absurd existence by continuing to trick him. He is advised: 'espérala sedienta/ y atrápala en tu aljibe' ('sit down and wait for her, and catch her in your water cistern') (p.174). Pierrot, it seems, is capable of capturing the reflection, but not the essence. Here is Pierrot the fool, mocked and reviled by the moon.

In 'Cantilena' Pierrot emerges as both simpleton and deceiver. A number of examples of the former have already been noted, while the latter is highlighted through the exposure of his pretentious affectation. The pomposity with which he addresses the moon is ridiculed by ordinary people:

> La platitud plebeya
> con imbécil apodo,
> clasifica el gran modo
> de tu prosopopeya. (p.171)

> The common people in their simplicity give an imbecile nickname to your pompous grandiloquence.

Pierrot's penchant for writing poetry to his beloved is referred to as the 'lírico embuste/ con que la llamas linda' ('the lyrical fraud with which you call her beautiful') (p.173), while the lines 'escríbele una resma/ de epitalamios y odas' ('write her a ream of wedding songs and odes') (p.173) are sarcastic in tone.

The Pierrot of 'Odeleta a Colombina' ('Mini ode to Columbine') is even more absurd than his counterpart in 'Cantilena'. The mime he performs for Columbine is the direct result of his drunken state: this is a poem in which, as we shall see, the grotesque predominates over the sentimental. As in 'Cantilena' Pierrot is satirised chiefly through the juxtapositon of his pretensions with the absurdity of the figure he cuts. For example, in the sixth stanza he groans and calls Columbine 'Clori', 'plagiando una oda vieja' (p.176) ('plagiarising an ancient ode'). The poetic name and form are clearly inappropriate to the whining mime with its foolish jumble of words ('necio mixtifori' - p.176), while a little later his love is referred to as 'unskilled in poetic verbiage' ('poco ducho/ del poético ripio' -p.176).

So far we have seen a dual attitude to Pierrot in Lugones's work. His love eventually wins through in 'El Pierrot negro', but his pretentious seriousness is ridiculed in 'Cantilena a Pierrot' and 'Odeleta a Colombina'. Another poem from *Taburete de máscaras*, 'A las máscaras' ('To Masks'), contains a Laforguian mixture of the sublime and the mundane in the following description of depersonalised Pierrots:[18]

> Pobres Pierrots sin luna,
> que en erótico albur,
> desdeñan la fortuna
> papando un bol de azur. (p.155)

> Poor moonless Pierrots who scorn fortune in an erotic game of chance by gulping down a bowl of the azure.

There is a similarity to the following lines from 'Odeleta a Colombina':

> En la sombra infinita
> donde su luz extingue,
> la luna echará un pringue
> vivaz, de carpa frita;

> Y amagará la hartura,
> cuando en torno a esa carpa,
> trinando como un arpa
> pulule la fritura. (p.179)

> In the infinite shadow where it extinguishes its light, the moon will cover the fried carp in boiling oil; and it will threaten satiety, when the fried fish swarms around that carp, trilling like a harp.

Here, the prosaic description of fish frying is juxtaposed with poetic images like 'infinite shadow' and 'trilling like a harp' to produce, as in the description of the Pierrots in 'A las máscaras', a comic effect.

In the sixteen-line poem 'El pierrotillo' the poet's attitude to his Pierrot is not so obviously mocking as it is in 'Cantilena a Pierrot', 'Odeleta a Colombina' and 'A las máscaras'. For example, it is not clear whether the diminutive of the title is mocking or endearing. Pierrot tries to turn the tables on his unfaithful mistress the moon by cocking a snook at her. She then responds by kicking him up the backside and sending him into space: the poem ends with the following lines:

> Un puntapié
> Le manda allá
> Y se
> Va... (p.166)

A kick sends him there, and he disappears...

Nonetheless, although the poet's attitude is ambiguous, the 'pierrotillo' belongs clearly to the line of pathetic clowns which are often found in Symbolist and post-Symbolist poetry.

A frequently-noted feature of Lugones's poetry is the urban settings he employs. In some of his *commedia* works he deliberately juxtaposes these with the idealised country scenes associated with Darío and earlier *modernismo*. The final scene of 'El Pierrot negro', for instance, takes place in a Watteau-like country gathering in which Arlequín, Colombina and Polichinela are entertainers, in contrast with the description of the slum-dwellings which in their turn are set against a *modernista* sunset in the first scene. 'A las máscaras' is a blend of the Watteau *Fêtes galantes* and the urban carnival, and is a satire of both. The satire is achieved through the juxtaposition of an elegant country setting and a sordid urban environment. One can contrast, for instance, the following two stanzas:

> Máscaras blancas, únicas
> joyas del dominó,
> bajo lunares túnicas
> o chaponas Watteau. (p.154)

White masks, unique jewels of the carnival costumes, beneath lunar tunics or Watteau-style blouses;

and:

> Colombinas en crisis
> bajo turbio farol,
> asoleando sus tisis
> con barato arrebol. (p.155)

Columbines in crisis beneath the dim street lamp, sunning their tuberculosis with cheap rouge.

The sensuality of the country gathering ('nucas gusto a champaña,/senos al new-mown-hay') ('necks which taste of champagne, breasts of new-mown hay') (p.155) is counterbalanced by the cacaphony of the:

> Divergentes oboes
> sin sombra de compás;
> bizarros cacatoes
> bajo cosmos de gas. (p.155)

Divergent oboes without the shadow of a beat, strange cockatoos beneath gas cosmos

Lugones has here subverted the harmony of music one normally associates with *modernismo,* and inserted a twentieth-century urban landscape into the Watteau-like country settings, subverting the latter. His picture of the city environment contrasts sharply with that of Darío in his carnival poems; for Lugones that very prosaic element so despised by earlier *modernistas*, is an integral part of poetry.[19]

The love which characterises Lugones's presentation of the *fêtes galantes* and the carnival in 'A las máscaras' is ritualistic and theatrical:

> Corazones galantes,
> que en comedia de amor
> pierden (*agítese antes*
> *de usarse*) su candor. (p.156)

> Gallant hearts, which in love's comedy lose (*shake before using*) their candour.

The italicised 'stage direction', which emphasises the ritualistic element, typifies Lugones's cynical humour. Love is also essentially deceitful, and the carnival frivolous, a point made by Lugones in an earlier stanza with his cynical, elegant humour:

> Beso que en fútil salsa
> condimenta el desliz,
> precio de perla falsa
> por una hora feliz. (p.155)

> A kiss which flavours the indiscretion with a futile sauce, the price of a false pearl for one hour of happiness.

Here the theme of the one-night carnival stand, treated with sentimentality by Darío in 'El faisán', is witheringly satirised by Lugones: the image of the 'futile sauce' adding spice to the affair anticipates the extension of the image to satirize ritual in the 'shake before using' image.

Expectations of a Bakhtinian eulogy of primitive carnival spontaneity in 'A las máscaras' are dashed when the primitiveness too is artificial:

> Berrea una comparsa
> su epilepsia común,
> en primitiva farsa
> de cafres de betún.

A masquerade bellows its common epilepsy, in a primitive farce of shoe-blacked negroes.

The characters of the *commedia*, with their usual adaptability and malleabilty, move between country and urban settings, suffering a crisis of identity in the process. Pierrot, in particular, loses his purity though not his innocence. His posturings are often pathetic, and his gestures empty, as in the following description from 'Odeleta a Colombina':

> Esbozan sus afanes
> mímicas morondangas
> que amplían en sus mangas
> alados ademanes. (p.175)

His yearning sketches a mimed nonsense, which puffs out winged gestures in his sleeves.

The empty gesture and word are features of Lugones's portrayal of the *commedia*, particularly in 'Odeleta a Colombina', where several characters are parodied. Arlequín is an empty posturer, Lugones emphasising his hand and arm gestures:

> Arlequín mequetrefe,
> con su mano afable y luenga,
> te subraya su arenga
> finchado como un jefe. (p.175)

Good for nothing Arlequín, with his long, affable hand, emphasises his harangue, puffed up like a boss.

In the following stanza, Lugones seems to anticipate Valle-Inclán, who developed an aesthetic of the grotesque in which he often brilliantly satirised the traditional honour code of Spain:

> Arlequín, con remedos
> de militar sainete,
> para un lance a florete
> se ensortija los dedos. (p.178)

> Arlequín, in a parody of a military farce, puts rings on his fingers in preparation for a fencing foil.

The most grotesque of the *commedia* characters is Polichinela, whose traditional function as a violent, drunken lecher is treated with Lugonian humour. Again from 'Odeleta a Colombina':

> Y el gran Polichinela,
> rojo como una antorcha,
> a tu salud descorcha
> su frasco de mistela.
>
> Como un hechizo corre
> su erótico menjurje,
> y su joroba surge
> bella como una torre. (p.177)

> And the great Polichinela, red as a torch, uncorks his bottle of *mistela* and drinks to your health. His erotic brew flows like a magic spell, and his hump rises, as beautiful as a tower.

One may contrast Polichinela's actions here with the innocent deeds of Darío's *commedia* figures in 'Canción de carnaval'. The eroticism hinted at in the final phrase is continued in the following stanza:

Que asiéndote a su cuello
con audacias modernas,
le oprimes con tus piernas
como a un feliz camello. (p.177)

He holds you to his neck with modern audacity, and you squeeze
him with your legs as if he were a cheerful camel.

Lugones's Polichinela is a far more daring creation than his briefly-sketched
counterpart in 'Canción de carnaval', in terms both of his actions and of the
language in which he is evoked.

Valle-Inclán: *La marquesa Rosalinda*

Striking and ambitious imagery, then, is one of the most impressive
features of Lugones's presentation of the *commedia*. Another is his undermining of
the *commedia* characters, although his attitude to Pierrot is somewhat ambiguous. A
similar ambiguity towards Arlequín is a feature of Valle-Inclán in *La marquesa
Rosalinda* (*The Marchioness Rosalinda*). I have demonstrated elsewhere how he is
a composite of the sentimental figure who appears in Marivaux's work and the
roguish, unsentimental don Juan, beloved of writers like Apollinaire and Jacob.[20]
He is in many ways a contradictory character, a 'personaje enigmático' as Rubio
calls him.[21] He is the source of much of the play's verbal humour, particularly in
the deadpan punning with which he deflates Colombina. For example, in the first
act he satirizes Colombina's anger at his interest in Rosalinda:

COLOMBINA	¡Señor!... ¡Señor!... ¡Que haya burlado Con tanto arte, A Pierrot por este malvado!
ARLEQUIN	Eso se dice en un aparte.[22]
COLOMBINA	Good Lord! To think that I've deceived Pierrot so skilfully for this wretch!

ARLEQUIN	That should be said in an aside.

and

COLOMBINA	¡La madama se ha de acordar de Colombina!
ARLEQUIN	Llora bajo si has de llorar!
COLOMBINA	¡Tanto cinismo me asesina! (p.103).
COLOMBINA	Madame will remember Colombina!
ARLEQUIN	Weep quietly if you've got to weep!
COLOMBINA	All this cynicism is killing me!

Here, as with Lugones, language is an unsettling, disruptive force.

If Arlequín shows scant regard for Colombina's feelings, in his attitude to Rosalinda he comes closer to the tradition of the sentimental Harlequin, 'poli par l'amour', to use Marivaux, words, as, for example in his words of love to her in the second act:

Vuelve a hacer musicales las fuentes y las brisas
Con el teclado armónico de tus divinas risas,
Que enseñan la primera lección de sus escalas
Al ruiseñor, cuando abre en el nido las alas
Y tu mano lunaria, el esquife de plata
De mi ensueño, conduzca a oír la serenata
De las liras, enfermas de aquel celeste mal,
Que el narigudo Ovidio llamó mal autumnal. (p.176)

Make the fountains and the breezes musical again, with the harmonious keyboard of your divine laughter, which gives the first scales lesson to the nightingale when she opens her wings in her nest. And let your lunar hand, that silver skiff of my fantasy, lead us to hear the serenade of the lyres, sick with that heavenly sickness which big-nosed Ovid called autumnal.

These lines, which are written in verse, are full of stock *modernista* imagery, but, apart from the reference to Ovid's large nose, without any hint that they are being spoken with anything but seriousness. Arlequín seems convinced of the validity of his magical dream world. However, in this same scene Valle displays the ambiguity in his presentation of Arlequín that he maintains throughout the play. When Rosalinda suggests that she might flee from the palace and join the troupe of players, Arlequín, far from painting a romantic picture of the wandering life, is more concerned about the effect that the constant travelling will have on Rosalinda's 'poor bones' ('pobres huesos') (p. 177). He displays the same humorous practicality in attributing the change in Rosalinda's husband (from a tolerant man *a la francesa* to a Calderonian man of honour) to a change of diet:

> ¡La sobreasada de las Islas Baleares!
> ¡El marisco gallego, que es de tanto deleite!
> ¡Y ese queso manchego tan metido en aceite!
> ¡Y el de Burgos! ¡Y aquel vino rancio y espeso
> Que reclama la boca tras de morder el queso!
> ¡Y el jamón y los embutidos de los charros. (p.178)

> Balearic sausage! Galician shellfish, which is so exquisite! And that Manchegan cheese marinated in olive oil. And the Burgos variety! And that thick mellow wine which the mouth demands after tasting the cheese. And the Salamancan ham and sausages!

One is never sure to what extent Arlequín is really in love, and how far he is involved in an adventure. He is simultaneously a detached cynic and a romantic dreamer, but a 'soñador desengañado' ('a disillusioned dreamer'), as Rubio calls him.[23] He exemplifies one of the most striking features of *La marquesa Rosalinda*, namely that it is a blend of apparent opposites, 'a harmony of opposites' ('una armonía de contrarios'), as Arlequín himself describes life at one point in the play (p.172).

He is indeed a complex and multi-faceted character. He sees his own role as an ambassador of paganism, a worldy-wise lover who has had adventures the length and breadth of Europe. With his colour and his mysterious international past, he provides a contrast to the narrow provincialism of Catholic Spain, which was the butt of Valle-Inclán's satire in several of his works. He represents temptation in the form of pagan, European, non-Spanish tradition to which Rosalinda is attracted before she rejects him and clings once more to orthodox Spanish morality.[24] As well as being a pagan, Arlequín fulfils his *commedia* role as a devil figure, or at least is viewed as such by the Spanish courtiers, for whom he is an alien force. Rubio also puts forward the interesting speculation that Arlequín is a kind of all-seeing *über-régisseur,* a projection of the author himself: 'una proyección del propio dramaturgo, convertido en demiurgo que controla la ficción a su antojo'[25] ('a projection of the dramatist himself, converted into a demigod who controls the story at his will'). This interpretation accords well with Valle's ideas on the role of the playwright as a puppet-master in control of and detached from his actors/ characters.

And yet there is a side to Arlequín which resembles the lovestruck Pierrot, especially in his soliloquy to the moon which closes Act 1. The soliloquy, whose sentimentality is counterbalanced by an element of the grotesque, is an almost exact version of a Valle-Inclán poem entitled 'A la luna: monólogo de Pierrot', which was published in *Nuevo Mundo* in 1911. As Rubio says:

> Su contenido se ajusta mucho más a la tradición de Pierrot, a quien los simbolistas habían convertido en un personaje soñador y desengañado, que no a Arlequín, que en la tradición tenía otras características... El propio Arlequín de Valle aparece dotado de un carácter soñador, no sólo en esta situación, sino en varios otros momentos de la farsa; soñador, eso sí, desengañado e irónico.[26]

> Its content is much more in tune with the tradition of Pierrot, whom the Symbolists had transformed into a disillusioned dreamer, than with Harlequin, who traditionally possessed different characteristics... Valle's Arlequín appears to be a dreamer, not only in this situation, but also at other moments of the farce; a dreamer, albeit disillusioned and ironic.

It could be purely coincidental that Pierrot recites the *Nuevo Mundo* monologue and Arlequín the second version, and that Valle-Inclán is not conscious of the quite distinct history of these two *commedia* characters. On the other hand, perhaps it indicates indecision on the part of the author, or the creation of a deliberate ambiguity between *art arlequin* and *art pierrot*. *La marquesa Rosalinda* is often cited as typical of Valle's transitional phase, as he abandons *modernismo* in favour of more socially-oriented literature. The Pierrot/Arlequín dichotomy could be interpreted as reinforcing the notion of the play as a crossroads work, between the Symbolist/*modernista* aesthetic and the new direction of Expressionism and the grotesque that Valle's work was to take in the post-Great War years.[27]

The way forward is pointed by Valle's careful use of exaggerated gesture, comparable to Lugones's in *Lunario sentimental*, and by cultivated theatricality.[28] Some of Arlequín's gestures, for instance, as well as his language, are almost self-parodying, as if he were conscious that he his playing a role. The following stylised stage-direction is an excellent example:

> Arlequín hace la pirueta,
> Saludando al modo de Francia,
> Y evoca un ritmo de opereta
> Con el ritmo de su elegancia. (p.222)
>
> Arlequín pirouettes, bowing in the French fashion, and evokes the rhythm of an operetta with the rhythm of his elegance.

This description accords well with the play's stylised theatricality, and the spectators are constantly reminded that what they are watching is not a naturalistic representation of life but theatre.[29] The *commedia dell'arte* provides Valle with the perfect vehicle for his portrayal of theatricality. The players' arrival in the *carro* in the opening scene indicates the beginning of the performance, and Arlequín's reference to hanging up his mask and returning to the cart because his role is complete closes the play and underlines the fiction of what has gone before, the 'beautiful lie' ('bella mentira') of the prologue. Valle-Inclán has destroyed the simple distinction which had been drawn by such writers as Banville, Benavente and Darío between 'real' life and an imaginary, idealised world of which the *commedia dell'arte* is a part. It is with this perspective in mind that one must view the various refences to *ensueño* in the play.

If there is more than a little of the nineteenth-century Pierrot in Arlequín, then the Pierrot of the play is a grotesque, puppet-like character, whom the author subjects to his pre-*esperpento* grotesque dehumanisation. He is the cuckolded victim of an affair between his wife Colombina and Arlequín, and attempts to restore his honour by challenging Arlequín to a duel. However, this duel turns out to be a farce, and as well as reinforcing Valle's satire of the honour theme, is a further illustration of the artificiality of the spectacle. The sword which Pierrot gives to Arlequín is not a real but a theatrical one, and is made not of steel but of tin. The exchange between these two characters which concludes the 'duel' provides the *coup de grâce* to any expectations that we may be about to witness a tragic outcome:

ARLEQUIN	¡Señor Pierrot, mi acero es hojalata!
PIERROT	¿No me podrás matar?
ARLEQUIN	Así lo espero, Que espada de teatro nunca mata.
PIERROT	¡Pues no puedo matarte, ni la muerte Recibir de tus manos de payaso, Para filosofar sobre mi suerte Me vuelvo a la carreta, paso a paso! (pp. 232-3)

ARLEQUIN	Mr Pierrot, my steel is tin!
PIERROT	Won't you be able to kill me?
ARLEQUIN	I hope not. A theatrical sword never kills.
PIERROT	Since I cannot kill you, nor receive death at your clown's hands, I shall return step by step to the cart to philosophise on my destiny.

This exchange, reminiscent of the satire of honour in the description of Arlequín in 'Odeleta a Colombina' and of militarism in the shape of the Captain of Benavente's

Los intereses creados, but very different from the description of the duels in Carrere's *Bohemia sentimental* and Zamacois's *Noche de máscaras* (discussed in chapter 4), encapsulates the essential theatricality of *La marquesa Rosalinda*, as the clowning metaphor deflates potential tragedy or melodrama. Valle-Inclán was later to develop this perspective into an aesthetic of the grotesque in some of the *esperpentos*. However, this aesthetic has not yet reached its full potential. Rather like Valle's first *esperpento*, *Luces de bohemia (Bohemian Lights)* (1920), *La marquesa Rosalinda* maintains a fine balance between sentimentality and the grotesque.

The grotesque is present in Valle's depiction of the court characters, and in stage directions which refer to the *commedia* characters, particularly Pierrot, Polichinela and Colombina, but also Arlequín on occasions, as in the following example:

> Arlequín saluda burlando,
> Con una pirueta grotesca.
> Colombina funambulesca,
> Aparece manoteando.
>
> Hace un vuelo por el jardín
> Con un ritmo de marioneta,
> Que recuerda la comedieta
> Del retablo de Fagotín. (pp. 167-8)

> Arlequín bows in a mocking fashion, with a grotesque pirouette. The grotesque Colombina appears waving her hands. She skips across the garden with the rhythm of a marionette, which recalls the 'retablo' of Fagotín.

Here Arlequín is ironiser ('saluda burlando') and ironised ('pirueta grotesca'), while Colombina cuts an absurdly comic figure, as she advances waving her hands in a way which recalls some of Lugones's descriptions of his *commedia* characters.The marionette reference is a clear indication of dehumanisation and anticipates the *esperpentos*, while 'la comedieta del retablo de Fagotín' is typical of Valle-Inclán's use of popular source material.[30]

A strong shift of emphasis has been observed in this chapter. This is most starkly illustrated in Benavente's *La ciudad alegre y confiada*, in which all the subtlety of *Los intereses creados* has been lost. Deflation and bitterness dominate Manuel Machado's *commedia* poems, which contain perhaps the sharpest and most chilling destruction of illusion. Nevertheless, it is Lugones and Valle-Inclán who really break new ground as far as the presentation of the *commedia* in Hispanic literature is concerned. Both authors, while maintaining a certain balance between sentimentality and the grotesque, undermine their *commedia* characters with sophisticated humour and by emphasising the theatrical nature of their behaviour. At the same time they turn on their head such Romantic and *modernista* clichés as the relationship between Pierrot and the Moon.[31]

---

1 *Antología crítica de la poesía modernista* (Madrid: Hiperión, 1985), p.20, p.24.

2 *Ibid.*, p.34.

3 Manuel y Antonio Machado, *Obras completas* 5th edn (Madrid: Plenitud, 1967), p.35. Further quotations from Manuel Machado's poetry are taken from this edition, and the corresponding page references are given in the body of the text.

4 It seems likely that these lines are a satire of the Watteau-like world of Rubén Darío's well-known poem 'Sonatina', from *Prosas profanas*.

5 Gordon Brotherston, *Manuel Machado: A Revaluation* (Cambridge: CUP, 1968), p.85.

6 A parallel may be drawn with some of the press reviews of the *commedia* and carnival which were discussed in chapter 2.

7 Brotherston uses the term to equate with *modernista*.

8 Brotherston, p. 32.

9 Similarities will be noted with García Lorca's *commedia* drawings (see chapter 6).

10 Rubén Darío, *Obras completas*, p. 1057.

11 *La ciudad alegre y confiada*, in *Obras completas*, III, 1125-1214 (p. 1131). Subsequent references are given in the main body of the text.

12 *Drama y sociedad en la obra de Benavente (1894-1914)* (New York: Anaya Las Américas, 1974), pp.246-47. Once more the reaction against the *commedia* in post-Great War Spain which was referred to in chapter 2 comes to mind.

13 Brotherston, p. 37.

14 Leopoldo Lugones, *Lunario sentimental*, ed. by Jesús Benítez (Madrid: Cátedra, 1988), p. 303. All quotations from Lugones are taken from this edition, and the corresponding page references are given in the body of the text.

15 The town/country question will be examined in more detail later in the chapter.

16 In the prologue to the first edition of *Lunario sentimental*, Lugones emphasises the role of imaginative imagery in the work: 'hallar imágenes nuevas y hermosas, expresándolas con claridad y concisión, es enriquecer el idioma, renovándolo a la vez...el lugar común es malo, a causa de que acaba perdiendo toda significación expresiva por exceso de uso; y la originalidad remedia este inconveniente, pensando conceptos nuevos que requieren expresiones nuevas' ('by finding new and beautiful images, and expressing them with clarity and concision, one enriches the language and renews it at the same time...the commonplace is bad, because it ends up losing all expressive meaning through over-use; originality solves this problem, through thinking of new concepts which require new expressions' (cited in Benítez ed, p.92). Critics often refer to Lugones's original use of imagery, in particular metaphor. Lugones' fellow-Argentinian, the poet and short-story writer Borges, is full of praise for Lugones's use of metaphor, and was influenced by it: see Jorge Luis Borges, *Leopoldo Lugones* (Buenos Aires: Pleamar, 1965), p.33.

17 'Aquel símbolo sagrado de los románticos está para siempre desterrado, y se ha convertido en un astro domesticado o urbanizado. Objeto y blanco de la ironía de Lugones es el planeta muerto, sin vida y sin sentimiento' ('that sacred symbol of the Romantics has been banished for ever, and has become a domesticated, urbanised star. The dead planet, lifeless and without feelings, is the object of Lugones's irony') ('Notas para un estudio comparativo de Lugones y Valle-Inclán [*Lunario sentimental y La pipa de Kif*]', *Boletín-Biblioteca Menéndez Pelayo*, 56 [1980], 315-45 [p.327]). Benítez, however, believes that the Lugones moon has a slightly different purpose: 'Lugones ha pretendido hacer belleza (que para él era sinónimo de bien) utilizando símbolos del mal - como la luna - en una especie de conjuro neutralizador con el que aspira a conseguir una meta tan deseada como es la unión de opuestos' ('Lugones aimed to produce beauty [which for him was a synonym of good] by using symbols of evil - such as the moon - in a kind of neutralising spell with which he aspired to achieve his highly treasured goal of the union of opposites') (Benítez ed, p.58).

18 For similarities between Laforgue and Lugones, see Raquel Halty Ferguson, *Laforgue y Lugones: dos poetas de la luna* (London: Támesis, 1981).

19 The Mexican critic and poet Octavio Paz sees the Lugonian presentation of an urban environment as a characteristic of later *modernismo*: 'el modernismo había poblado el mar de tritones y sirenas, los nuevos poetas viajan en barcos comerciales y desembarcan, no en Citera, sino en Liverpool; los poemas ya no son cantos a las cosmópolis pasadas o presentes, sino descripciones más bien amargas y reticentes de barrios de la clase media; el campo no es la selva ni el desierto, sino el pueblo de las afueras...ironía y prosaísmo: la conquista de lo cotidiano maravilloso' ('*modernismo* had filled the sea with Tritons and mermaids, the new poets travel in commercial boats and land, not in Citera, but in Liverpool; the poems are no longer songs to past or present cities, but rather bitter and ironical descriptions of middle-class suburbs; the countryside is not the jungle or the desert, but an outlying town...irony and the commonplace: the conquest of the wonder of everyday reality') (from 'Traducción y metáfora', in *Los hijos del limo* [Barcelona: Seix Barral, 1974], pp.115-41 [p.114]).

20 David George, 'Harlequin Comes to Court: Valle-Inclán's *La marquesa Rosalinda*', *Forum for Modern Language Studies*, vol. XIX no. 4 (1983), 364-74.

21 Jesús Rubio Jiménez, 'Los primeros textos de *La marquesa Rosalinda* y otras páginas olvidadas de Valle-Inclán', *Boletín de la Fundación Federico García Lorca*, 7-8 (December 1990), 25-44 (p.36). Rubio discusses the various versions of the play, including the fragment published in *Por esos mundos* in December 1911.

22 Ramón del Valle-Inclán, *La marquesa Rosalinda*, ed. by Leda Schiavo (Madrid: Espasa Calpe, 1992), p.101. All quotations from the play are taken from this edition, and the corresponding page references are given in the body of the text.

23 'Los primeros textos', p. 28.

24 A parallel will be detected with the poetry of Manuel Machado. One will also recall the critic Antonio de Zayas, who identified the *commedia dell'arte* with decadent forign culture (see chapter 4).

25 'Los primeros textos', p. 33.

26 *Ibid.*, pp.42-43.

27 I am aware that it would be facile to claim that there is in Valle's theatre a smooth development from *modernismo* to drama which has as one of its main concerns a criticism of Spanish society. For instance, two of the *Comedias bárbaras, Aguila de blasón* and *Romance de lobos*, which portray the decadence of the Galician rural nobility, belong to 1907 and 1908 respectively. Nevertheless, many critics do regard *La marquesa Rosalinda* as a work in which Valle questions some *modernista* precepts. For example, the foremost British specialist on Valle-Inclán's theatre, John Lyon, writes: 'the general tone of the play suggests a half-nostalgic farewell to the dream world of *Modernismo*' (*The Theatre of Valle-Inclán* [Cambridge: CUP, 1983], p.73). See also John Lyon, 'Valle-Inclán: Between Symbolism and the Absurd', *ALEC*, 19 (1992), 145-62. The hybrid nature of *La marquesa Rosalinda* is emphasised by Rubio, who describes Arlequín as a 'simbiosis de elementos procedentes de distintas culturas' ('symbiosis of elements from different cultures') ('Los primeros textos', p.34).

28 For a detailed analysis of the subtle and highly complex theatricality of *La marquesa*, see Xavier Peter Vila, 'Valle-Inclán and the Theater' (unpublished doctoral thesis, Princeton University, 1985), chapter 2.

29 Pring-Mill's comments on Calderón's drama are apposite here: 'hasta se puede acrecentar la verosimilitud del mensaje con una destrucción intencionada de dicha ilusión [teatral], obligándonos a reconocer la artificialidad de las convenciones teatrales cuyo empleo estamos observando' ('the verisimilitude of the message can even be increased with a deliberate destruction of this [theatrical] illusion, forcing us to recognise the artificiality of the theatrical conventions whose use we are observing') (Robert D.F. Pring-Mill, 'Calderón de la Barca y la fuerza ejemplar de lo poetizado', in *Hacia Calderón: sexto coloquio anglogermano*, ed. by Hans Flasche, 2 vols [Wiesbaden: Franz Steiner Verlag, 1981], II, 1-15 [pp.7-8]).

30 On carnivalization in Valle-Inclán, see Iris M. Zavala, *La musa funambulesca. Poética de la carnivalización en Valle-Inclán* (Madrid: Orígenes, 1990).

31 Curiously, Vila, while providing several examples of how 'Romantic and *fin de siècle* motifs and images are wrenched from their original context, and placed in situations that burlesque the original' ('Valle-Inclán and the Theater', p.75), does not make the point that the *commedia* is itself one such motif.

Chapter 6

From Destruction to Renewal: *Commedia* and Mask in García Lorca

In the works examined in chapter 3 the *commedia* was part of a generally comforting conception of popular culture. Although the commercialism of contemporary Spanish drama was challenged, the emphasis was on the comic and the farcical. The Harlequin figure of *El retablillo de don Cristóbal*, for example, was part of a cheery popular theatrical tradition which could bring a breath of fresh air to the stultified bourgeois theatre and shake it out of its complacent rut.

A much more disturbing picture of the *commedia* emerges from this chapter, in which I concentrate exclusively on García Lorca, on his drawings and a filmscript as well as his theatre. Four questions will concern us: the use of mask, and the interplay between mask and face; gesture, mime and movement; the disturbing, unsettling presence of the dehumanised Harlequin figure; and, finally, the regeneration which can be brought about after the false masks have been destroyed.

The drawings

As a prelude to my discussion of the plays *Así que pasen cinco años* and *El público* and the filmscript *Viaje a la luna*, I shall consider some of Lorca's many drawings on the Clown/Pierrot (the more numerous) and the Harlequin themes. The Pierrot or clown drawings are mainly traditional, in that the face or mask is sad. A number of them, such as the *Payaso de rostro desdoblado* (*Clown with the Split*

Face) (1927) have a double mask, a technique which, according to Santos Torroella, Lorca owed to Dalí, himself the author of a series of paintings and drawings on the Harlequin theme.[1] Like the Dalí Harlequins, the Lorca Pierrots or clowns are usually self-portraits. As we saw in chapter 1, the clown or Pierrot was a favourite subject of self-portrait in art and poetry of the late nineteenth and early twentieth centuries, and the Lorca versions are traditional in their melancholy (see the example in fig.14). Typically, however, Lorca undermines the tradition in that both face and mask are usually revealed, in a process of unmasking that recalls the discussions on the subject in *El público*. The most difficult of the Pierrot drawings, *Pierrot priápico* (1932-36) is traditional in that it is a self-portrait of the artist and deals with the theme of sexual impotence and frustration (see fig. 12). However, its form is modern and is obviously influenced by Dalí and Miró.

There are at least five Lorca drawings of Harlequins, all of which belong to the period 1927-28. To judge from the collar of his costume, the *Arlequín desdoblado* (*Split Harlequin*) of 1927 is more akin to a Pierrot than to a Harlequin (see fig.13). Like a number of Lorca's Pierrot and Clown drawings, he has a superimposed mask, separate from the face, and hard to distinguish from it. The two Harlequin drawings which most resemble each other are *Arlequín veneciano* (*Venetian Harlequin*) and *Arlequín*, which is subtitled *Poesía* (*Poetry*) (see fig. 15 for the latter). According to Santos Torroella, there is a certain resemblance between these and Dalí's *Arlequín* of 1926-27 and other Dalí drawings of the period.[2]

The interplay between black and white which characterises the rather menacing *Arlequín* is associated with death, and with duality and balance, by Mario Hernández:

> El arlequín, con mucho de imagen de la muerte [...] está concebido como fina escultura metálica sostenida por un vástago cenjjtral que descansa en diminuta base...Lo definitorio del arlequín, su traje, está aludido mediante mitades contrapuestas de luz y de sombra....Una concepción semejante, aun desde otra perspectiva, presenta el poema titulado

ARLEQUíN
Teta roja del sol
Teta azul de la luna.

Torso mitad coral,
mitad plata y penumbra.[3]

The harlequin, to a large extent a symbol of death... is conceived as
a delicate metal structure, supported by a central stem which rests on
a tiny base... The harlequin's defining feature, his costume, is
evoked through two halves of light and shadow which are set
against each other.... A similar concept, although from a different
perspective, is found in the poem entitled 'Arlequín':

Red breast of the sun.
Blue breast of the moon.
A torso which is half coral,
and half silver and shadow.

In some ways the strangest and most beautiful of the Lorca Harlequin
drawings is *Arlequín ahogado (Drowned Harlequin)* (1927-28) (see fig.16). The
drowning motif is, of course, a common one in Lorca's poetry, and the spider's
web in which Arlequín is trapped in this drawing is another image of frustration and
helplessness, a very different picture of Harlequin to that of the self-confident
trickster of *Así que pasen cinco años*.[4] The repetition of masks is another feature of
Arlequín ahogado (Drowned Harlequin), with three rather than two faces or masks
on this occasion. The mask here is clearly negative, a frightening expression of a
narcissistic projection of self. The mask cannot be cast off, which produces the
same sense of helplessness that Lorca associates with drowning.

Así que pasen cinco años

With these ideas on mask and identity in mind, as well as the complexity of
the *commedia* figures in the drawings, we can examine: *Así que pasen cinco años
(When Five Years Have Passed)* (1931), *Viaje a la luna (Trip to the Moon)* (1929-

30) and *El público* (*The Public* or *The Audience*) (1929-30). Arlequín appears in *Así que pasen cinco años* as one of several non-human characters, who also include a clown, a mannequin and various masks. When Arlequín first enters at the start of Act 3, his movements are stylised, and like those of a ballet-dancer: 'acciona de modo plástico, como un bailarín' [5] ('he moves in an expressive way, like a ballet-dancer'). We should remember the albeit limited impact the Diaghilev troupe had in Spain in the 1910s, and Lorca may also have had in mind Picasso's designs for the Russian ballet's performances of Stravinsky's music in *Pulcinella* and *Petroushka*.[6]

Arlequín and the Clown belong to a circus which is in a wood. Francisco García Lorca explains:

> La significación del Payaso y el Arlequín en la obra se justifica por el hecho de que en el bosque donde la acción se desarrolla hay un circo y, diseminados, los armatostes, carros y jaulas de animales. Algún valor simbólico tiene el que estos obstáculos, como vemos después, estén cerrando senderos y salidas. El bosque, sitiado por el circo, obliga de algún modo a los demás personajes a formar parte de él.[7]

> The significance of Clown and the Harlequin in the work is justified by the fact that in the wood where the action takes place there is a circus, with huge pieces of furniture, carts and animal cages scattered around. The fact that these obstacles, as we see later, block off paths and exits, must have some symbolic value. The wood, besieged by the circus, forces the other characters to form a part of it.

The inclusion of such paratheatre as ballet and circus within the text of a play is, as I observed in chapter 1, common practice in Surrealism and Dada, as well as in the later Theatre of the Absurd, in works such as *Waiting for Godot*. These extra-theatrical forms bring a new dimension to theatre, and, as we have already seen, were part of the reaction against Naturalism, at the same time as popular manifestations such as *commedia*, mime and circus were considered to be agents for revitalising drama, restoring the links with a more ancient form of ritual that bourgeois-dominated cultures had lost. The circus routine of Arlequín and Clown in

Act 3, Scene 1 is also linked to the play within a play technique, which is part of Lorca's exploration of the relationship between actors and audience that finds fuller expression in *El público*.[8]

Arlequín carries two masks, which he can change at will. As a non-human character, he has no emotions and is able to play with and tease the various 'human' characters with whom he comes into contact. In this he is typical of many a post-Romantic Harlequin, the detached, cynical observer of the world. There are certain similarities between him and Arlequín of Valle-Inclán's *La marquesa Rosalinda*, although Lorca goes further than Valle in that the latter's Arlequín does, at least to a degree, become emotionally involved with Rosalinda. This does not, however, invalidate Gwynne Edwards's point that 'these figures [i.e. Harlequin, Clown and others], for all their puppet-like appearance, move us emotionally, for in them we see paraded before us those issues to which we cannot be indifferent, for they are things that affect us most and that lie at the very core of our existence - joy, love, sorrow, death'. He is also right in saying that 'human beings become the helpless victims of their [the Clown's and Harlequin's] merciless and deadly clowning, pawns in the grotesque game of life'.[9]

The role of Harlequin, clown and mask is to disturb and confuse human beings, and shake us out of our complacency. We must be made to face up to our fears and tear away our masks, and it is the function of the theatre to provoke us into doing this. These non-human clowning figures therefore have a positive role to play, although it is not until *El público* that this positive element becomes clearer. We are dealing, in other words, with universal themes, which characters of the *commedia*, who are perceived as belonging to no specific place or time, are ideally suited to convey. They have to be dehumanised to enable Lorca to convey the theme of humans as pawns, at the mercy of fate. Similarities will be observed with Valle-Inclán, although Lorca places more emphasis on the sinister than on the comic grotesque, and with *Bodas de sangre* (*Blood Wedding*), in which the Moon and the Beggar Woman, like Arlequín and the Clown in *Así que pasen cinco años*, are the manipulators of human lives. As Andrew Anderson writes of the characters of *La zapatera prodigiosa*, 'his or her plight demands little sympathy', and, quoting Davis, 'the comic spirit of farce [...] tends to debar empathy for its victims'.[10]

In *Así que pasen cinco años* the first human character to be tormented by Arlequín is the Young Girl, who is searching for her lover. His tone when addressing her is variously humorous and ironic ('gracioso' and 'irónico') (p.562). He calls to the Clown to come, 'a voces y como si estuviera en el circo' ('loudly, and as if they were in a circus') (p.563). There then follows a scene in which the two jokers pretend that they are in the circus, and frighten the Young Girl. Arlequín plays a two-stringed violin and intones in a deliberately forced voice, mocking the Young Girl further. She is frightened by reality ('asustada de la realidad') (p.565). She finally goes offstage, her innocence destroyed by the mocking pair. Arlequín here is in many ways the opposite of Banville's Romantic creation, for far from transporting human beings to a magical world, he destroys the romantic illusions of the innocent young girl. As in *Viaje a la luna*, he is a corruptor of innocents.

At one point, the Clown addresses the audience: '*al público. Buenas noches*' ('*to the audience. Good night*') (p.564), which on the one hand heightens the sense of theatricality and on the other involves the audience in the action: there is a more complex manifestation of this technique in *El público*. The whole scene invloving Arlequín and the Clown is highly theatrical:

> ARLEQUÍN   ¿Dónde? ¿A qué?.
> PAYASO   A representar.
>   Un niño pequeño
>   que quiere cambiar
>   en flores de acero
>   su trozo de pan........
> ARLEQUÍN (*adoptando una actitud de circo y como si los oyese el niño*)
>   Señor hombre, venga (p.566).
>
> ARLEQUÍN   Where? Why?
> CLOWN   To put on a play. A little child who wants to
>   exchange his piece of bread for flowers of steel...
> ARLEQUÍN (*adopting a circus pose, as if the child were listening to them*)
>   Come along, sir.

The Arlequín/Clown scene is followed by another one in which a human character is mocked by a masked figure: this time the First Mask is the mocker and the Typist the mocked. Arlequín and Clown then return to the stage to play with and confuse the Young Man. Arlequín tries to bar the latter's way out of the wood, to his considerable irritation.[11] The Young Man fails to see the funny side of a circus routine carried out by the two:

> PAYASO (*Dando una bofetada de circo al Arlequín*) ¡Toma casa!
> ARLEQUÍN (*Cae al suelo, gritando*) ¡Ay, que me duele, que me duele!
> PAYASO (*Al Joven*) Venga.
> JOVEN (*Irritado*) Pero me quiere usted decir qué broma es ésta? Yo iba a mi casa, es decir, a mi casa, no; a otra casa, a.....(p.572)

> CLOWN (*Giving a circus slap to the Harlequin*) Take that!
> ARLEQUÍN (*Falls to the ground, shouting*). Oh, it hurts, it hurts!
> CLOWN (*To the Young Man*) Come on.
> YOUNG MAN (*Annoyed*) What sort of joke is this? I was going home, I mean not to my house, to another house, to... .

The reference to the circus recalls, for instance, Benavente's essays on the subject, but the circus routine between the Clown and Arlequín is threatening and is very different from Benavente's idealised approach to the subject.

The Young Man now turns to see the Typist. They have been brought together rather as Leonardo and the Bride were by the Moon and the Beggar Woman in *Bodas de sangre* and, in a scene reminiscent of the meeting between the two lovers in Act 3, Scene 2 of that play, they declare their love for one another. The next exchange between them and another masked figure, the Yellow Mask, which is set in the same library as in Act 1, shows the Young Man declaring the urgency of his love in contrast to the attitude of the Typist, in a reversal of their role

in Act 1. The fact that the same tragic fate awaits the Young Man as will befall
Leonardo is suggested in the final scene of Act 3, Scene 1. Arlequín and Clown
are, like the Moon and the Beggar Woman, symbols of death. This point is
highlighted by Arlequín's wearing a green and black costume, which are not
colours normally associated with him: these colours, of course, often symbolise
death in Lorca's work. The description of Clown's head, which is powdered and
which 'da una sensación de calavera' ('looks like a skull') (p.563), similarly
evokes death.

In *Así que pasen cinco años*, then, the *commedia* and other masked
characters are dehumanised figures, not belonging to any one era, and therefore
ideally suited to conveying universal themes and to destroying a sense of
Naturalism in the theatre.[12] They are not timebound, limited by social conventions,
or mortal as are the human beings they cruelly mock. However, despite his lack of
humanity, Arlequín has not yet undergone the degree of dehumanisation to which
he is subjected in *Viaje a la luna* and *El público*.

Viaje a la luna

C.B.Morris claims that the inspiration for *Viaje a la luna* came from Lorca's
visits to Luna Park on Coney island, which included among its attractions A Trip to
the Moon, 'a cyclorama which enjoyed enormous success at the Buffalo Exposition
in 1901.'[13] The *commedia* , of course, has a long association with the moon,
principally through the figure of Pierrot, the white-faced moon worshipper. I
examined in chapter 5 Lugones's satire of the Pierrot/Moon relationship. The
Lorcan trip to the moon, however, contains none of the humour that typifies
Lugones and Valle-Inclán, as well as Lorca's own farces, and the *commedia* figure,
in this case Arlequín, disturbs but does not amuse. In fact, Harlequin as such does
not appear in *Viaje a la luna*; we have instead merely a harlequin costume, a *traje de
arlequín*.[14] This costume first appears in the introduction, sequence 26:

> Un hombre de la bata le ofrece un traje de arlequín, pero el muchacho rehúsa. Entonces el hombre de la bata lo coge por el cuello, el otro grita, pero el hombre de la bata le tapa la boca con el traje de arlequín.

> A man in a dressing gown offers him a harlequin costume, but the boy refuses it. Then the man in the dressing gown grabs him by the neck, he screams, but the man in the dressing gown covers his mouth with the harlequin costume.

This violent action seems to symbolise the sexuality which the man tries to force on the boy when the latter rejects his advances. As in *Así que pasen cinco años*, the harlequin, albeit only via his costume in this case, is linked with the familiar Lorcan theme of the destruction of innocence.

Utrera sees Arlequín as one of a series of symbols of the boy's crisis of identity:

> Los símbolos que aparecen desde el traje de arlequín hasta los peces agónicos, sugieren la crisis de identidad de un muchacho expresada por medio de un clima angustioso en el que predomina la violencia y la sexualidad.[15]

> The symbols which appear, from the harlequin costume to the dying fishes, suggest the identity crisis of a boy expressed through an anguished climate dominated by violence and sexuality.

The harlequin costume makes another appearance in sequence 41:

> La cámara desde abajo enfoca y sube la escalera. En lo alto aparece un desnudo de muchacho. Tiene la cabeza como los muñecos anatómicos con los músculos y las venas y los tendones. Luego sobre el desnudo lleva dibujado el sistema de la circulación de la sangre y arrastra un traje de arlequín.

> The camera focuses from below and goes up the stairs. At the top a nude figure of a boy appears. His head is like that of anatomical

puppets with muscles and veins and tendons. The blood circulation system is drawn above the nude figure, and he is dragging along a harlequin costume.

The vision of the naked boy dragging along the harlequin costume parallels the painful removal of the harlequin and other costumes by the Director in Scene 3 of *El público*, while the graphic exposition of veins and tendons is matched by that play's harsh exposure and analysis of bare essentials contained in the image of the X-ray.

The final appearance of the harlequin costume begins in sequence 49. A harlequin enters a bar and begins dancing there with an almost naked girl. The veins man enters the bar in sequence 50, gesticulating desperately, an action which is followed in sequence 53 by an image of the girl, now dressed in the innocent colour of white, fleeing along a New York street with the harlequin. The following sequences develop the relationship between the girl and the boy harlequin:

55. Se disuelve sobre un ascensor donde un negrito vomita. La muchacha y el arlequín suben en el ascensor.
56. Suben en el ascensor y se abrazan.
57. Plano de un beso sensual.
58. El muchacho muerde a la muchacha en el cuello y le tira violentamente de sus cabellos.
59. Aparece una guitarra. Y una mano rápida corta las cuerdas con unas tijeras.
60. La muchacha se defiende del muchacho y éste, con gran furia, le da otro beso profundo y pone los dedos pulgares sobre los ojos, como para hundir los dedos en ellos.
61. Grita la muchacha y el muchacho, de espaldas, se quita la americana y una peluca y aparece el hombre de las venas.
62. Entonces ella se disuelve en un busto de yeso blanco y el hombre de las venas la besa apasionadamente.
63. Se ve el busto de yeso con las huellas de labios y huellas de manos.

55. It dissolves into a lift where a Negro vomits. The girl and the harlequin go up in the lift.
56. They go up in the lift and embrace each other.
57. Shot of a sensual kiss.
58. The boy bites the girl on the neck and pulls her hair violently.

59. A guitar appears. And a hand swiftly cuts the strings with a pair of scissors.
60. The girl defends herself from the boy who furiously gives her another deep kiss and places his thumbs over her eyes as if to plunge them in.
61. The girl screams and the boy, with his back to her, takes his jacket and a wig off, and the veins man appears.
62. She then dissolves into a white plaster bust and the veins man kisses her passionately.
63. The plaster bust is seen, with the lip and hand marks.

Disguise, metamorphosis and identity, features which are more fully and subtly treated in *El público*, are present in the above sequences. The corrupt veins man disguises himself as a boy harlequin in order to deceive the girl. Perhaps Lorca had in mind here the Picasso paintings of his son Paolo dressed in harlequin costume, which suggests innocence, although it is Santos Torroella's view that Lorca's *commedia* drawings, at least, were more influenced by Dalí than by Picasso. In *Viaje a la luna*, instead of representing innocence, the costume is associated once more with sexual violence, although the boy harlequin is, of course, only the veins man in disguise. It is possible that he wears the disguise in order to deceive the young girl. At the same time, the boy and the man need not be two different characters but two sides of one, as in *El público* where the different aspects of the same person are constantly shown as characters strip off costumes. The double or multiple masks of the drawings also come to mind.

The girl in *Viaje a la luna* is variously projected as virtually unclothed and dressed in white, both symbols of innocence, and is prepared to accept the young boy, clothed in what she believes is the innocent harlequin costume. However, once the true nature (violent) and the true identity (the veins man) of the boy harlequin are revealed to the girl, she is metamorphosed into a plaster bust, which the veins man, soon to die, can only kiss in frustrated desperation. Love in the New York setting is stripped of its innocence, and the 'popular' Arlequín of the idealised rural environment of *El retablillo de don Cristóbal* has been corrupted and dehumanised by his journey from country to town. His innocence is more apparent than real, and he is as menacing as he was in *Así que pasen cinco años*. As Morris says:

> The harlequin figure who moves through *Viaje a la luna* - and who reappears in *El público* - is more at home in the canvases of Picasso than in this city of violence, and Lorca denied the harlequin suit the remotest chance of provoking amusement when he imagined it thrust into the boy's mouth...we realize that the clown has been transformed in Lorca's mind into a sensualist and a sadist. The harlequin is clearly not what we think he ought to be.[16]

Morris is obviously correct to point to the transformation of the Harlequin/Clown, but is surely mistaken in having preconceived notions of what he ought to be. Utrera falls into the same trap when he writes:

> La figura del arlequín es más habitual en los cuadros de Picasso que en la violenta ciudad neoyorquina en la que el poeta vive; por ello, la ropa del clown, antes que incitadora a la risa, está utilizada como objeto portador de agresividad.[17]

> The figure of the harlequin is more at home in the paintings of Picasso that in the violent city of New York in which the poet lives; therefore, the clown's costume, which previously evoked laughter, is used as a bearer of aggression.

The relationship between the *commedia* and the town/country question is, of course, rather more complex than Utrera indicates. The subtle interplay between urban and country environments in Lugones's *Lunario sentimental*, which was discussed in chapter 5, warns one to guard against the over-simplified conclusions of Utrera.[18]

El público

In *El público*, the *commedia* is once more linked with mask and identity, although Lorca explores these issues more fully here than in the texts so far considered. The harlequin costume which the Director is wearing in Scene 3, and which then speaks once he has cast it off, is one of several masks in the play. The whole question of mask is intimately connected with the regeneration of the theatre, and mask is seen both as destructive and creative, positive and negative.

As Ilie writes:

> Man's social role, so admirably civilized when not tested by tension, proves at critical points to be a flimsy mask behind which lurk characteristics that epitomize the physiology and behavior of lesser animals [...] in the modern metamorphosis, man's face and personality evolve according to the laws of culture. This is why the faceless figure and the mannequin are so typically Surrealistic in theme.[19]

Jerez-Farrán, however, insists that the masks and costumes of *El público* are Expressionist rather than Surrealist: 'Lorca parece indicar con este juego de máscaras y de trajes que la vida es un teatro y el hombre un actor que forzosamente finge un papel y se forja una personalidad ajena a él'[20] ('Lorca seems to indicate with this interplay of masks and costumes that life is a stage and man an actor who is forced to play a role and who forges a personality which is alien to him'). Cao, too, considers the influence of Expressionism on Lorca's theatre to have been considerable.[21] It seems to me that it can be argued that the mask and costume fulfil both a Surrealist and an Expressionist function: the former in the sense that they reveal the inner self, and the latter in that they encapsulate in a single vivid image the essence of the character.[22]

Until Scene 5 of *El público* the Director insists that the theatre should be a comfortable experience for the audience, not challenging their values in any way.

154

He insists that the mask is a necessary part of human society: 'en medio de la calle, la máscara nos abrocha los botones y evita el rubor imprudente que a veces surge en las mejillas'[23] ('in the middle of the street the mask fastens our buttons and avoids the unwise blush that sometimes appears on one's cheeks'), in contrast to the views of The First Man. At the same time, however, the Director is afraid of mask:

> ¿Qué hago con el público si quito las barandas al puente? Vendría la máscara a devorarme. Yo vi una vez a un hombre devorado por la máscara. Los jóvenes más fuertes de la ciudad, con picas ensangrentadas, le hundían por el trasero grandes bolas de periódicos abandonados, y en América hubo una vez un muchacho a quien la máscara ahorcó colgado de sus propios intestinos. (pp.41-43)

> What will I do with the audience if I take the railings away from the bridge? The mask would come and devour me. I once saw a man devoured by the mask. The strongest young people of the city, with bloodied pikes, forced great bundles of abandoned newspapers into his backside, and once upon a time in America there was a boy whom a mask hanged by his own intestines.

Also: 'no hay más que máscara...Si burlamos la máscara, ésta nos colgará de un árbol como al muchacho de América' ('there is only mask... If we cheat the mask it will hang us from a tree as it did to the boy from America') (p.105) . The horrific violence of this image is similar to the brutal one of the harlequin costume being stuffed into the boy's mouth in *Viaje a la luna*; despite their use of sometimes grotesque irony, there is nothing remotely like this in any of the authors discussed in chapter 5. The mask in *El público* is interpreted by Londré as 'societal convention and accepted morality, which the Director does not wish to antagonize'.[24] The Director is shocked and terrified at the idea of the mask's revenge, but the reaction of the First Man is '¡magnífico!' ('magnificent'). He is a passionate and aggressive defender of the idea of a theatre without masks, and an opponent of the views of the Director. When the Director reappears in the third Scene transformed into a white harlequin, he calls for 'teatro al aire libre!' ('open-air theatre') (p.103).[25] The White Horse insists that there is no longer a place for open-air theatre: 'No. Ahora hemos inaugurado el verdadero teatro, el teatro bajo la arena' ('No. Now we have inaugurated true theatre, the theatre beneath the sand') (p.103). The First Man insists that he has struggled with mask until he has finally seen the Director naked,'but Lorca soon suggests that he is oversimplifying matters. The Director peels off his harlequin costume to reveal underneath 'un sutilísimo traje de bailarina' ('a most delicate ballerina costume') (p.109), then Enrique's costume appears from behind the column: 'este personaje es el mismo arlequín blanco con una careta amarillo pálido'('this character is the same white harlequin with a pale yellow mask') (p.109), and the harlequin costume speaks the lines, repeated later, and vaguely reminiscent of words spoken by the Moon in *Bodas de sangre*: 'Tengo frío. Luz eléctrica. Pan. Estaban quemando goma' ('I am cold. Electric light. They were burning rubber') (p.109). The Director, having been metamorphosed from Arlequín to ballet-dancer, then takes off his ballet dress and throws it behind the column, after which it reappears speaking nonsense language.

At the same time as non-human 'characters' such as costumes are given a human characteristic like speech, so human beings are dehumanised. In Scene 3, for example, the Third Man refers to Julieta in the following terms: 'ésta no es mi amiga, ésta es una máscara, una escoba, un perro débil de sofá' ('this is not my friend, this is a mask, a broom, a feeble sofa dog') (p.113).[26] The following lines from Manuel Machado's poem 'La tragicomedia del carnaval', from *Confetti* (1935) also come to mind:

En la percha está colgado
el vestido de Arlequín,
que es, a cuadros, colorado,
verde, azul, blanco y carmín.
¿Y Arlequín?... ¡Se ha evaporado![27]

On the coat stand hangs Arlequín's costume, with its red, green, blue, white and rouge squares. And Arlequín?... He has evaporated!

156

The harlequin costume exhibits the same mocking nature as that of Arlequín in *Así que pasen cinco años*: at the end of Scene 3 the The First Man tries to embrace the harlequin costume, mistakenly believing it to be Enrique. The costume mocks him by echoing his words. The costume then seeks Enrique, but cannot find him. There are other complex frustrated searches involving human beings and costumes in this scene which is summed up as follows by Edwards:

> In this astonishing scene in which the characters search in vain not only for others but even for themselves, we are left with an impression of the uncertainty of everything, of love, of individual identity, and of the treachery of appearances and the shift and flux of all reality.[28]

The debate on whether the theatre should give the audience escapist entertainment or should involve them emotionally in the action is presented in a discussion between two students in Scene 5. The First Student expresses the view that the audience should not look behind the poet's fantasy, but let it continue to be fantasy. The Second Student agrees with him, saying: 'el público se ha de dormir en la palabra y no ha de ver a través de la columna las ovejas que balan y las nubes que van por el cielo' ('the audience must sleep on the word and must not see through the pillar the bleating sheep or the clouds which float across the sky') (p.131). The Fourth Student, however, disagrees with his colleagues. He is dismayed that the audience is rebellious because the Director has shown them what is going on behind the scenes. The First Student is not convinced by his argument, and makes the following point in its defence:

> Un espectador no debe formar nunca parte del drama. Cuando la gente va al acuario no asesina a las serpientes de mar ni a las ratas de agua, ni a los peces cubiertos de lepra, sino que resbala sobre los cristales sus ojos y aprende. (p.139)

> A spectator should never form part of the play. When the people go to the aquarium they do not kill the sea serpents or the water rats, or

the fishes covered with leprosy, but they slide their eyes over the glass and learn.

When the Director reappears in Scene 5, however, he has completely changed his ideas on the role of mask in the theatre. He no longer defends or is afraid of mask, but is convinced of the arguments that The First Man had forcefully put to him earlier in the play and that Fourth Student expounded to his colleagues earlier in Scene 5; that the theatre should not be afraid to rip away masks and deal with difficult or controversial subjects. His views are expressed in the dialogue between him and the Conjurer. The latter suggests that all fantasy is valid in the theatre, a viewpoint that the Director denies. He believes that in order that truth be discovered, the theatre must be destroyed, something that the audience cannot accept. Rather than defend the open air theatre, as he did earlier in the play, he firmly believes in the same theatre beneath the sand, the theatre of dark forces, as that advocated by The First Man.

The precise identity of open air theatre is difficult to ascertain. The most likely interpretation is that it is the commercial theatre of superficial entertainment to which Lorca was so opposed. In Edwards's words, open air theatre is 'a form of theatre that is concerned only with the presentation of the pleasant appearance of things',[29] and the Director, having passed through the identity crisis externalised in his wearing of the harlequin and the ballerina costumes, has moved by Scene 5 to the position defended by The First Man earlier in the play that theatre should not be afraid to strip away masks and costumes and deal with difficult issues, and with the often disturbing things that lie behind the external façade of human beings. It is, as Edwards writes: 'a shedding of masks, another search for individual identity beneath the guises with which we all conceal ourselves'.[30]

Typically of *El público*, however, the transformation to theatre 'beneath the sand' is not straightforward. Andrew Anderson quite rightly warns against seeing it in simple terms, and he criticizes María Clementa Millán for allegedly doing so in his review of her 1987 edition of the play:

> I felt that the distinction made between 'teatro al aire libre' and 'teatro bajo la arena' and their corresponding scenes too cut and dried; this is no simple opposition but rather a progression which may possibly only have culminated in the missing or excised 'Scene IV'.[31]

For Jerez-Farrán the new theatre so boldly advocated in *El público* is basically the same phenomenon as the 'poetry in theatre' advocated in the prologues to the farces and the Lorca interview ('que se levanta del libro'): 'Lorca cree que el teatro nuevo debe aceptarse por sus valores poéticos, por lo que cree apasionadamente que es el arte escénico "poesía que se levanta del libro"...'[32] ('Lorca believes that the new theatre should be accepted for its poetic values, and consequently he believes passionately that scenic art should be "poetry which gets up from the book"...'). At the same time, as Londré points out, the 'conversion' of the Director to 'new theatre' is not as complete as it seems:

> In Scene 6 the Director argues vehemently for a theatre beneath the sand, but then his actions belie his words. He sells out to sleight-of-hand trickery the moment he - like Peter denying Christ - tells the Lady in Black that he is not the one she should talk to about Gonzalo. The final betrayal of his true nature signals the beginning of the cold [*sic*] that kills the Director.[33]

Another cautionary note against seeing *El público* as an optimistic play is sounded by Feal, who argues that the dialogue between the Director and the Conjurer is essentially a monologue, with both characters conveying the same pessimistic message. Feal emphasises too the 'amontonamiento de figuras, que a su vez originan otras, en una serie inacabable de metamorfosis, cuyo objeto es precisamente encubrir la radical unidad, la radical soledad'[34] ('the piling up of figures, which in their turn give rise to others, in an endless series of metamorphoses, whose objective is precisely to cover up the radical unity, the radical loneliness'). He sees the old and the new theatres as one and the same thing, in that both concern life becoming death.[35] For Feal, the mask and costume are entirely negative: 'la multiciplicidad de trajes o máscaras, emancipados del personaje a quien revestían, provoca la visión de una desintegración de la personalidad, cuyos diversos aspectos no pueden ya ser conectados con un foco u origen común'[36] ('the multiplicity of costumes or masks, once divested of the character whom they were clothing, provoke the vision of a disintegration of the personality, whose diverse aspects can no longer be connected with a common source or origin').

Despite what Feal and Londré say, Lorca does hint that the mask could possess a positive dimension, which hinges on the duality that has long been a feature of the clown or fool figure in popular festival. Bakhtin, for instance, has pointed out the contradictions inherent in the role of the clown and the fool in medieval festivals:

> Clowns and fools...were not actors playing their parts on a stage, as did the comic actors of a later period, impersonating Harlequin, Hanswurst, etc., but remained fools and clowns always and whenever they made their appearance. As such they represented a certain form of life, which was real and ideal at the same time. They stood on the borderline between life and art, in a peculiar mid-zone as it were; they were neither eccentrics nor dolts, neither were they comic actors. Thus carnival is the people's second life. Festivity is a peculiar quality of all comic rituals and spectacles of the Middle Ages.[37]

As Belleau points out in an article on the carnivalesque in Bakhtin:

> La carnavalisation implique trois régimes d'antagonismes simultanés:
> 1) Dans la culture populaire: systeme interne d'oppositions et de permutations de type binaire: le cul et la tete, la mort et la vie, l'injure et la louange, etc.
> 2) Le discours ambivalent de la culture carnavalesque populaire vs. le discours unilatéral de la culture dite officielle.

160

3) La transposition textuelle des deux premiers systemes par la carnavalisation.[38]

Carnivalisation implies three types of simultaneous antagonisms:
1) In popular culture: an internal system of oppositions and permutations of the binary type: the backside and the head, life and death, insult and praise, etc.
2) The ambivalent discourse of popular carnivalesque culture versus the unilateral discourse of so-called official culture.
3) The textual transposition of the first two systems through carnivalisation.

The ambivalence of much Lorcan imagery is, of course, a commonplace, and although it is not my intention to enter into this question here, we should remind ourselves of the duality of the Harlequin figure in the drawing *Arlequín* and the poem of the same title. It would not be unreasonable to suggest that a similar duality could apply to the harlequin, mask and costume in *El público*. The role of disguise in the form of the costume and the mask has, as has been observed, crucially changed by Scene 5, coinciding with the Director's changed views on the theatre. The Conjurer calls him 'man of mask' ('hombre de máscara') (p.151), but the Director has different views on disguise:

Cuando los trajes hablan, las personas vivas son ya botones de hueso en las paredes del calvario. Yo hice el túnel [bajo la arena] para apoderarme de los trajes, y, a través de ellos, enseñar el perfil de una fuerza oculta cuando ya el público no tuviera más remedio que atender lleno de espíritu y subyugado por la acción. (p.155)

When the costumes speak, living people are knots of bone on the walls of Calvary. I constructed the tunnel [beneath the sand] in order to have power over the costumes, and through them to reveal the features of a hidden force when the audience would have no choice but to pay attention with intelligence, captivated by the action.

He is no longer afraid of disguise, but has learnt to be the master of the costume through his symbolic journey through the tunnel beneath the sand. Costumes are not now a negative force, but a means to achieve an end ('through them'). Perhaps, as in the work of a number of late nineteenth- and early twentieth-century poets where the *commedia*, and in particular the figure of Pierrot, has therapeutic or regenerative force,[39] mask can fulfil the same function in Lorca's concept of 'new' drama.

While regeneration in *El público* is more complex and certainly more painful than it is in *El retablillo de don Cristóbal* and in the other authors discussed in chapter 3, it is still through popular tradition that it could be achieved. The Director's struggle with mask and to journey beneath the sand symbolises the new path, in which mask and costume must become more dynamic. Although the Director may be, as Londré points out, a traitor to the new cause,[40] all hope is not lost, and transformation through a new definition of mask and costume may be possible.

A free expression of love is seen to be the key to the transformation. Interestingly, open air theatre seems to be associated with heterosexual love: harassed by The First Man in the first scene on the question of the role of theatre, the Director seeks to take refuge in the stereotyped female recipient of heterosexual love, Elena:

> DIRECTOR Elena! Elena!
> HOMBRE 1 (*Fuerte*) No llames a Elena.
> DIRECTOR Y por qué no? Me ha querido mucho cuando mi teatro estaba al teatro libre. ¡Elena! (p.49)

> DIRECTOR: Elena! Elena!
> FIRST MAN: (*Forcefully*) Don't call Elena.
> DIRECTOR: And why not? She loved me deeply when my theatre was in the open air. Elena!

This attempted denial of his homosexuality is, as is well known, soon exposed, and later in the play an obvious link seems to be established between 'true' love uninhibited by society's masks, and the regeneration of the theatre through a redefined costume/mask: 'Eso es precisamente lo que se hace en el teatro. Por eso yo me atreví a realizar un dificilísimo juego poético en espera de que el amor rompiera con ímpetu y diera nueva forma a los trajes' ('This is precisely what happens in the theatre. This is why I was bold enough to carry out a very difficult poetic game in the hope that love would break open the costumes and give them a new form') (p.155). The 'old' costumes, symbolised once more by the harlequin costume, are swept away, even exorcised, to be replaced by the new: this seems to me to be the symbolic significance of the tired, feeble harlequin costume's being pushed off the stage by the Servant just before the end of the play.

Lorca's use of the harlequin figure in the works examined in this chapter places him firmly in the *art arlequin* line described by Max Jacob. The sentimentality of the *art pierrot* has entirely disappeared, as Lorca takes dehumanisation further than either Lugones or Valle-Inclán. This harlequin figure is not central to Lorca's texts in the same way that he and other *commedia* figures are to those of most of the other authors already examined, but is instead a dehumanised and judgemental figure. In *Así que pasen cinco años*, *Viaje a la luna* and *El público*, Lorca has taken the views on the regeneration of the theatre through the *commedia* and other forms of popular theatre a radical and disturbing step further.

---

1 Rafael Santos Torroella, 'Barradas-Lorca-Dalí: temas compartidos', in *Federico García Lorca: dibujos*, ed. by Mario Hernández (Barcelona: Caixa de Barcelona, 1986), pp. 39-53. This volume contains reproductions of Lorca's drawings exhibited in Granada, Madrid and Barcelona in 1986, and all the drawings referred to in the present article are contained in it. A fuller collection of Pierrot and Harlequin drawings is contained in Mario Hernández, *Libro de los dibujos de Federico García Lorca* (Madrid: Tabapress/Fundación Federico García Lorca, 1990). Santos Torroella analyses Dalí's *Arlequín* of 1927, which is a self-portrait and which Santos Torroella compares with another Dalí self-portrait, *Autoretrato desdoblándose en tres*, in his *La sangre es más dulce que la miel (las épocas lorquiana y freudiana de Salvador Dalí)* (Barcelona: Seix Barral, 1984), p.96, p.205. Further useful comments on the drawings are in Helen Oppenheimer, *Lorca: the Drawings* (London: The Herbert Press, 1986). On the question of *desdoblamientos*, or *döppelganger*, in *Así que pasen cinco años* and *El público*, see Antonio F.Cao, *Federico García Lorca y las vanguardias: hacia el teatro* (London: Támesis, 1984), pp. 83-85. The question of the other self is also, of course, clearly reminiscent of Unamuno. Mario Hernández suggests another possible significance of the *rostro desdoblado* in Lorca's drawings: 'como en el *Payaso de rostro desdoblado*, en la *Leyenda* Lorca sugiere, en línea con Dalí, la interrelación en un mismo ser del mundo de la vigilia y del sueño, o de muerte y vida' ('as in the *Clown with the Split Face*, in *Legend* Lorca suggests, in line with Dalí, the interrelation in a single being of wakefulness and sleep, of death and life') (Mario Hernández, *Libro de los dibujos de Federico García Lorca*, p.68).

2 'Barradas-Lorca-Dalí', in *Federico García Lorca: dibujos* pp. 49-50.
3 Ibid., p.156. The poem entitled 'Arlequín' which is quoted by Hernández is from *Canciones (Songs)*. Both *Arlequín* and *Arlequín veneciano* bear a striking resemblance to the drawing *Danza macabra (Macabre Dance)* (1927-28), whose title suggests primitive culture as a source. The poem 'Danza de la muerte' ('Dance of Death'), from *Poeta en Nueva York*, also comes to mind.
4 Cf the 'araña' image in 'La monja gitana' in its double meaning of 'chandelier' and 'web', but, above all, as an image of imprisonment. On the drowning motif, see C.Brian Morris, ' "Agua que no desemboca" ', in *"Cuando yo me muera"...: Essays in Memory of Federico García Lorca*, ed. by C.Brian Morris, pp. 159-89. See also, Nigel Dennis, 'Lorca in the looking-glass: on mirrors and self-contemplation', in *Ibid.*, pp. 41-55.
5 *Obras completas*, II, 560. Further quotations from *Así que pasen cinco años* are taken from this volume of *Obras completas*, and the corresponding page references are given in the body of the text.
6 On the limited impact of Diaghilev and Picasso, as well as the experimental work of Jacques Copeau, on Spanish drama, see *Epoca contemporánea (1914-1939)*, ed. by V. G. de la Concha, which is vol. VII of *Historia y crítica de la literatura española*, ed. by F. Rico (Barcelona: Crítica, 1984), p. 536. On the *commedia* and circus in Picasso, see, for example, Anthony Blunt and Phoebe Pool, *Picasso: The Formative Years* (London: Studio Books, 1962), p.6 and pp. 20-22; Douglas Cooper, *Picasso Theatre* (London: Weidenfield and Nicholson, 1968), p. 15, *passim*; and Roland Penrose, *Picasso: His Life and Work*, 3rd edn (Berkeley: University of California Press, 1981), pp.110-11. The Picasso paintings referred to in the course of this chapter are reproduced in Josep Palau i Fabré, *Picasso*, trans. by Kenneth Lyons (Chartwell: New Jersey, 1981). Alberti also mentions Diaghilev in Madrid in his autobiography: 'el ballet ruso de Diagilev continuaba asombrando al mundo y removiendo a su paso los ámbitos artísticos' ('the Russian ballet continued to astonish the world, shaking up artistic circles wherever it went') (*La arboleda perdida* [Barcelona: Seix Barral, 1975 (reprint)], p.125).
7 Francisco García Lorca, *Federico y su mundo*, 2nd edn. (Madrid: Alianza, 1981), p. 329.
8 For an interesting exploration of the technique in *Así que pasen cinco años*, see Joaquín Roses-Lozano, 'Códigos sígnicos y discurso teatral en *Así que pasen cinco años*', *ALEC*, 14 (1989), 115-41.
9 *Lorca: The Theatre Beneath the Sand* (London and Boston: Marion Boyars, 1980), p. 117, p. 110.
10 Andrew A. Anderson, *García Lorca: 'La zapatera prodigiosa'* (London: Grant & Cutler/Támesis, 1991), p.97.
11 Ricardo Doménench considers this scene to be a model for the Bridegroom/Beggar Woman scene in Act 3 of *Bodas de sangre*: see 'Aproximación a *Así que pasen cinco años*', in *Estudios en honor a Ricardo Gullón*, ed. by Luis T.González-del-Valle and Darío Villanueva (Lincoln, Nebraska: Society of Spanish and Spanish-American Studies, 1984), pp.101-14 (p.104).
12 Similar sentiments are expressed by Andrew A. Anderson à propos of *La zapatera prodigiosa*: 'Lorca's treatment of traditional sources and precedents, therefore, is certainly not academic and not necessarily reverential: as in his 1930s productions of Golden Age plays with La Barraca, he is here concerned to emphasise that which is universal and timeless, and to make the traditional material readily accessible to modern audiences' (*García Lorca: 'La zapatera prodigiosa'*, p.29). The following résumé by Martin Esslin is also relevant here: 'The modern movement in painting and the Theatre of the Absurd meet in their rejection of the discursive and narrative elements, and in their concentration on the poetic image as a concretization of the inner reality of the conscious and subconscious mind, and the archetypes by which it lives' (*The Theatre of the Absurd* [Harmondsworth: Penguin, 1968], p.382). The Harlequin and the Clown are clearly examples of the archetypes which Esslin has in mind.
13 C.B.Morris, *This Loving Darkness*, pp. 129-30. It could be that Lorca also knew of another film with a remarkably similar title to that of his own, the French film director Georges Méliès's

Le Voyage dans la Lune (1902). Méliès was 'rediscovered' by the Surrealists in the 1920s: see *Cinema. A Critical Dictionary. The Major Film Makers*, ed. by Richard Round, 2 vols (London: Secker and Warburg, 1980), I, 394 and 396, and II, 676-81. Agustín Sánchez Vidal is sceptical about this latter influence: see his 'El viaje a la luna de un perro andaluz', in *Valoración actual de la obra de Federico García Lorca* (Madrid: Casa de Velázquez/Universidad Complutense, 1988), p.144.

14 I have consulted both the original manuscript and the Marie Laffranque edition of the filmscript (Loubressac: Braad, 1980). All my quotations are from the original manuscript (Biblioteca de España MSS, 22584 38), and the sequence numbers are cited in the body of the text. I am most grateful to Dr John London for showing me a copy of the manuscript edition.

15 Rafael Utrera, *García Lorca y el cinema*, pp. 64-65.

16 *This Loving Darkness*, p. 134.

17 Utrera, p. 81.

18 On Lorca's use of the urban landscape see Kristine Ibsen, 'The Illusory Journey: García Lorca's *Viaje a la luna*', in *The Surrealist Adventure in Spain*, ed. by C.Brian Morris, pp.225-39.

19 Paul Ilie, *The Surrealist Mode in Spanish Literature* (Ann Arbor: University of Michigan Press, 1968), p. 107, p. 111.

20 Carlos Jerez-Farrán, 'La estética expresionista en *El público* de García Lorca', *ALEC*, 11 (1986), 111-27 (p. 123).

21 *Federico García Lorca y las vanguardias*, p. 44.

22 The most sensible point in the debate on whether Lorca is a Surrealist or an Expressionist is, it seems to me, made by Andrew A. Anderson, writing specifically on the use of the *commedia* in *Así que pasen cinco años*: 'the *commedia dell'arte*-derived characters would be at home in almost any of the broadly avant-garde arts of the early twentieth century (but not particularly in either Expressionism or Surrealism)' ('Bewitched, Bothered and Bewildered: Spanish Dramatists and Surrealism', in *The Surrealist Adventure in Spain*, ed. by C.Brian Morris, p.263).

23 *El público y Comedia sin título* (Barcelona, Seix Barral, 1978), p. 105. All further quotations from this play are from this edition, and the corresponding page references are given in the body of the text.

24 Felicia Hardison Londré, *Federico García Lorca* (New York: Frederick Ungar, 1984), p. 42.

25 Apropos of the stage mechanics of this scene, Londré writes: 'the Men place a screen at stage center and push the Director behind it. He reappears at the other end as a boy dressed in white satin with a white ruff at the neck. In *The Audience* and in his filmscript *A Trip to the Moon*, Lorca refers to this outfit as a "White Harlequin Costume", although he must have envisioned what we would call a Pedrolino or Pierrot costume' (*Federico García Lorca*, p.42). Londré could possibly be correct, but it has already been observed that the distinctions between Harlequin and Pierrot are sometimes blurred, as in Valle-Inclán and elsewhere in Lorca's work, and one does not have to look any further than Picasso's 1923 *Harlequin* to see a Harlequin with an almost white costume.

26 Bárbara Sheklin Davis has pertinent things to say about the deliberate confusion between human and non-human characters in Surrealist drama: 'la coexistencia de personajes reales o irreales es otro aspecto de la contradicción intencional de la obra surrealista. Como los autores creían que era su deber pintar los niveles más profundos de la existencia humana - y como ya no estaban restringidos por la necesidad de justificaciones racionales - pusieron personajes fantásticos en la escena: medios seres, muertos, personajes literarios, hasta Dios. Mientras las personas se universalizaban hasta la abstracción, las abstracciones se personifican [...] Mientras las personas se deshumanizan, lo no-humano se hace humano' ('the coexistence of real and unreal characters is another aspect of the deliberate contradiction of the Surrealist work. Since the authors believed that it was their duty to portray the deepest levels of human existence - and as they were no longer restricted by the need for rational justifications - they introduced fantastic characters onto the stage: half beings, literary figures, even God. While people were being universalized to abstraction, abstractions were being personified [...] While people were being dehumanised, the non-human was made human' ('El teatro surrealista español', in *El surrealismo*, ed. by Víctor García de la Concha

[Madrid: Taurus, 1982], pp.327-51 [p.346]). The empty costume and the half being appear in a number of Spanish works of the 1920s and 1930s, such as Alberti's *El hombre deshabitado* (*The Uninhabited Man*) (1931), and Gómez de la Serna's *Los medios seres* (*The Half Beings*) (1929).

27 Manuel y Antonio Machado, *Obras completas*, p. 235

28 *Lorca: The Theatre Beneath the Sand*, p. 78.

29 *Ibid.*, p. 69.

30 *Ibid.*, p. 78.

31 *BHS*, 66 (1989), 296-97 (p. 297). Furthermore, a contemporary theatre critic, Luis Araquistain, did not see even commercial theatre and minority art theatre as mutually exclusive, writing 'de estos teatros de minorías salen a la larga los directores, autores y comediantes que han de renover los teatros de muchedumbres' ('in the long run, it is from these minority theatres that the directors, authors and actors who will renew the theatre of the masses will emerge') (*La batalla teatral* [Madrid: CIAP, 1930], p. 73).

32 'La estética expresionista', p. 124.

33 Londré, pp. 55-56.

34 Carlos Feal, 'El Lorca póstumo: *El público y Comedia sin título*', *ALEC*, 6 (1981), 43-62 (p.52).

35 *Ibid.*, p. 58.

36 *Ibid.*, p. 50.

37 *Rabelais and his World*, p. 8.

38 André Belleau, 'Carnavalesque pas mort?', in *Bakhtine mode d'emploi, Etudes Françaises*, 201 (Montreal: Les Presses de l'Université de Montréal, 1983), pp.37-44 (p. 39). One may recall the tension between body and mind leading up to and during the 'liberated' mask scene in *Yerma*.

39 For a study of the figure of Pierrot as therapeutic agent, see Pauline Hueurre, 'Etude du personnage de Pierrot', chapter 4. See also Richard Sheppard's analysis of the therapeutic role of mythical and magical figures in Dada that was quoted in chapter 1.

40 *Federico García Lorca*, p. 56.

Conclusion

Over the centuries, the *commedia* has acted as a kind of cultural barometer, and late nineteenth- and early twentieth-century Hispanic literature is no exception in this respect. The rapid and radical changes in cultural temper during the first three decades of the twentieth century are reflected in the changing perceptions of the *commedia*, as *modernismo* passed into Modernism and the avant-garde. From being an essentially post-Romantic and Symbolist image, the *commedia* became one of the most paradigmatic symbols both of Modernism's concern to 'make it new' and of its sense of life's absurdity and dehumanisation.

Although the *commedia* never developed along neat chronological lines, it has been possible to trace a shift in emphasis from *art pierrot* to *art arlequin*, to use Max Jacob's terminology. Writers who were critical of the legacies of both Symbolism and Naturalism turned to the *commedia* as to other forms of popular theatrical culture like the circus and the carnival for a source of renewal of what they considered to be an ailing national culture.

It has emerged that the *commedia* form has lent a loose unity to widely disparate works. Nonetheless, this is clearly a unity based on a series of contrasts, of which four stand out. First, there is a contrast between individuality and collectivity. Pierrot the lonely, rejected outsider personifies the former, while the theatrical innovators discussed in chapter 3 conceive the *commedia dell'arte* as a complete entity, just as they view the theatre itself as a total experience in which no one element predominates. Nonetheless, Harlequin does acquire an almost archetypal significance in some of these writers as a universal comic type which has its counterpart in the idea of Pierrot as a symbol of the suffering but dandified outsider.

Secondly, a contrast between innocence and corruption has been noted, as the harlequin and clown figures, who represent a kind of naive spirituality in Benavente (in the circus essays), Darío, Gómez Carrillo, Carrere and Rusiñol, become menacing, even frightening in some of Lorca's works. This second contrast is linked closely to a third, which involves the town and the countryside. The country settings of Watteau's *Fêtes galantes*, which were so influential in the development of the *commedia* in the eighteenth and the nineteenth centuries, permeate early *modernista* writing in Latin America and Spain. Even when urban settings are used, they tend to be idealised. This is especially true of the *modernista* vision of Paris which for writers like Gómez Carrillo is merely the setting for nostalgic Pierrot mime plays. A more ironical awareness of the city and its contrast with the *fêtes galantes* tradition is displayed by Lugones, while a degrading urban environment provides the backcloth to Lorca's disturbing harlequin figures in *Viaje a la luna*.

The second and the third set of contrasts outlined above are underpinned by the fourth area, where the values of the on occasions sickly sentimentality associated with the nineteenth-century Pierrot are supplanted by the more detached but more artistically creative mode associated with Harlequin. Writers such as Gómez Carrillo, Mota and Zamacois generally identify with the Pierrot figure, sometimes to an exaggerated degree. This would account for the appropriateness, even the inevitability, of the ironic manner adopted by Lugones and Valle-Inclán. A sense of perspective is applied to what had previously been uncritical acceptance of the Romantic and Symbolist Pierrot model. The spirituality reflected in the vertical movement is brought down to earth by a deliberately prosaic deflation of idealism. However, the language of some of Machado's poems, and of *Lunario sentimental* and *La marquesa Rosalinda* is certainly not prosaic. Indeed, one of the most striking features of Lugones and Valle-Inclán is their imaginative, often brilliant use of language.

Closely connected with the brilliant imagery which is frequently utilised to deflate *commedia* characters is theatricality, an important feature of Hispanic writers' portrayal of the *commedia*, particularly following Lugones's *Lunario sentimental*. This is linked with perspectivism, and is most evident in Valle-Inclán's *La marquesa Rosalinda* and Lorca's *El público*. Both these plays use the *commedia* as one of several paratheatrical elements in order to explore questions such as the play-within-a-play, and the relationship between the actors and the audience. In so doing, they are at the forefront of the avant-garde movement, and also anticipate the Theatre of the Absurd.

Indeed, numerous points of contact between Hispanic *commedia* literature and its European counterpart have been observed. The variety and contrasts in the Hispanic world were also present in the non-Hispanic world. For instance, the Decadent Pierrot of French Symbolism is clearly the source of the version of Pierrot that appears in writers like Darío and Gómez Carrillo. The revaluation of the *commedia* as part of a process of theatrical renewal that one discovers in Baroja, Gual and others has its parallel in Craig in England, Blok and Meyerhold in Russia, and Copeau in France.

Not only has this study set the Hispanic instances of the *commedia* within a wider context, it has also effectively highlighted certain trends within late nineteenth- and early twentieth-century Spanish, Catalan and Latin America literature. It has been observed how the changes within *modernismo*, as well as the demise of Catalan *modernisme* and its replacement by *noucentisme*, are worked out through the Pierrot figure. The socio-political ramifications of the latter conflict - although not spelt out by Rusiñol and Mestres - are implicit, as are those of Benavente's *La ciudad alegre y confiada*. Nevertheless, politics is generally notable for its absence in the *commedia* works: the genre is often appreciated by writers of the period for its timeless qualities and for its lack of historical specificity.

Finally, a study of the *commedia* has made it possible to emphasise the originality of some of the best writers of a great period of Hispanic literature. Benavente, for instance, now rather out of fashion with critics and public alike, is clearly a writer who was steeped in the *commedia* traditions. His treatment of the subject is varied, ranging from the standard *modernista* version, though at a very early date in *Cuento de primavera*, through the subtle and complex *Los intereses creados*, to the polemical but less interesting *La ciudad alegre y confiada*. In addition, an analysis of *Cuento de primavera* permits a critical questioning of the standard view that the early Benavente is essentially a Naturalist.

Like Benavente, Manuel Machado is not nowadays a fashionable writer, but once more an examination of his writing on the *commedia* permits one to appreciate a poet of quality. The same is true of Lugones, who, in a series of brilliant images, deflates the Pierrot figure and gives a sense of perspective to *modernista* sentimentality. But, like the Benavente of *Los intereses creados* and Machado, Lugones treats the *commedia* in an ambiguous and subtle way, and there is a duality in his approach to his subject.

The same is true of Valle-Inclán in *La marquesa Rosalinda*. There are many literary resonances in this work, but Valle ingeniously blends them into an original whole in which sentimentality is perfectly balanced by an element of grotesque distortion. As with Benavente, it is possible by focusing on the *commedia* to appreciate an important aspect of the development of his work in general and of his theatre in particular.

Lorca, Spain's best-known twentieth-century writer, finds in the *commedia* and analogous popular theatrical forms a source of inspiration and of potential theatrical renovation. He destroys the comforting Romantic images of Harlequin which are present even in theatrical innovators like Adrià Gual and Pío Baroja, and suggests that the destruction of tradition is a necessary prelude to the creation of a new type of theatre. His harlequin is more dehumanised and disturbing than any other *commedia* figure, but it also points the way most clearly to the future. The *commedia*, as ever throughout its long history, is in close touch with its roots but is constantly changing and renewing itself, as each new generation discovers its magic and adapts it to its own needs.

BIBLIOGRAPHY

PRIMARY SOURCES

BANVILLE, Théodore de. 'Arlequin', in *Critiques*, ed. by Victor Barrucand. Paris: Charpentier, 1917.

BANVILLE, Théodore de. *Odes funambulesques*. Paris: Libraire Alphonse Lemerre, n.d.

BAROJA, Pío. *Arlequín mancebo de botica*, in *Entretenimientos*. Madrid: Caro Raggio, n.d.

BECQUER, G.A. *Obras completas*. Barcelona: Ferma, 1966.

BENAVENTE, Jacinto. *Obras completas*. 11 vols., Madrid: Aguilar, 1940-1958.

BENAVENTE, Jacinto. *Los intereses creados*, ed. by José Díaz de Castro. Madrid: Espasa Calpe, 1990.

CARRERE, Emilio. *Retablo grotesco y sentimental*. Madrid: Mundo Latino, n.d.

DARIO, Rubén. *La vida de Rubén Darío escrita por él mismo*. Barcelona: Maucci, 1915.

DARIO, Rubén. *Obras completas*. 21 vols, Madrid: Biblioteca Rubén Darío, 1923-29.

DARIO, Rubén. *Obras completas*. 11th edn, Madrid: Aguilar, 1968.

GARCIA LORCA, Federico. *Lorca: Plays Two*, trans. by Gwynne Edwards. London: Methuen, 1990.

GARCIA LORCA, Federico. *La zapatera prodigiosa*, ed. by Mario Hernández. Madrid: Alianza, 1982.

GARCIA LORCA, Federico. *El público y Comedia sin título*. Barcelona: Seix Barral, 1978.

GARCIA LORCA, Federico. *Obras completas*. 3 vols, Madrid: Aguilar, 1986.

172

GARCIA LORCA, Federico. *Viaje a la luna*, ed. by Marie Laffranque. Loubressac: Braad, 1980.

GOMEZ CARRILLO, E. *La mujer y la moda. El teatro de Pierrot* , which is vol. 12 of *Obras completas*. 12 vols, Madrid: Mundo Latino, n.d.

GOMEZ CARRILLO, E. *Bohemia sentimental*. Paris: La Campaña, 1899.

GUAL, Adrià. *La serenata*, which is in vol. XVIII of *Lectura popular. Biblioteca d'autors catalans*. Barcelona: Ilustració Catalana, n.d.

GUAL, Adrià. *Arlequí vividor*. Barcelona: no publisher, 1912.

HERNANDEZ, Mario. *Libro de los dibujos de Federico García Lorca*. Madrid: Tabapress/Fundación Federico García Lorca, 1990.

LUGONES, Leopoldo. *Lunario sentimental,* ed. by Jesús Benítez. Madrid: Cátedra, 1988.

MACHADO, Antonio & Manuel. *Obras completas*. 5th edn, Madrid: Plenitud, 1967.

MARTINEZ SIERRA, G. *Teatro de ensueño*. 3rd edn, Madrid: Renacimiento, 1911.

MESTRES, Apel.les. *Gaziel/ Els sense cor*. Barcelona: Edicions 62, 1969.

PEREZ DE AYALA, R. de. *Las máscaras*, in *Obras completas*. 4 vols, Madrid: Aguilar, 1966.

RIVAS CHERIF, Cipriano de. 'Divagación a la luz de las candilejas', *La Pluma*, I (June-December 1920).

RIVAS CHERIF, Cipriano de. *Cómo hacer teatro*. Valencia: Pretextos, 1991.

RUDLIN, John and PAUL, Norman H (eds.). *Copeau: Texts on Theatre*. London and New York: Routledge, 1990.

RUSIÑOL, Santiago. *L'alegria que passa,* in *Teatre*. Barcelona: Edicions 62, 1981.

RUSIÑOL, Santiago, *La cançó de sempre*, in *Obres completes*. Barcelona: Selecta, 1947.

VALLE-INCLAN, Ramón del. *La marquesa Rosalinda*, ed. by Leda Schiavo. Madrid: Espasa Calpe, 1992.

VALLE-INCLAN, Ramón del. *Martes de carnaval*, ed. by Jesús Rubio Jiménez. Madrid: Espasa Calpe, 1992.

VERLAINE, Paul. *Œvres poétiques complètes*, ed. by Jacques Borel. Paris: Gallimard, 1962.

ZAYAS, Antonio de. 'El modernismo', in *Ensayos de crítica histórica y literaria*. Madrid: A. Marzo, 1907.

SECONDARY SOURCES

ANDERSON, Andrew A. 'Bewitched, Bothered and Bewildered: Spanish Dramatists and Surrealism, 1924-1936', in *The Surrealist Adventure in Spain*, ed. by C. Brian Morris. Ottawa Hispanic Studies, 6. Ottawa: Dovehouse, 1991, pp.240-81.

ANDERSON, Andrew A. *García Lorca: 'La zapatera prodigiosa'*. London: Grant & Cutler/Támesis, 1991.

ANDERSON, Reed. 'Prólogos and advertencias: Lorca's beginnings', in «*Cuando yo me muera*»: *Essays in Memory of Federico García Lorca*, ed. by C. Brian Morris. Lanham: University Press of America, 1988, pp.209-32.

ARAQUISTAIN, Luis. *La batalla teatral*. Madrid: CIAP, 1930.

BAKHTIN, Mikhail. *Rabelais and his World*, trans. by Helene Iswolksy. Cambridge, Mass: MIT, 1968.

BEAUMONT, Cyril W. *The History of Harlequin*. New York: Benjamin Blom, 1967 [reprint].

BLUNT, Anthony and POOL, Phoebe. *Picasso: The Formative Years*. London: Studio Books, 1962.

BORGES, Jorge Luis. *Leopoldo Lugones*. Buenos Aires: Pleamar, 1965.

BROTHERSTON, Gordon. *Manuel Machado: A Revaluation*. Cambridge: CUP, 1968.

CAIRNS, Christoper (ed.). *The Commedia dell'arte from the Renaissance to Dario Fo*. Lampeter/Lewiston/Queenston: The Edwin Mellen Press, 1989.

CAO, Antonio F. *Federico García Lorca y las vanguardias: hacia el teatro*. London: Támesis, 1984.

CARO BAROJA, Julio. *El carnaval*. Madrid: Taurus, 1979.

CARO BAROJA, Julio. *Los Baroja*. 2nd edn reprint, Madrid: Taurus, 1986.

COOPER, Douglas. *Picasso Theatre*. London: Weidenfield and Nicholson, 1968.

DE LA CONCHA, V.de (ed.). *Epoca contemporánea (1914-1939)*. Vol. VII of *Historia y crítica de la literatura española*, ed. by F. Rico. Barcelona: Crítica, 1984.

DIAZ-PLAJA, G. *Las estéticas de Valle-Inclán*. Madrid: Gredos, 1965.

DOMENECH, Ricardo. 'Aproximación a *Así que pasen cinco años*', in *Estudios en honor a Ricardo Gullón*, ed. by Luis T.González-del-Valle and Darío Villanueva. Lincoln, Nebraska: Society of Spanish and Spanish-American Studies, 1984, pp.101-14.

DOUGHERTY, Dru. 'The Semiosis of Stage Decor in Jacinto Grau's *El señor de Pigmalión*', *Hispania*, 67 (1984), 351-57.

DOUGHERTY, Dru. 'Talía convulsa: la crisis teatral de los años 20', in Robert Lima and Dru Dougherty, *2 ensayos sobre teatro español de los 20*. Murcia: Universidad de Murcia, 1984, pp.87-155.

EDWARDS, Gwynne. *Lorca: The Theatre Beneath the Sand*. London and Boston: Marion Boyars, 1980.

EVANS, George. 'Lesage and D'Orneval's *Théâtre de la foire*, the *commedia dell'arte* and power', in *Studies in the Commedia dell'Arte*, ed. by David J. George and Christopher J. Gossip, pp.107-20.

FABREGAS, Xavier, *Història del teatre català*. Barcelona: Millà, 1978.

FEAL, Carlos. 'El Lorca póstumo: *El público* y *Comedia sin título*', *ALEC*, 6 (1981), 43-62.

FISHER, James. 'Commedia Iconography in the Theatrical Art of Edward Gordon Craig', in *The Commedia dell'arte from the Renaissance to Dario Fo*, ed. by Christopher Cairns. Lampeter/Lewiston/Queenston: The Edwin Mellen Press, 1989, pp. 245-75.

FISHER, James. *The Theatre of Yesterday and Tomorrow: Commedia dell'arte on the Modern Stage*. Lampeter/Lewiston/Queenston: The Edwin Mellen Press, 1992.

GARCIA LORCA, Francisco. *Federico y su mundo*. 2nd edn, Madrid: Alianza, 1981.

GEORGE, David J. and GOSSIP, Christopher J. (eds.). *Studies in the Commedia dell'Arte*. Cardiff: University of Wales Press, 1993.

GEORGE, David. 'Commedia dell'arte and Mask in Lorca', in *Lorca, Poet and Playwright*, ed. by R.Havard. Cardiff: University of Wales Press, 1992.

GEORGE, David. '*Commedia dell'arte* in Rubén Darío and Leopoldo Lugones', in *Studies in the Commedia dell'Arte*, ed. by David J. George and Christopher J. Gossip, pp.161-83.

GEORGE, David. 'Harlequin Comes to Court: Valle-Inclán's *La marquesa Rosalinda*', *Forum for Modern Language Studies*, vol. XIX no. 4 (1983), 364-74.

GEORGE, David. 'Notes sobre Apel.les Metsres i la Commedia dell'arte (a propòsit de *Blanc sobre blanc*)', *Els Marges*, 24 (1982), 121-24.

GEORGE, David. 'The *commedia dell'arte* and the Circus in the Work of Jacinto Benavente' *Theatre Research International*, vol. VI, no. 2 (1981), 92-108.

GIBSON, Ian. *Federico García Lorca*. 2 vols, Barcelona: Grijalbo, 1985.

GLENDINNING, Nigel. 'Some Versions of Carnival: Goya and Alas', in *Studies in Modern Spanish Literature and Art Presented to Helen F.Grant*, ed. by Nigel Glendinning. London: Támesis, 1972, pp.65-78.

GRANT, Helen F. 'El mundo al revés', in *Hispanic Studies in Honour of Joseph Manson*, ed. by Dorothy M.Atkinson and Anthony H.Clarke. Oxford: Dolphin, 1972, pp.119-37.

GRIFFITHS, Bruce. 'Sunset: from *commedia dell'arte* to *comédie italienne*', in *Studies in the Commedia dell'Arte*, ed. by David J. George and Christopher J. Gossip, pp. 91-105.

HALTY FERGUSON, Raquel. *Laforgue y Lugones: dos poetas de la luna*. London: Támesis, 1981.

HARDISON LONDRE, Felicia. *Federico García Lorca*. New York: Frederick Ungar, 1984.

HARROW, Susan. 'From Symbolism to Modernism - Apollinaire's Harlequin-Acrobat', in *Studies in the Commedia dell'Arte*, ed. by David J. George and Christopher J. Gossip, pp.199-236.

HECK, Thomas F. *Commedia dell'arte: a Guide to the Primary and Secondary Literature*. New York and London: Garland, 1988.

HIGGINBOTHAM, Virginia. *The Comic Spirit of Federico García Lorca*. Austin: University of Texas Press, 1976.

HUEURRE, Pauline Baggio. 'Etude du personnage de Pierrot'. Unpublished doctoral thesis, Stanford University, 1976.

IBSEN, Kristine. 'The Illusory Journey: García Lorca's *Viaje a la luna*', in *The Surrealist Adventure in Spain*, ed. by C.Brian Morris. Ottawa: Dovehouse, 1991, pp.225-39.

ILIE, Paul. *The Surrealist Mode in Spanish Literature*. Ann Arbor: University of Michigan Press, 1968.

JACOBS, G. 'The *Commedia dell'arte* in Early Twentieth-century Music: Schoenberg, Stravinsky, Busoni et Les Six', in *Studies in the Commedia dell'Arte*, ed. by David J. George and Christopher J. Gossip, pp.227-45.

JEREZ-FARRAN, Carlos. 'La estética expresionista en *El público* de García Lorca', *ALEC*, 11 (1986), 111-27.

JONES, W.Gareth. '*Commedia dell'arte*: Blok and Meyerhold, 1905-1917', in *Studies in the Commedia dell'Arte*, ed. by David J. George and Christopher J. Gossip, pp.185-97.

KING, Russell P. 'The Poet as Clown: Variations on a Theme in Nineteenth-Century French Poetry', *Orbis Litterarum*, 33 (1978), 238-52.

LEA, K.M. *Italian Popular Comedy*. 2 vols, Oxford: Clarendon 1934.

LEHMANN, A.G. 'Pierrot and fin de siècle', in *Romantic Mythologies*, ed. by I. Fletcher. London: Routledge & Kegan Paul, 1967, pp.209-23.

LIMA, Robert. 'The *Commedia dell'arte* and *La marquesa Rosalinda*', in *Ramón del Valle-Inclán: A Critical Appraisal of His Life and Works*, ed. by Anthony Zahareas. New York: Las Americas, 1968, pp. 386-415.

LYON, John. 'Valle-Inclán: Between Symbolism and the Absurd', *ALEC*, 19 (1992), 145-62.

LYON, John. *The Theatre of Valle-Inclán*. Cambridge: CUP, 1983.

MARFANY, Joan-Lluís. *Aspectes del modernisme*. 5th edn, Barcelona: Curial, 1982.

178

MENARI, Piero. 'Un texto inédito de Lorca para guiñol: Cristobical', *ALEC*, 11 (1986), 13-37.

MORRIS, C.B. *This Loving Darkness*. Oxford, OUP [for University of Hull Press], 1980.

NIKLAUS, Thelma. *Harlequin Phoenix*. London: The Bodley Head, 1956.

OLIVER, William L. 'Lorca: The Puppets and the Artist', *Tulane Drama Review*, VII (1962), 76-95.

OLIVIO JIMENEZ, José. *Antología crítica de la poesía modernista*. Madrid: Hiperión, 1985.

OPPENHEIMER, Helen. *Lorca: the Drawings*. London: The Herbert Press, 1986.

ORTIZ GRIFFIN, Julia. *Drama y sociedad en la obra de Benavente (1894-1914)*. New York: Anaya Las Américas, 1974.

PALACIO, J. de. 'La Posterité du Gaspard de la Nuit', in *Max Jacob I - Autour du poème en prose, Revue des Lettres Modernes*. Paris: Minard, 1973.

PALAU I FABRE, Josep. *Picasso*, trans. by Kenneth Lyons. Chartwell: New Jersey, 1981.

PAZ, Octavio. 'Traducción y metáfora', in *Los hijos del limo*. Barcelona: Seix Barral, 1974, pp.115-41.

PENROSE, Roland. *Picasso: His Life and Work*. 3rd edn, Berkeley: University of California Press, 1981.

PHILLIPS, Allen W. 'Notas para un estudio comparativo de Lugones y Valle-Inclán (*Lunario sentimental* y *La pipa de Kif*)', *Boletín-Biblioteca Menéndez Pelayo*, 56 (1980), 315-45.

RICHARDS, Kenneth and Laura. *The Commedia dell'arte*. Oxford: Basil Blackwell, 1990.

ROSES-LOZANO, Joaquín. 'Códigos sígnicos y discurso teatral en *Así que pasen cinco años*', *ALEC*, 14 (1989), 115-41.

RUBIO JIMENEZ, Jesús. 'Los primeros textos de *La marquesa Rosalinda* y otras páginas olvidadas de Valle-Inclán', *Boletín de la Fundación Federico García Lorca*, 7-8 (December 1990), 25-44.

RUBIO JIMENEZ, Jesús. 'Perspectivas críticas: horizontes infinitos. Modernismo y teatro de ensueño', *ALEC*, 14 (1989), 199-222.

RUDLIN, J. *Jacques Copeau*. Cambridge: CUP, 1986.

SANCHEZ VIDAL, Agustín. *Valoración actual de la obra de Federico García Lorca*. Madrid: Casa de Velázquez/Universidad Complutense, 1988.

SANTOS TORROELLA, Rafael. 'Barradas-Lorca-Dalí: temas compartidos', in *Federico García Lorca: dibujos*, ed. by Mario Hernández. Barcelona: Caixa de Barcelona, 1986, pp. 39-53.

SANTOS TORROELLA, Rafael. *La sangre es más dulce que la miel (las épocas lorquiana y freudiana de Salvador Dalí)*. Barcelona: Seix Barral, 1984.

SHEKLIN DAVIS, Bárbara. 'El teatro surrealista español', in *El surrealismo*, ed. by Víctor García de la Concha. Madrid: Taurus, 1982, pp.327-51.

SHEPPARD, Richard W. 'Tricksters, carnival and the magical figures of Dada poetry', *Forum for Modern Language Studies*, 19 (2) (1983), 116-25.

SHERGOLD, N.D. 'Ganassa and the *commedia dell'arte* in the Sixteenth-Century Spain', *MLR*, 51 (1956), 359-68.

SHERGOLD, N.D., VAREY, J.E., and DAVIS, Charles. *Fuentes para la historia del teatro en España, XI. Teatros y comedias en Madrid: 1699-1719. Estudio y documentos*. London: Támesis, 1986.

STAROBINSKI, Jean. *Portrait de l'artiste en saltimbanque*. Geneva: Albert Skira, 1970.

STOREY, Robert. *Pierrot: A Critical History of a Mask*. Princeton: Princeton UP, 1978.

SUAREZ MIRAMON, Ana. *Modernismo y 98*. Madrid: Cincel, 1980.

UCELAY, Margarita. 'La problemática teatral: testimonios directos de Federico García Lorca', *Boletín de la Fundación Federico García Lorca,* 6 (1989), 27-58.

URIBE, María de la Luz. *La comedia del arte*. Madrid: Destino, 1983.

UTRERA, R. *García Lorca y el cinema*. Sevilla: Edisur, 1982.

180

VAREY, J.E. & SHERGOLD, N.D. 'La tarasca de Madrid: un aspecto de la procesión del Corpus durante los siglos XVII y XVIII', *Clavileño*, 4 (1953), no.20, 21.

VAREY, J.E. 'Ganassa en la península ibérica en 1603', in *De los romances-villancico a la poesía de Claudio Rodríguez. 22 ensayos sobre las literaturas española e hispanoamericana en homenaje a Gustav Siebenmann*, ed. by José Manuel López de Abadia and Augusta López Bernasocchi. Madrid: José Esteban, 1984, pp.455-62.

VAREY, J.E. 'La creación deliberada de la confusión: estudio de una diversión de carnestolendas de 1623', in *Homenaje al Prof. William L.Fichter*. Madrid: Castalia, 1971, pp.745-54.

VAREY, J.E. 'The First Theatre on the Site of the Caños del Peral', *Dieciocho*, 9 (1986), 290-96.

VAREY, J.E. *Los títeres y otras diversiones populares de Madrid: 1758-1840.* London: Támesis, 1972.

VILA, Xavier Peter. 'Valle-Inclán and the Theater'. Unpublished doctoral thesis, Princeton University, 1985.

VILCHES DE FRUTOS, María Francisca, & DOUGHERTY, Dru. 'La renovación del teatro español a través de la prensa periódica: la página teatral del «Heraldo de Madrid» (1923-1927)', *Siglo XX/20th Century*, vol. 6, nos.1-2 (1988-89), 47-56.

VILCHES DE FRUTOS, María Francisca, & DOUGHERTY, Dru. *La escena madrileña*. Madrid: Fundamentos, 1990.

ZATTLIN, Phyllis. 'Metatheatre and the Twentieth-Century Spanish Stage', *ALEC*, 17, 1-2 (1992), 55-74.

ZAVALA, Iris M. *La musa funambulesca. Poética de la carnivalización en Valle-Inclán*. Madrid: Orígenes, 1990.

Index

182